Tattoo Bible

BOOK FOUR

Published by:

ArtKulture – an Imprint of Wolfgang Publications

Wolfgang Publications
PO Box 223
Stillwater, MN 55082

Legals

First published in 2025 by
ArtKulture an imprint of Wolfgang Publications Inc.
PO Box 223, Stillwater MN 55082

The information in this book is true and complete to the best of
our knowledge. All recommendations are made without any
guarantee on the part of the author or publisher, who also disclaim
any liability incurred in connection with the use of this data
or specific details.

We recognize that some words, model name and designations,
for example, mentioned herein are the property of the trademark
holder. We use them for identification purposes only. This is not
an official publication.

ISBN-25: 978-1-941064-73-3

Printed in USA

Acknowledgements

The long list of people who's work is included in Tattoo Bible Book Four:

Top of the List: The man who created, operated and managed a number of successful Tattoo Shops in Hawaii and Arizona in the days when Tattoo Shops were few and far between. During those years Jim Watson collected Flash from a large number of talented Tattoo Artists from around the world. Some years later Jim decided that those images should be used to make his Tattoo Bible Book One.

We would like to think the many talented named and unnamed artists who contributed to Tattoo Bible Book Four.

Jim Watson
John Devon
Tattoo Duke
Wade Swisher
Manny
D. Willis
CLMI
Sammy Lerma
Acosta
Chris Bailey
Tri
Hackett
Wade Wiley
Joe Zuniga
Johnny Lacheco
Dustin Golden
M. Robyn Birk
Turbo
Bill Emmert
Martin B
Jamie Burresss
Jim Watson
Andre' Davis
Beck

From the Publisher

I was sitting in my small office years ago with an artist in one corner and the bookkeeper in the other. At that time we were publishing a large variety of books: How-to books on customizing your Harley, forming sheetmetal, overhauling Triumphs, buy an old Honda, paint your Hot Rod or Motorcycle, and work with Composite Material.

Everything changed when I received a phone call from Jim Watson. Jim said he owned the biggest Tattoo Equipment shop in the US. He also said he had a large collection of Flash – and did I wanted to make a book with the images? I said yes, and six months later he shipped me an abundant collection of great images complete with the text for the front-section pages of the book.

 The images were colorful and organized. We put them in form for the printer, and soon Tattoo Bible Book One was available on the shelves at the bookstores and the internet.

Over the next couple of years we published Tattoo Bibles Two and Three. We also published a number of tattoo books with images and information compiled and author by Jim. Putting everything together was labor of love for Jim and was well received by artists all over the world.

NOW

Jim passed in November 2019, but I had the assistance of Jim's wife and long-time partner Cherie Mackenzie Watson. It was Cherie who sorted and selected the images for this latest book from the collection that Jim created over the decades when he was active as an acclaimed artist.

We think that you will enjoy Tattooo Bible Book Four with the same appreciation that you showed for the well received books One, Two and Three.

Chapters

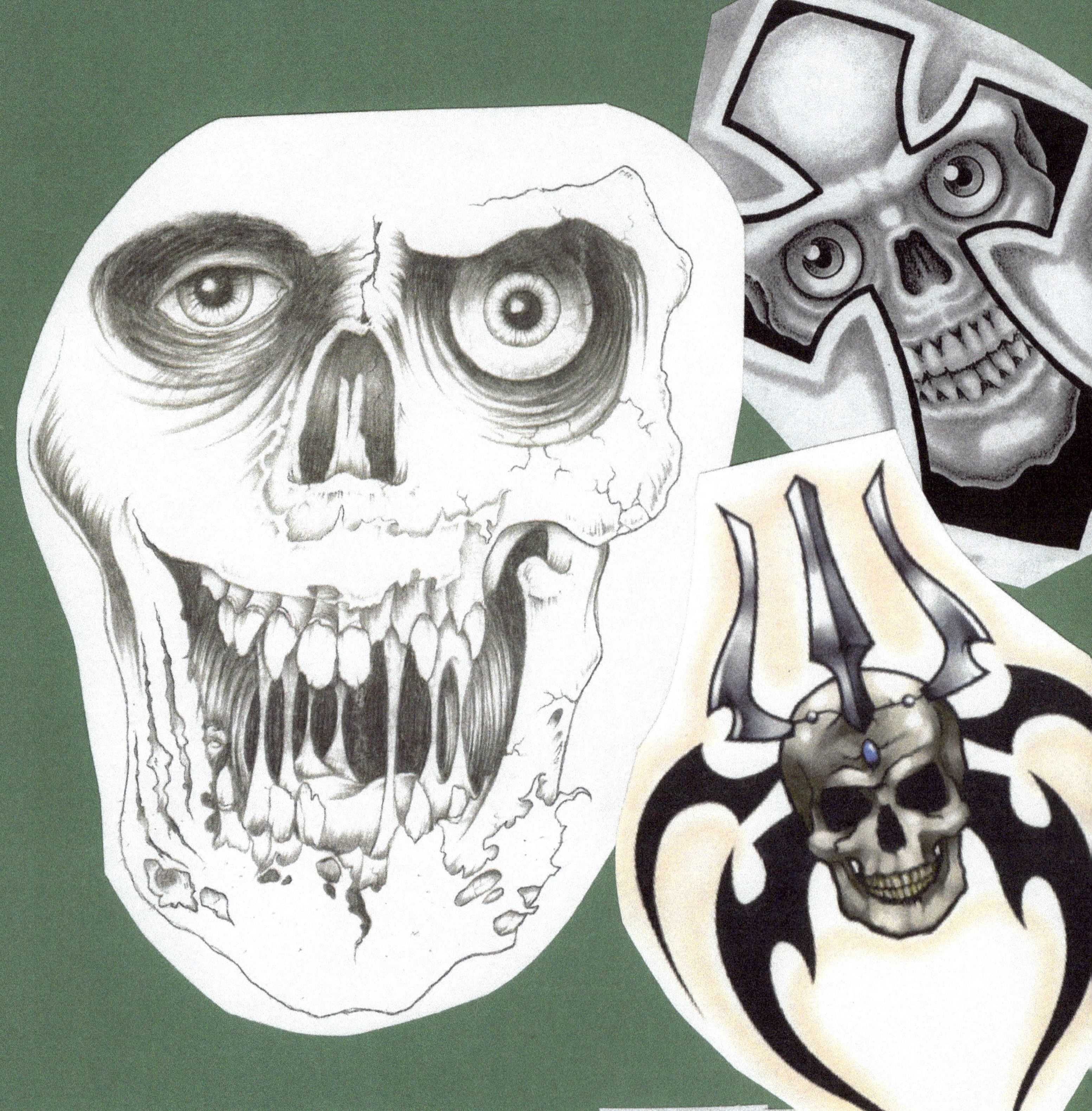

skulls

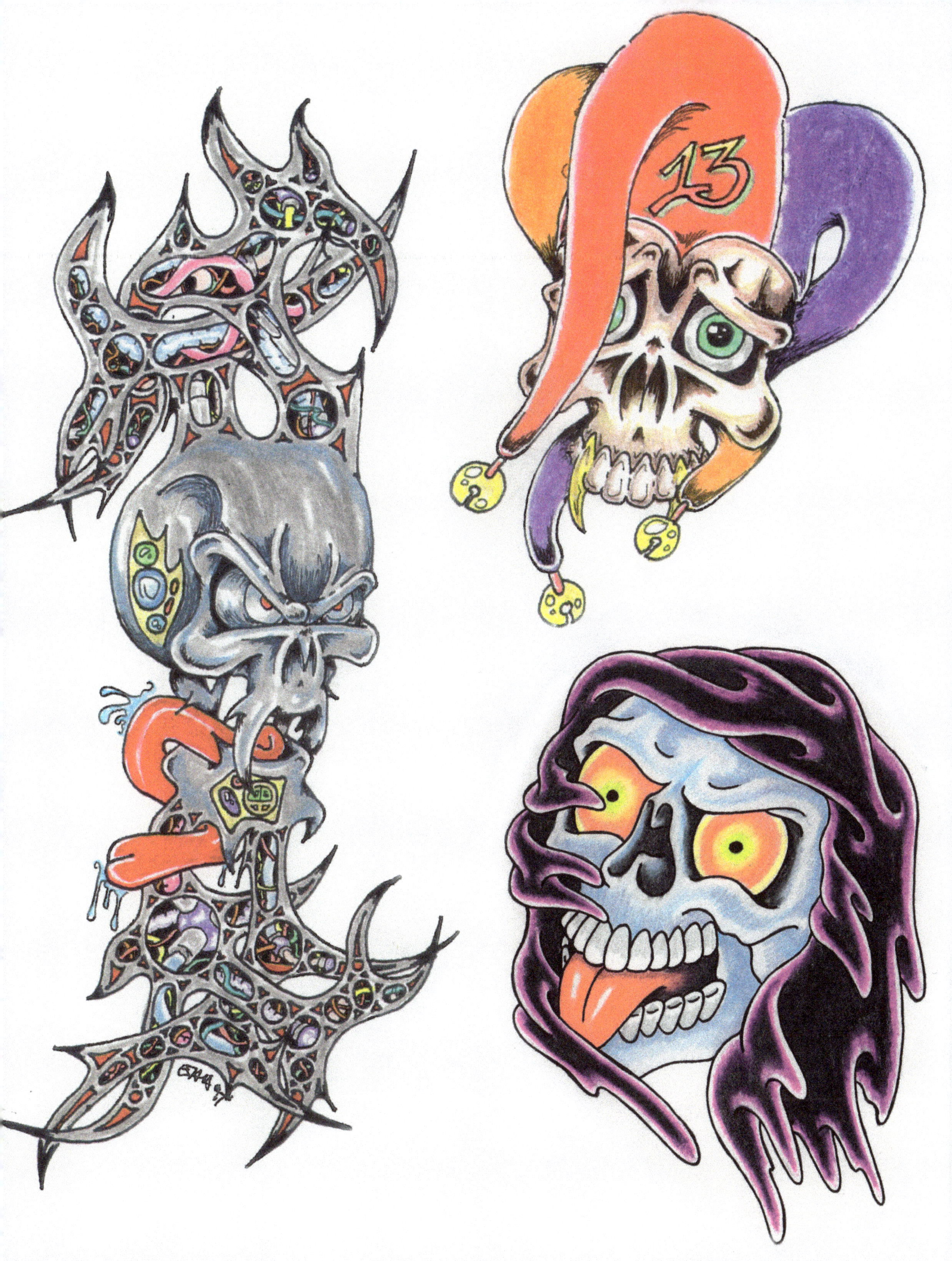
13

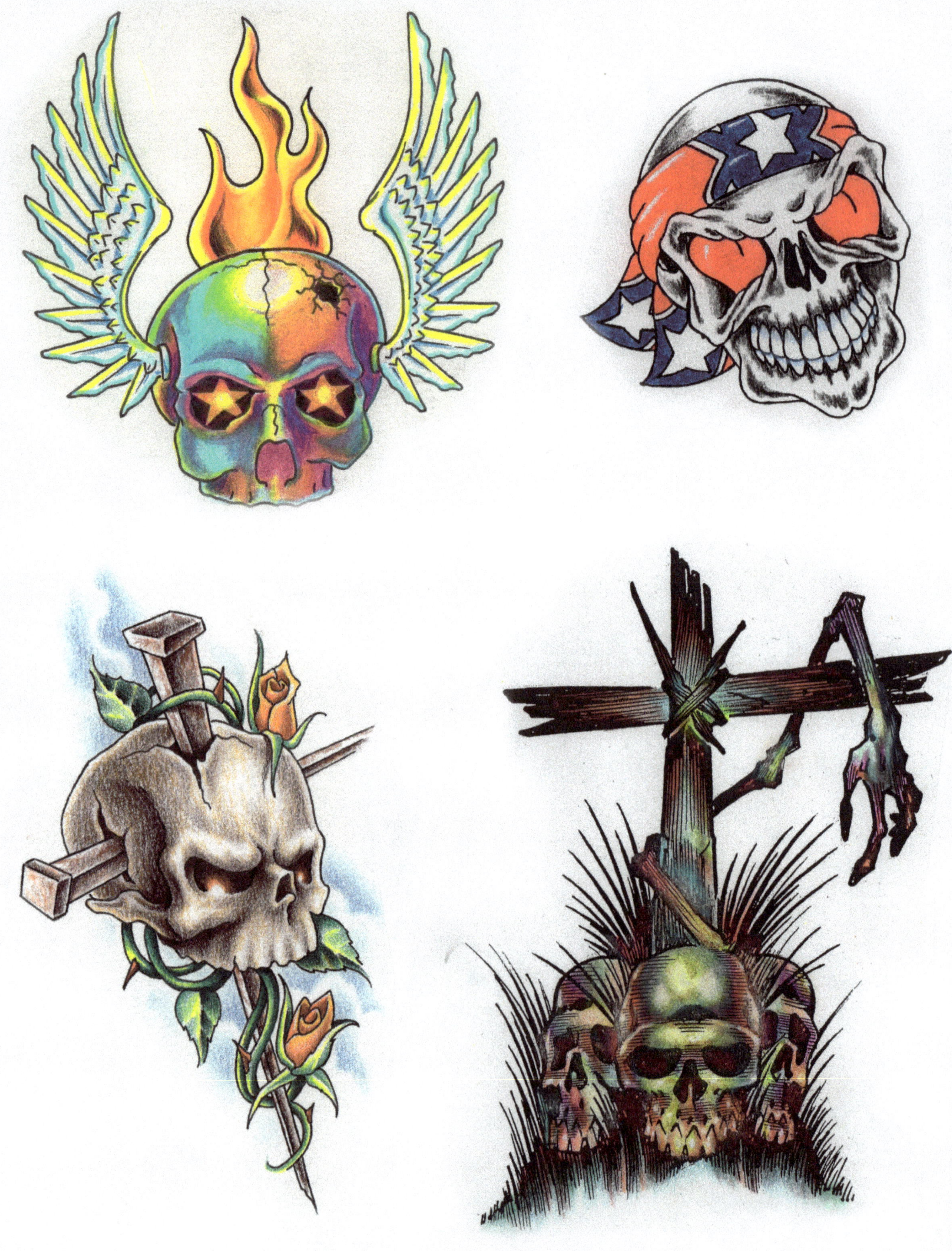

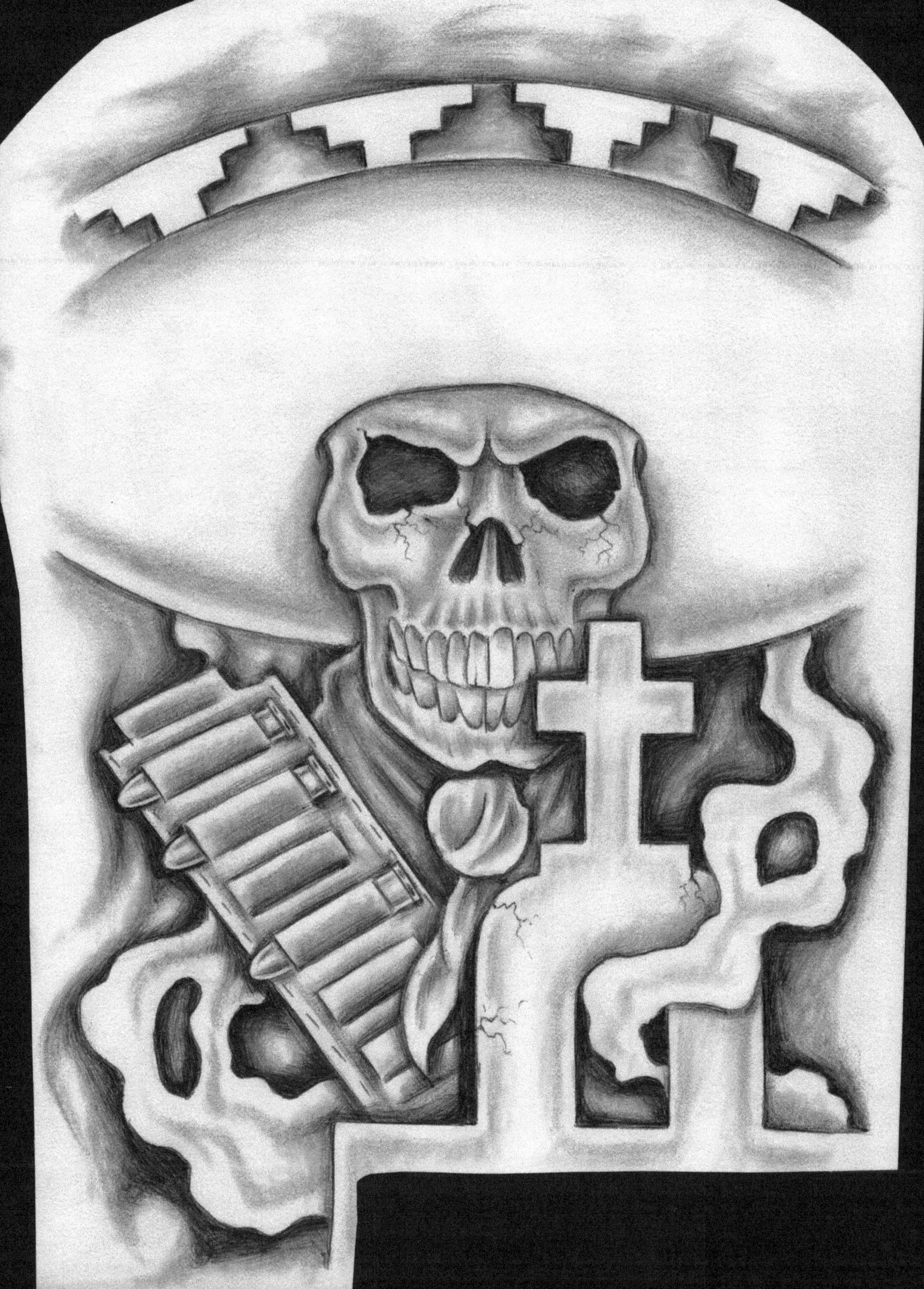

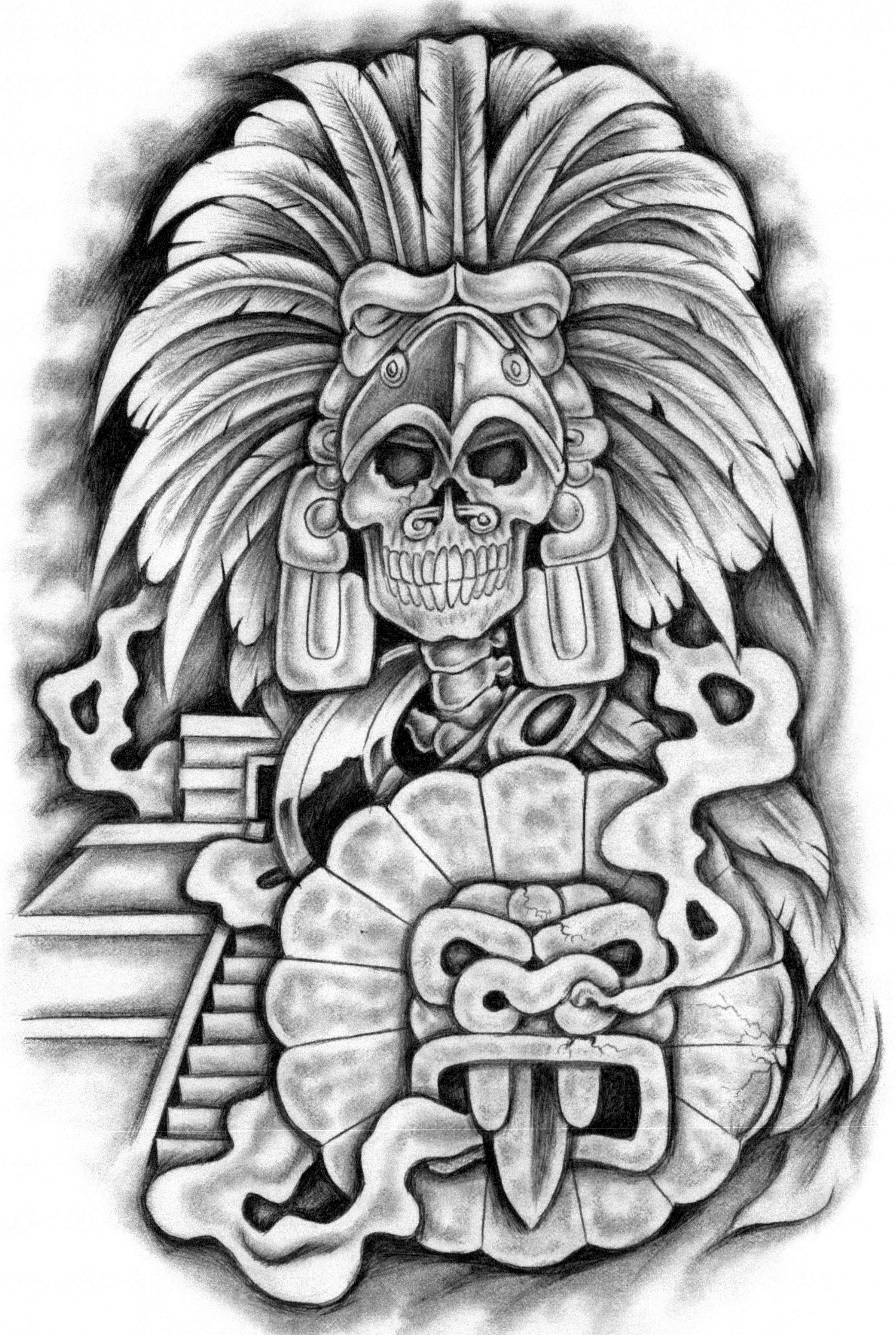

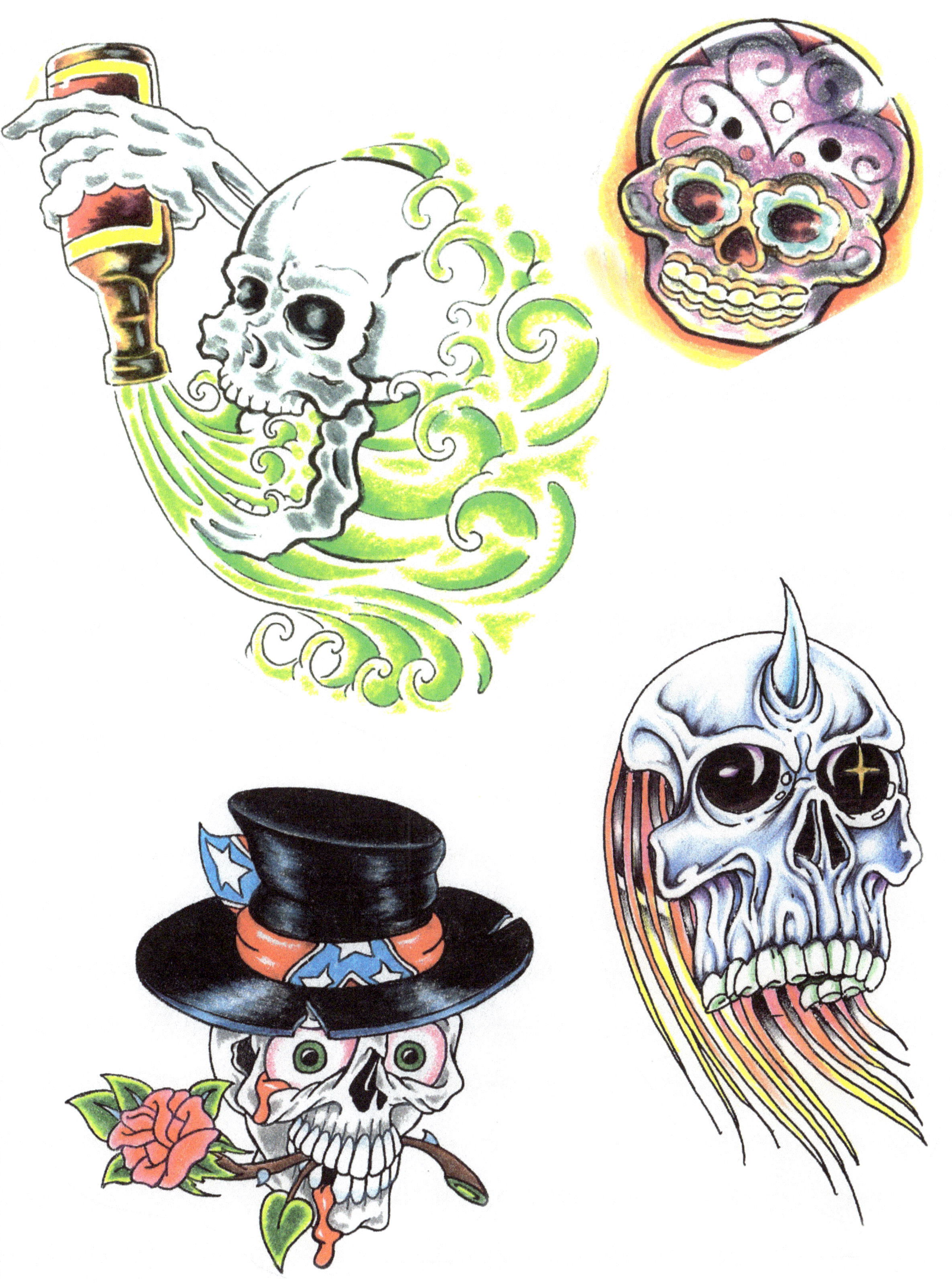

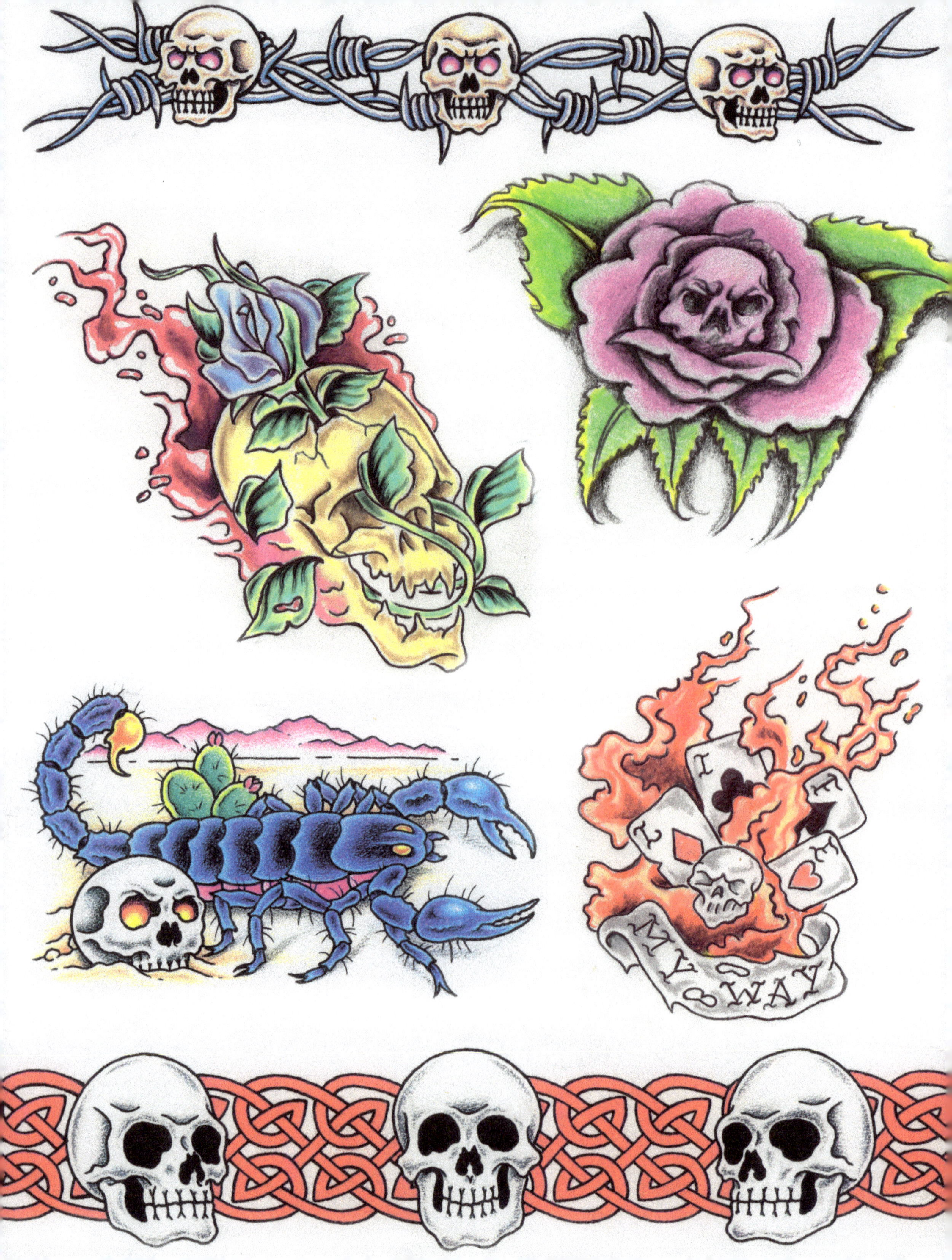
MY WAY

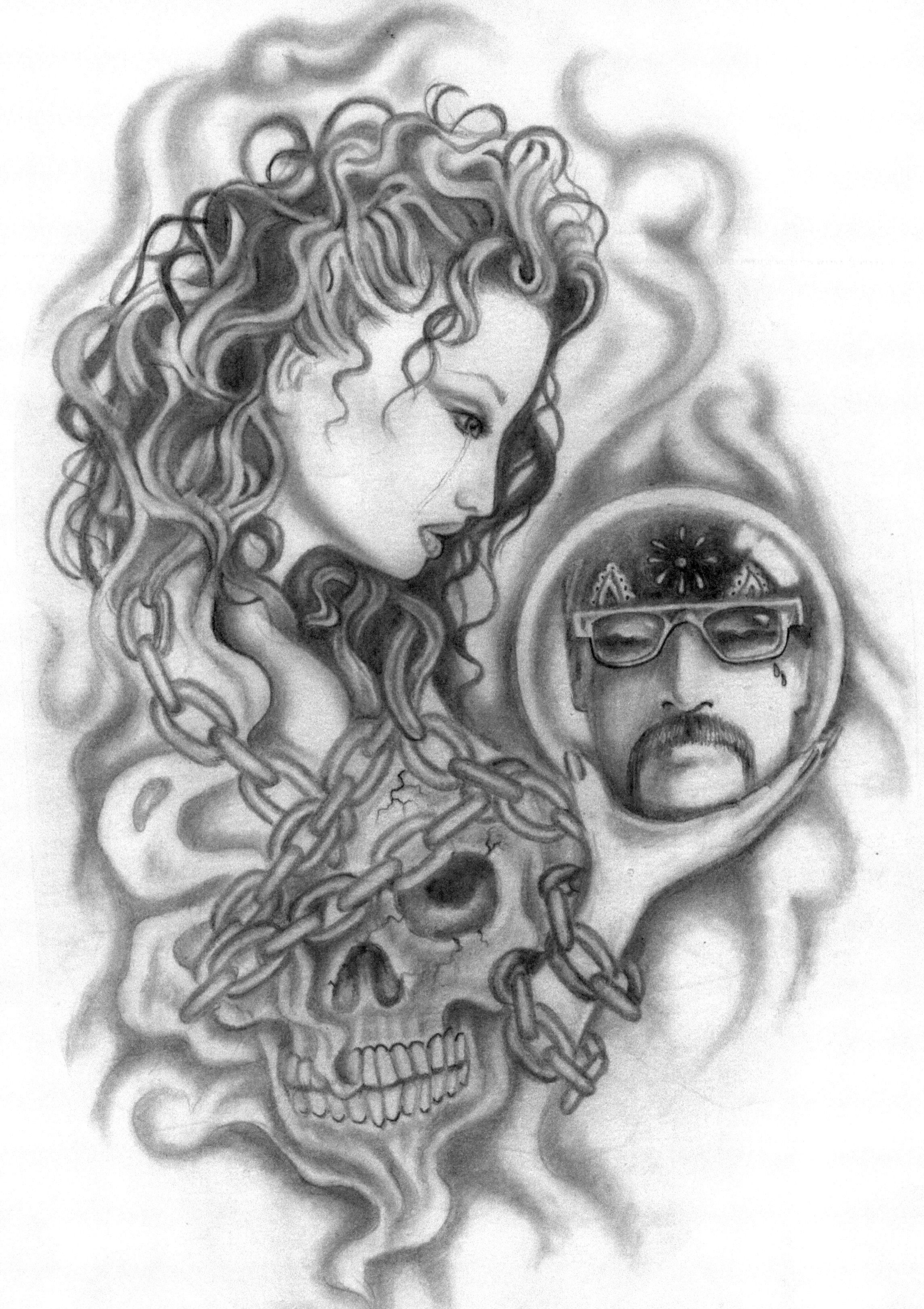

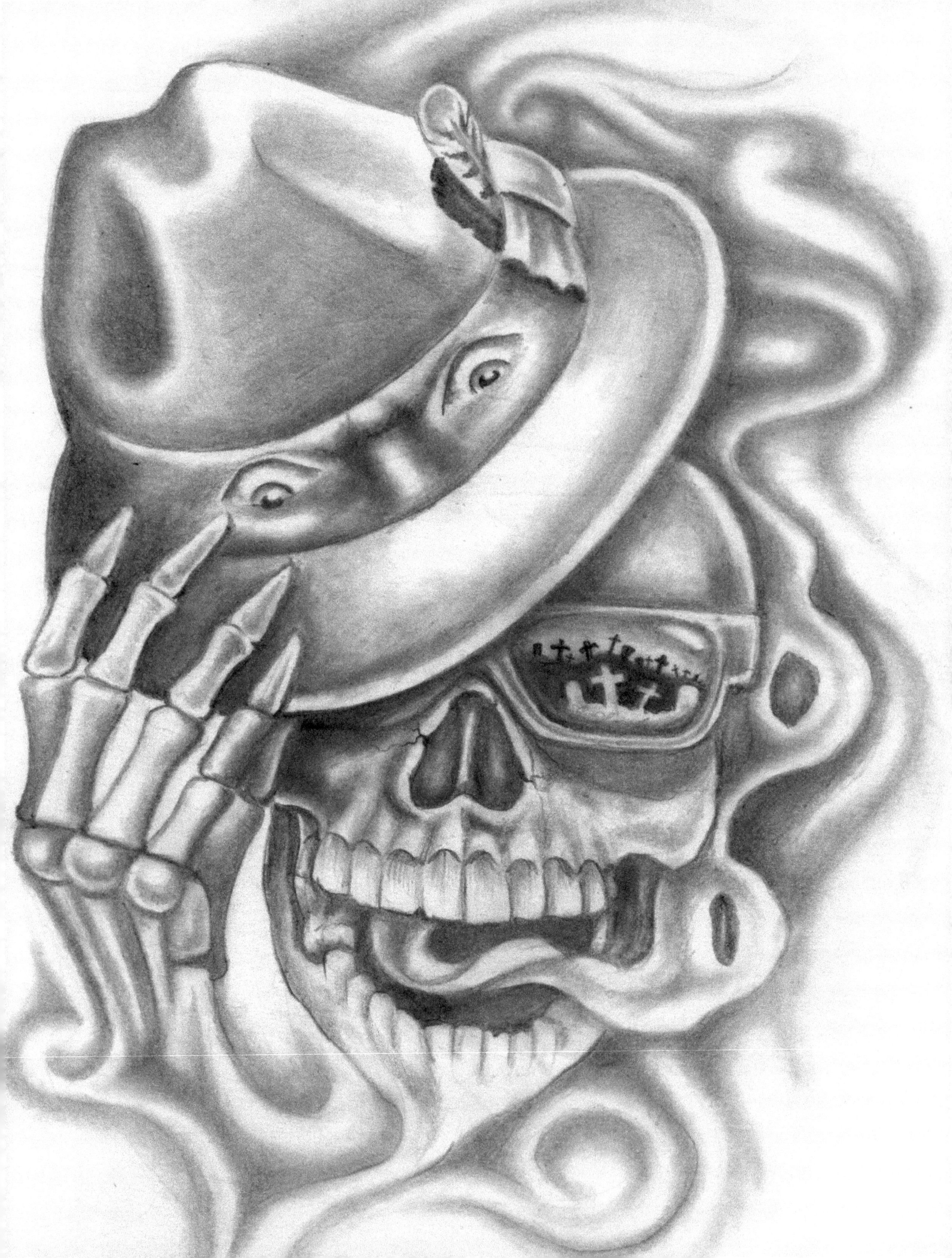

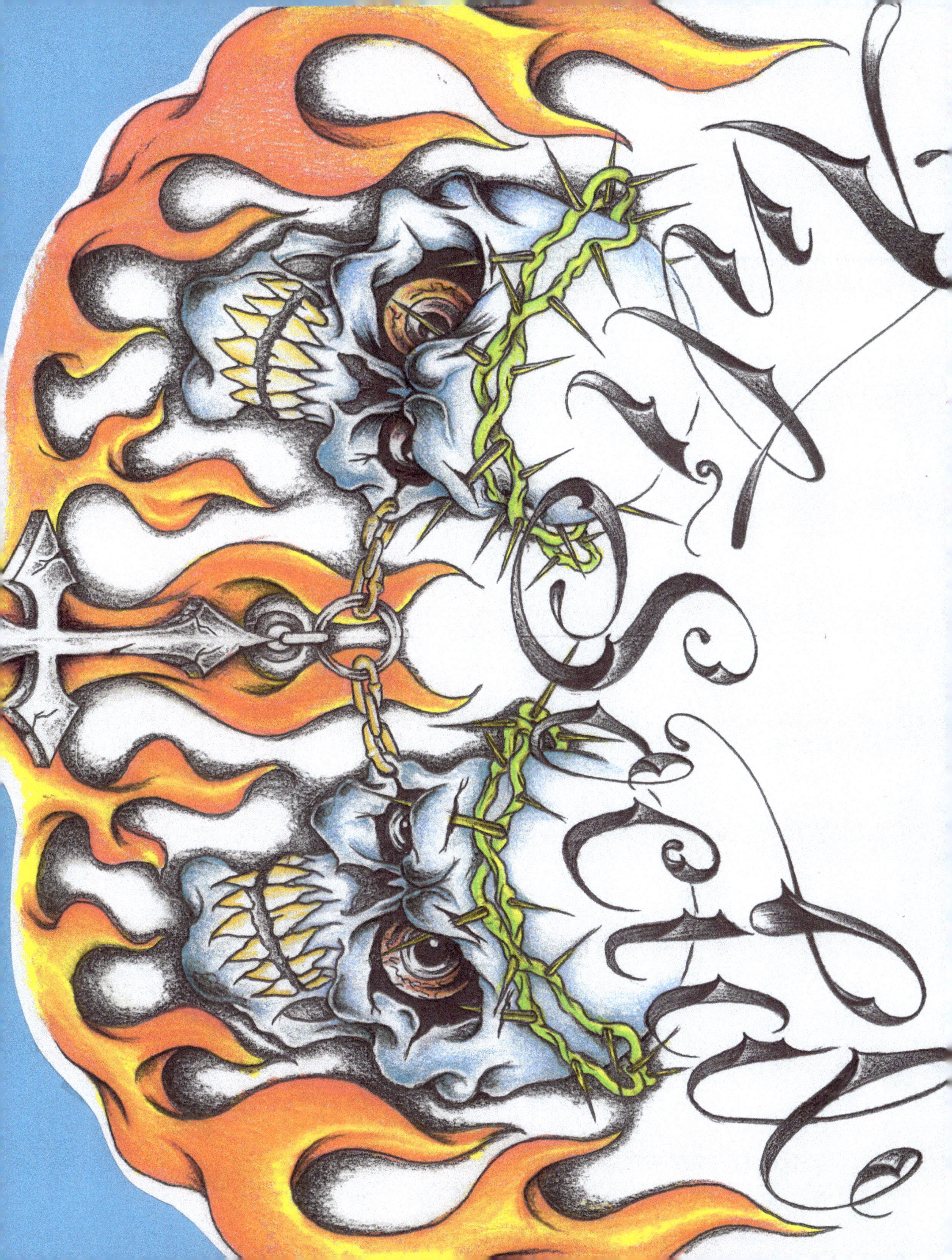

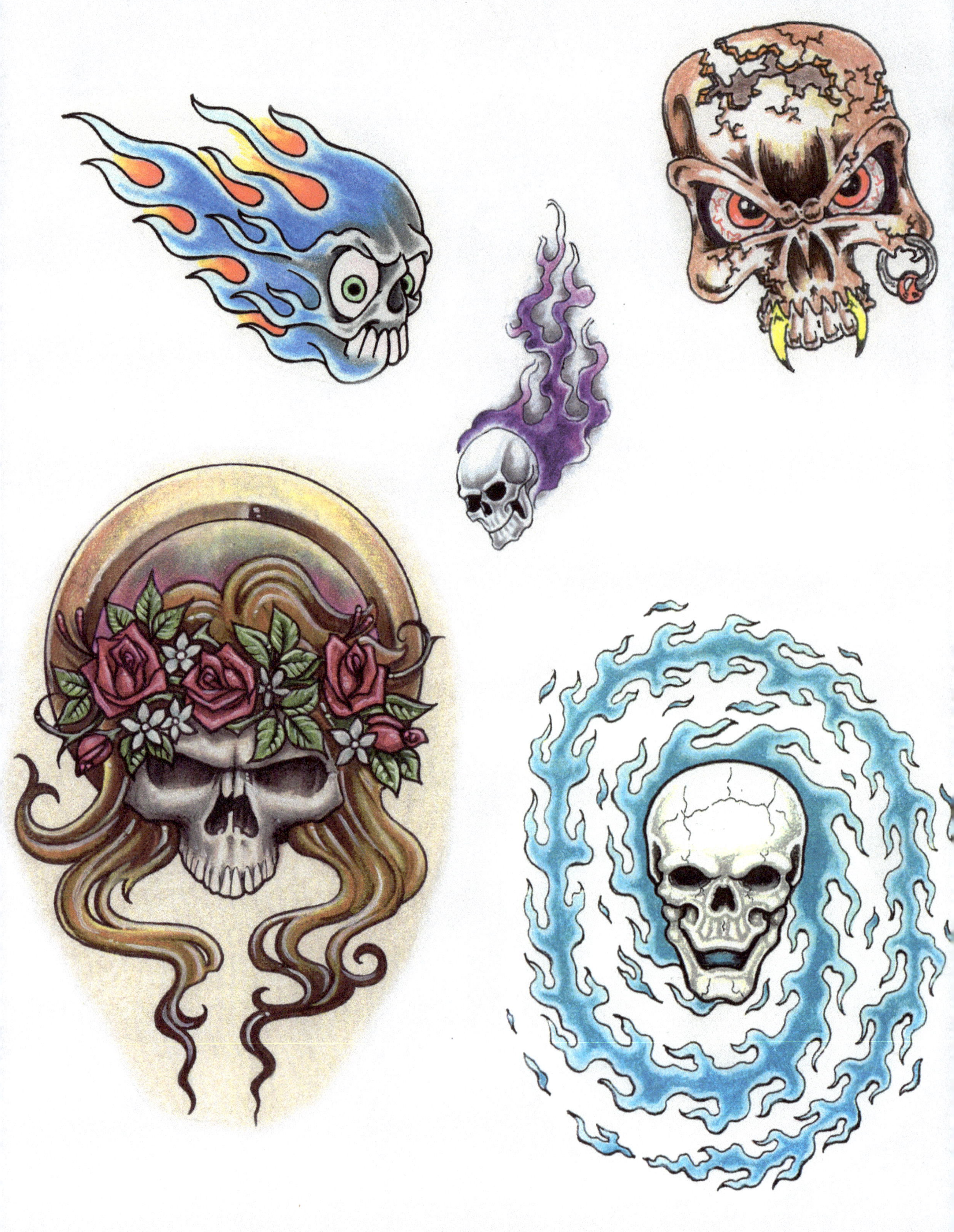

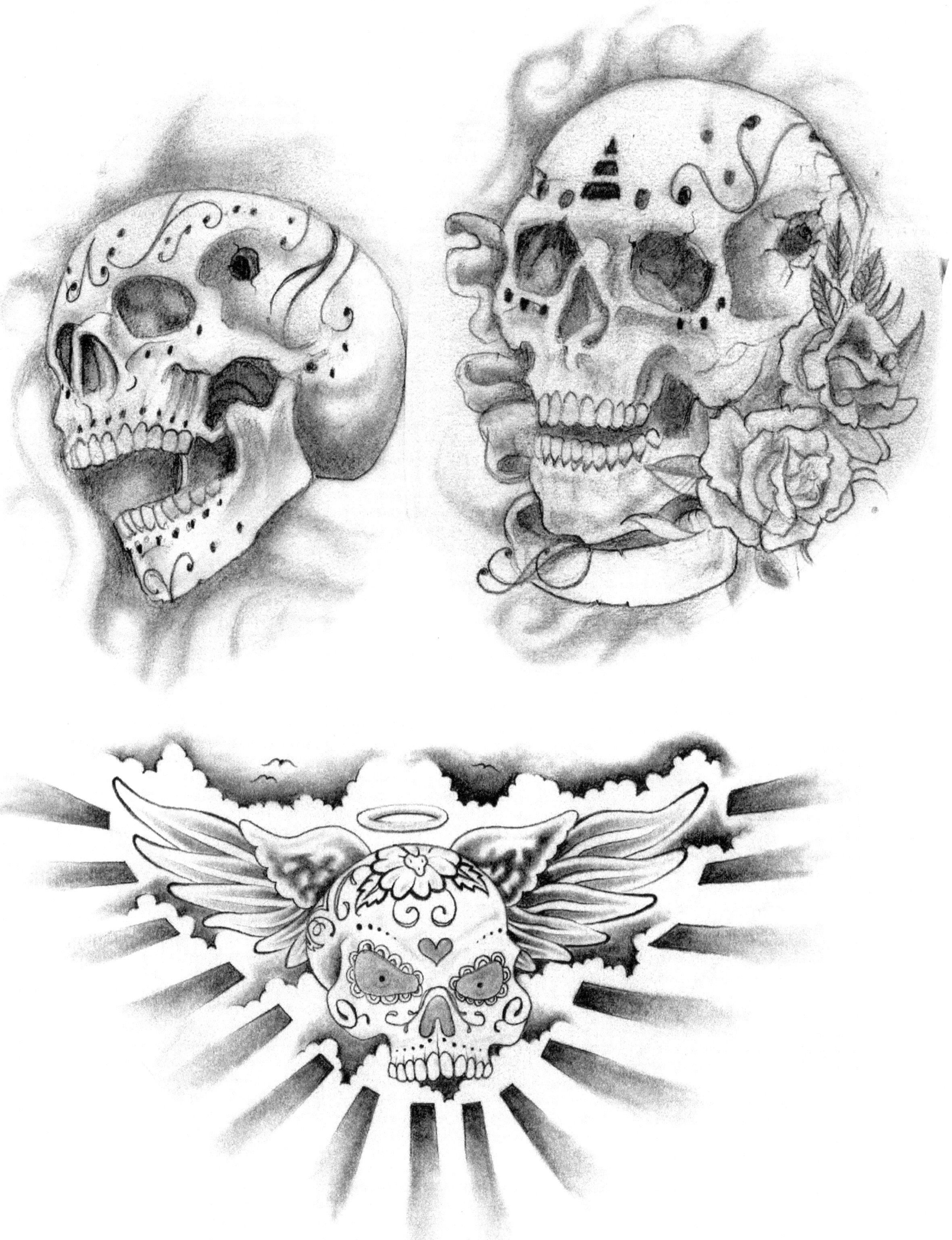

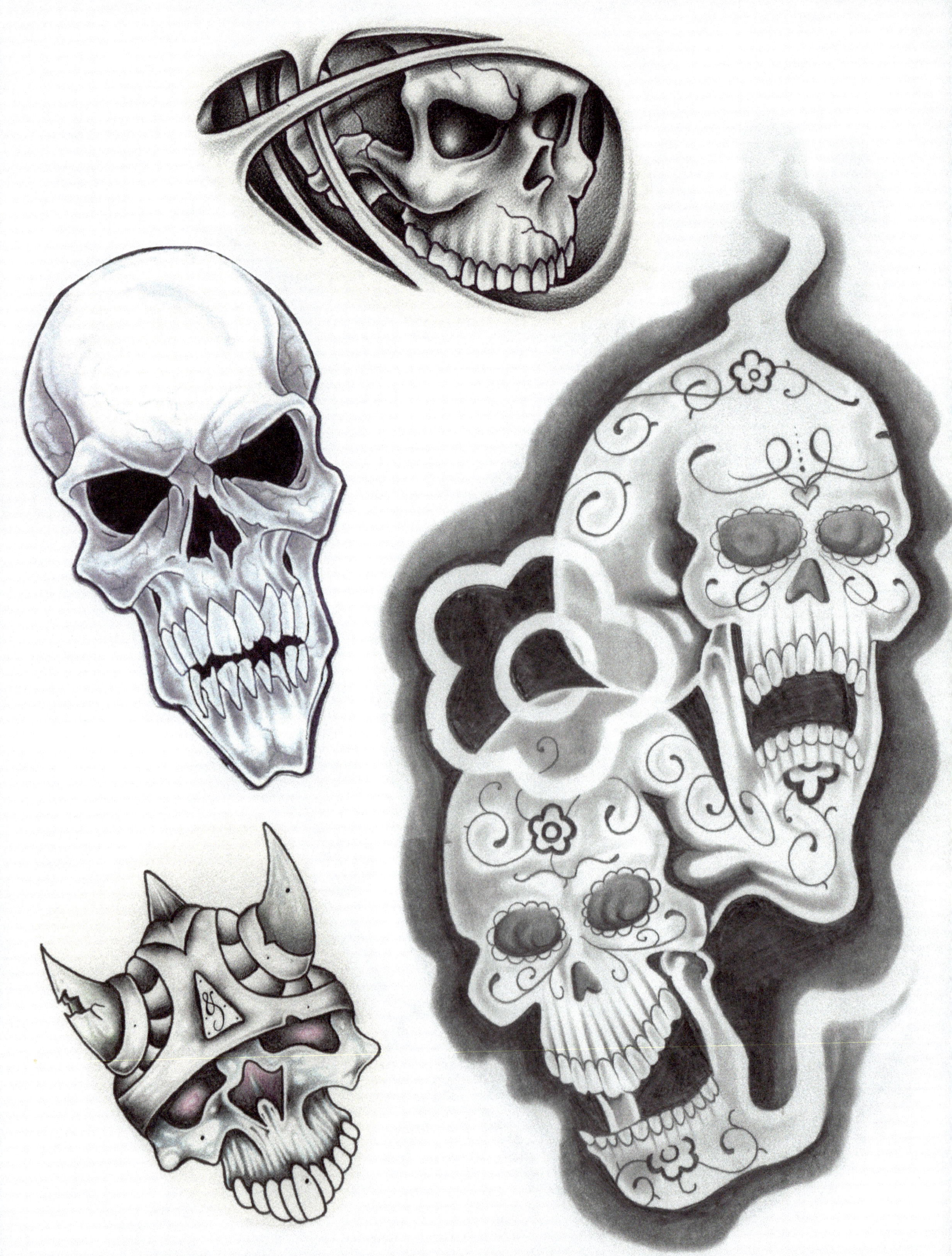

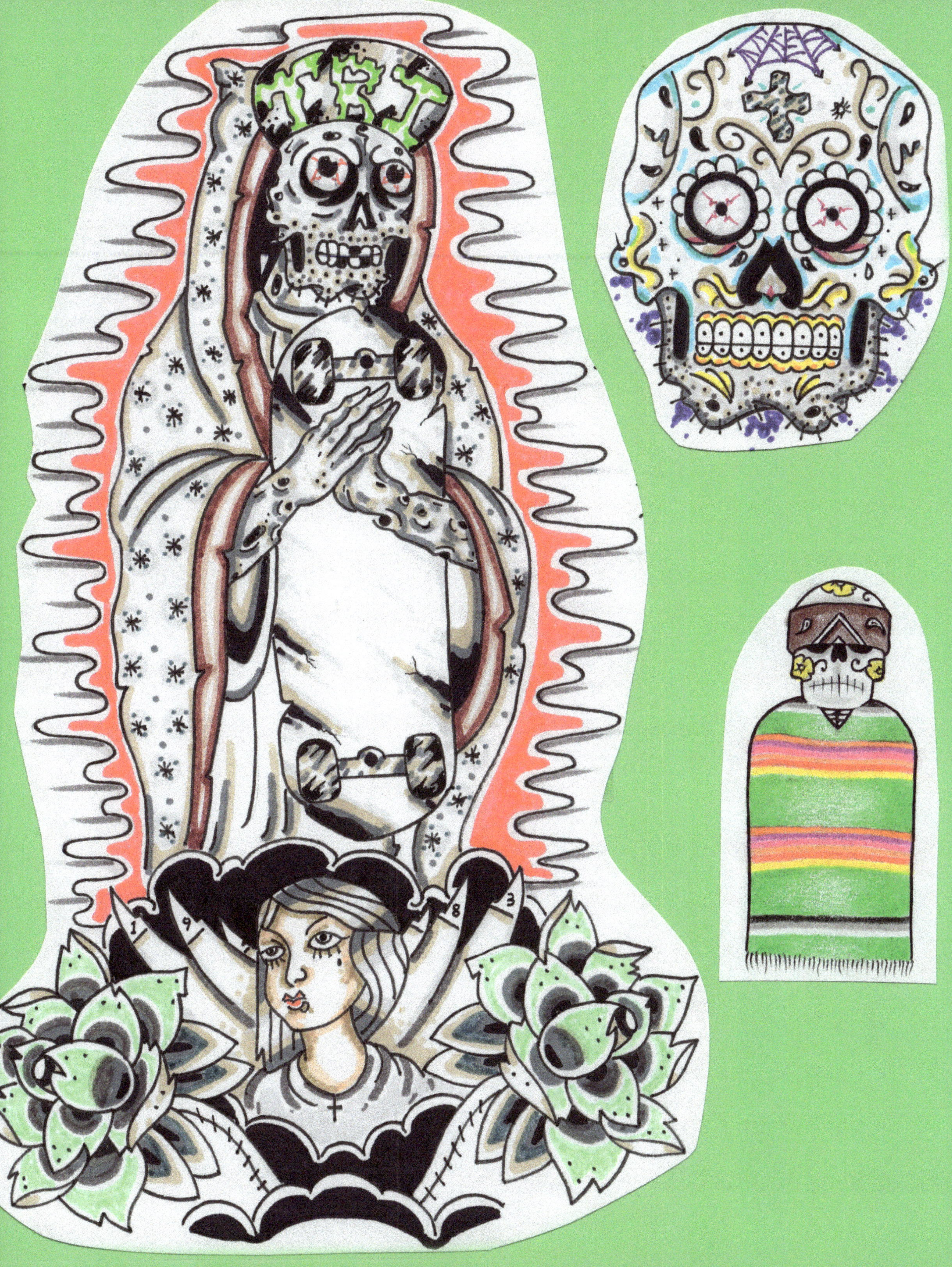

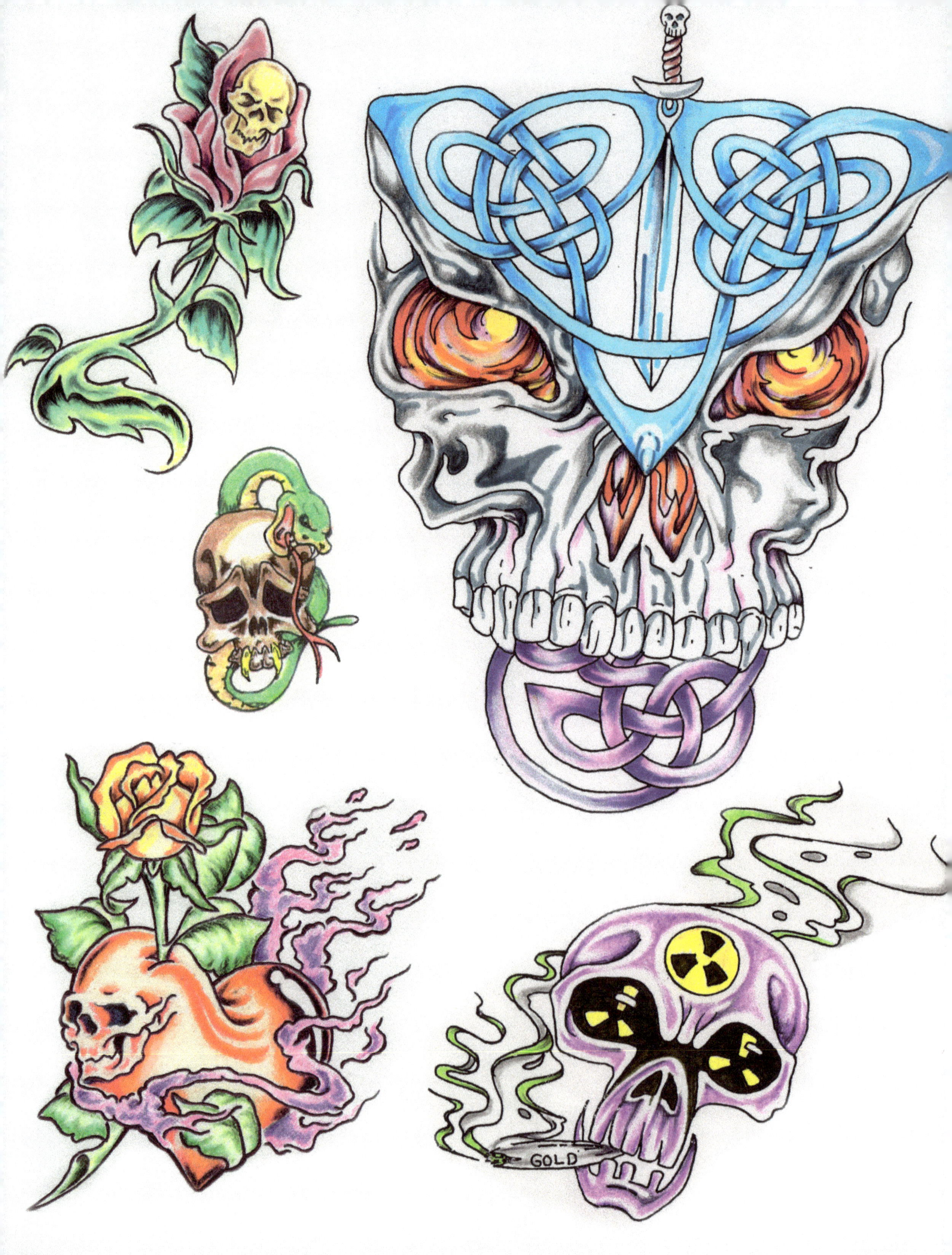
GOLD

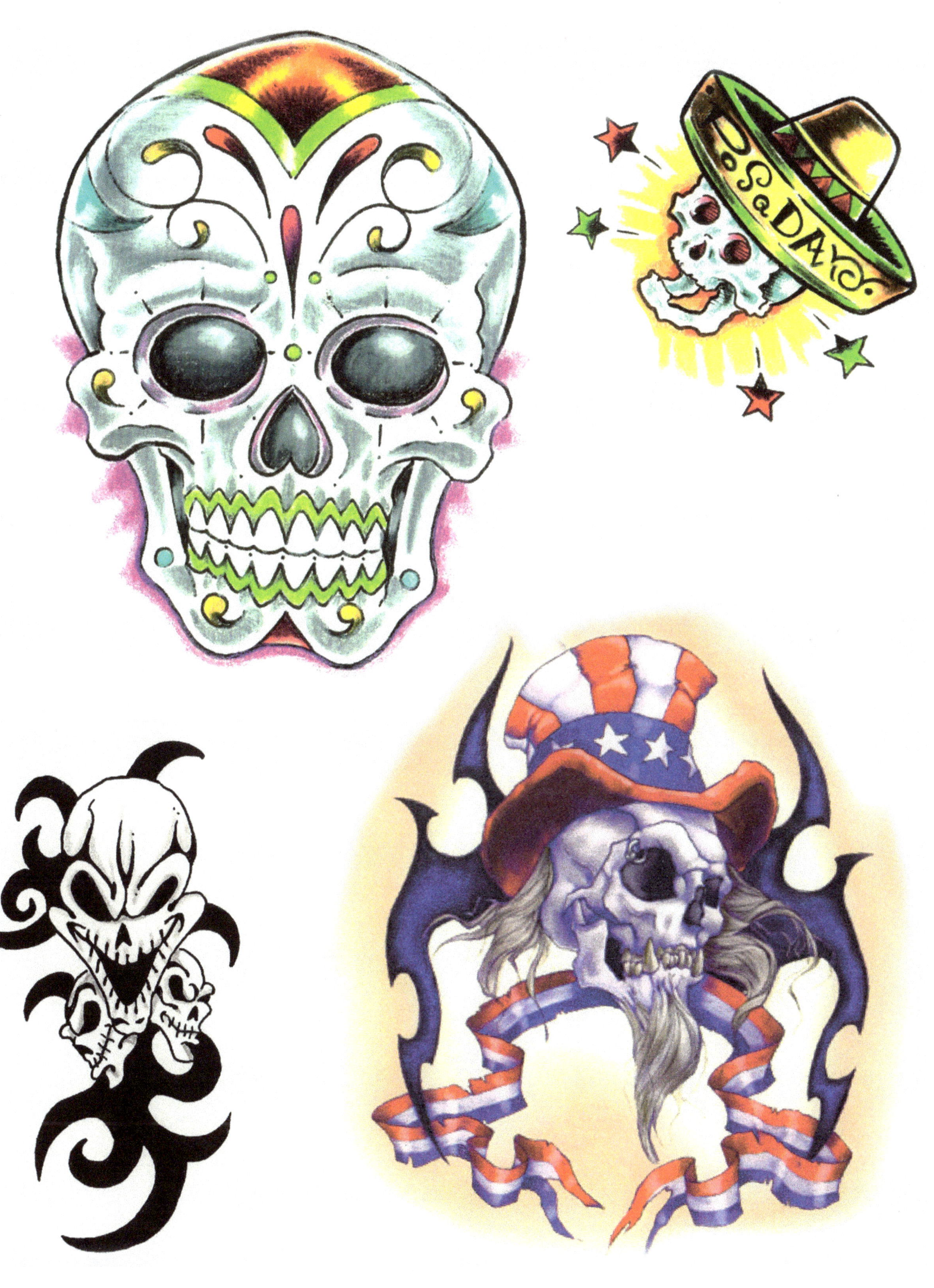
PoSaDAY

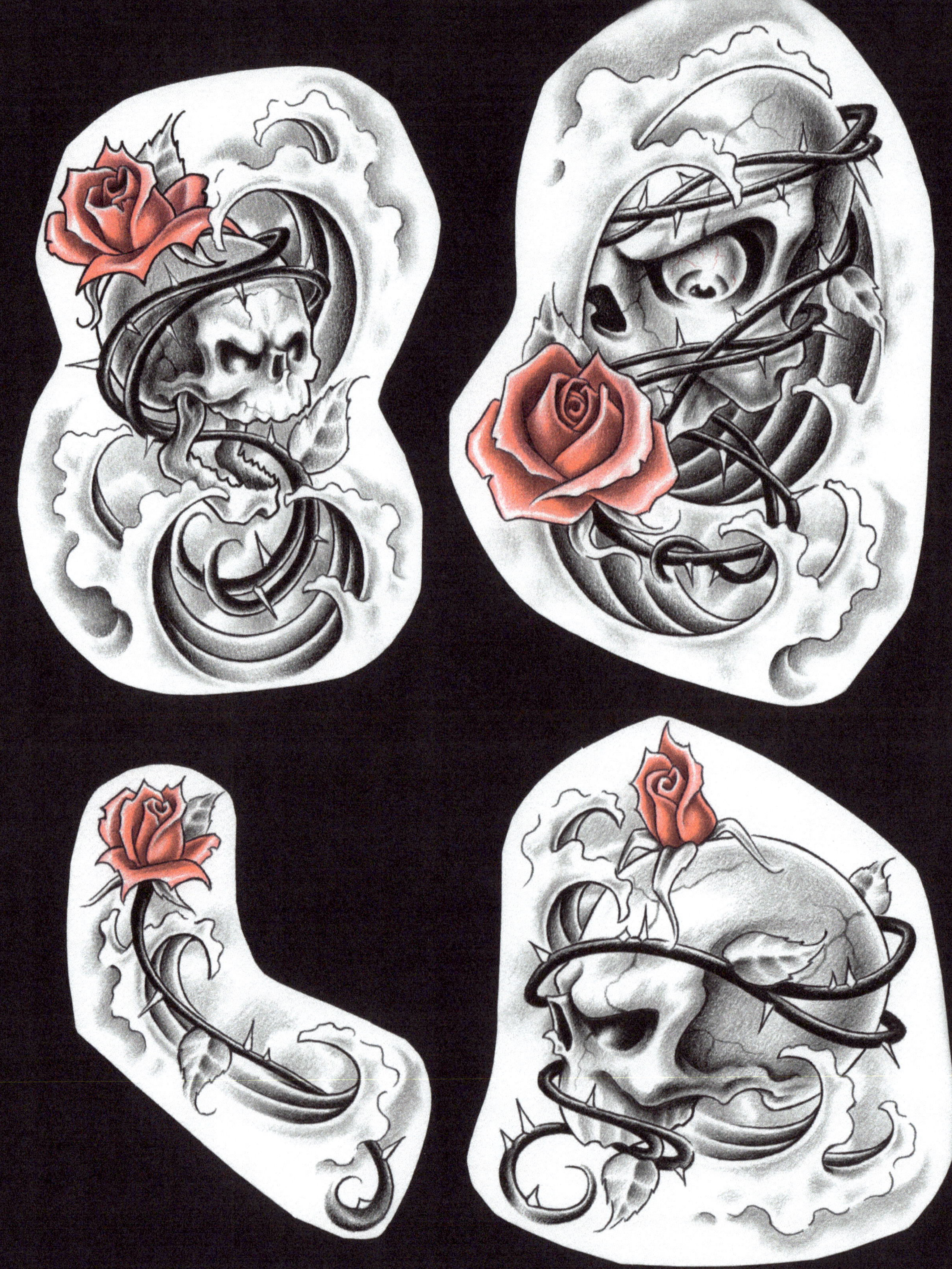

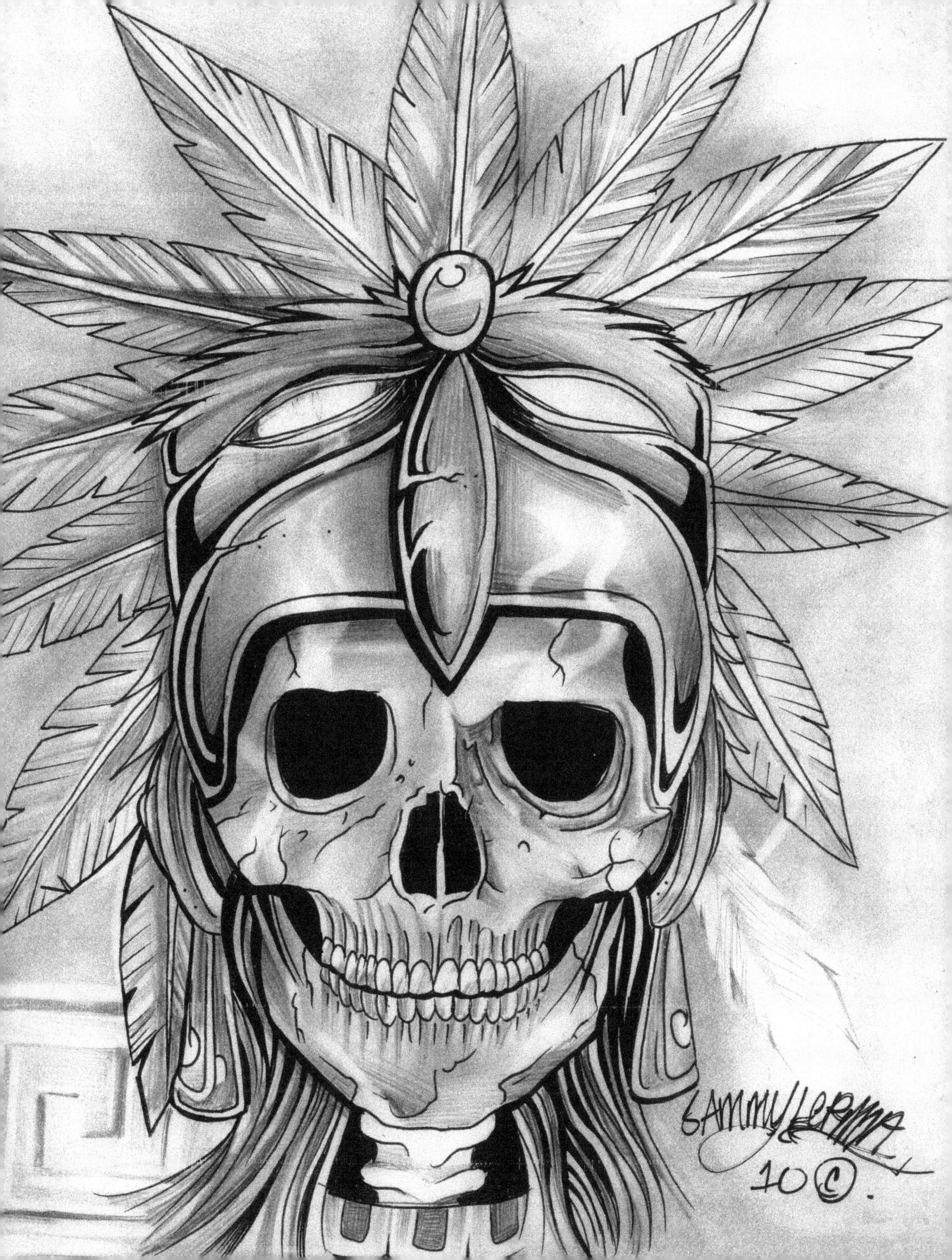
Sammy Lerma
10 ©

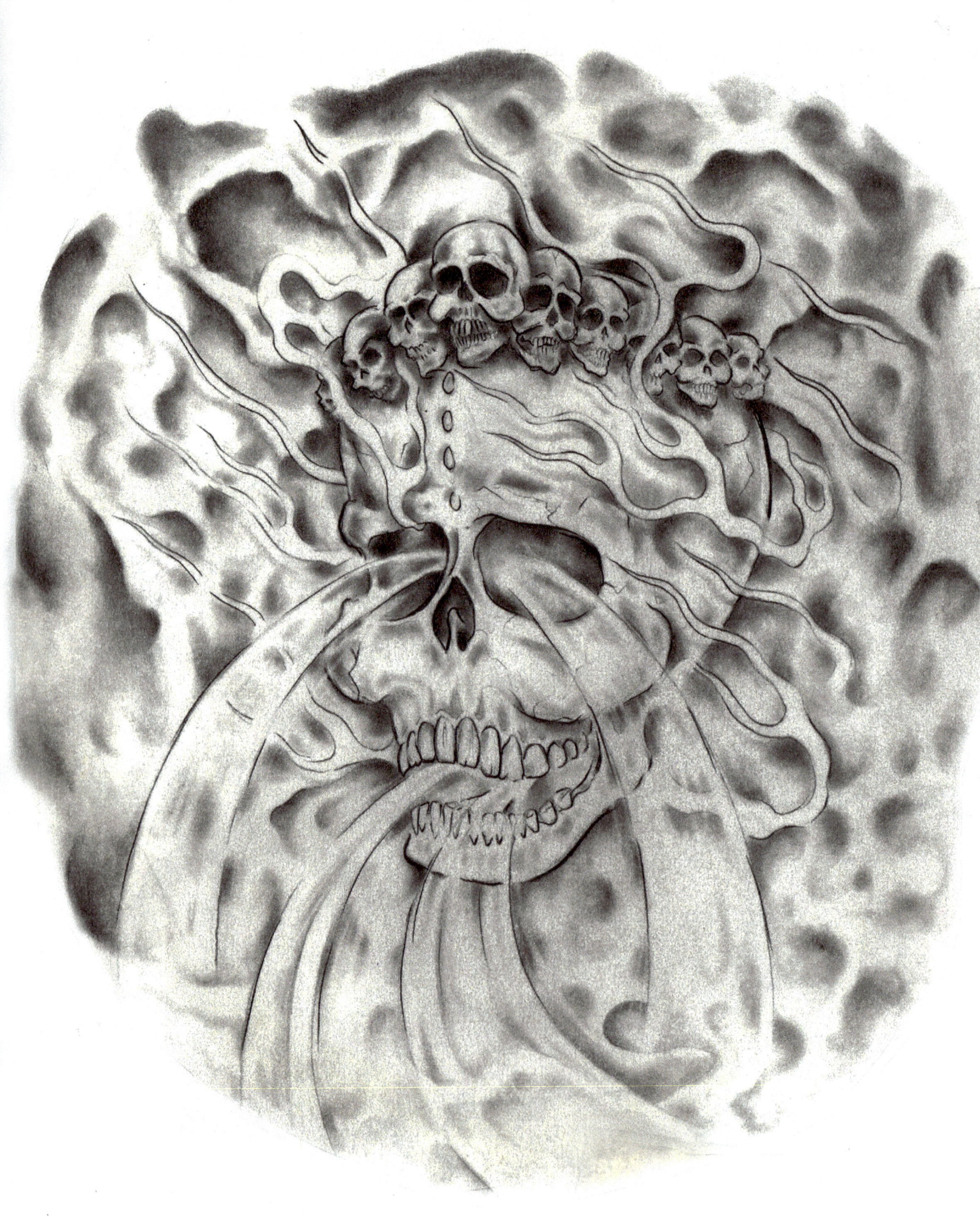

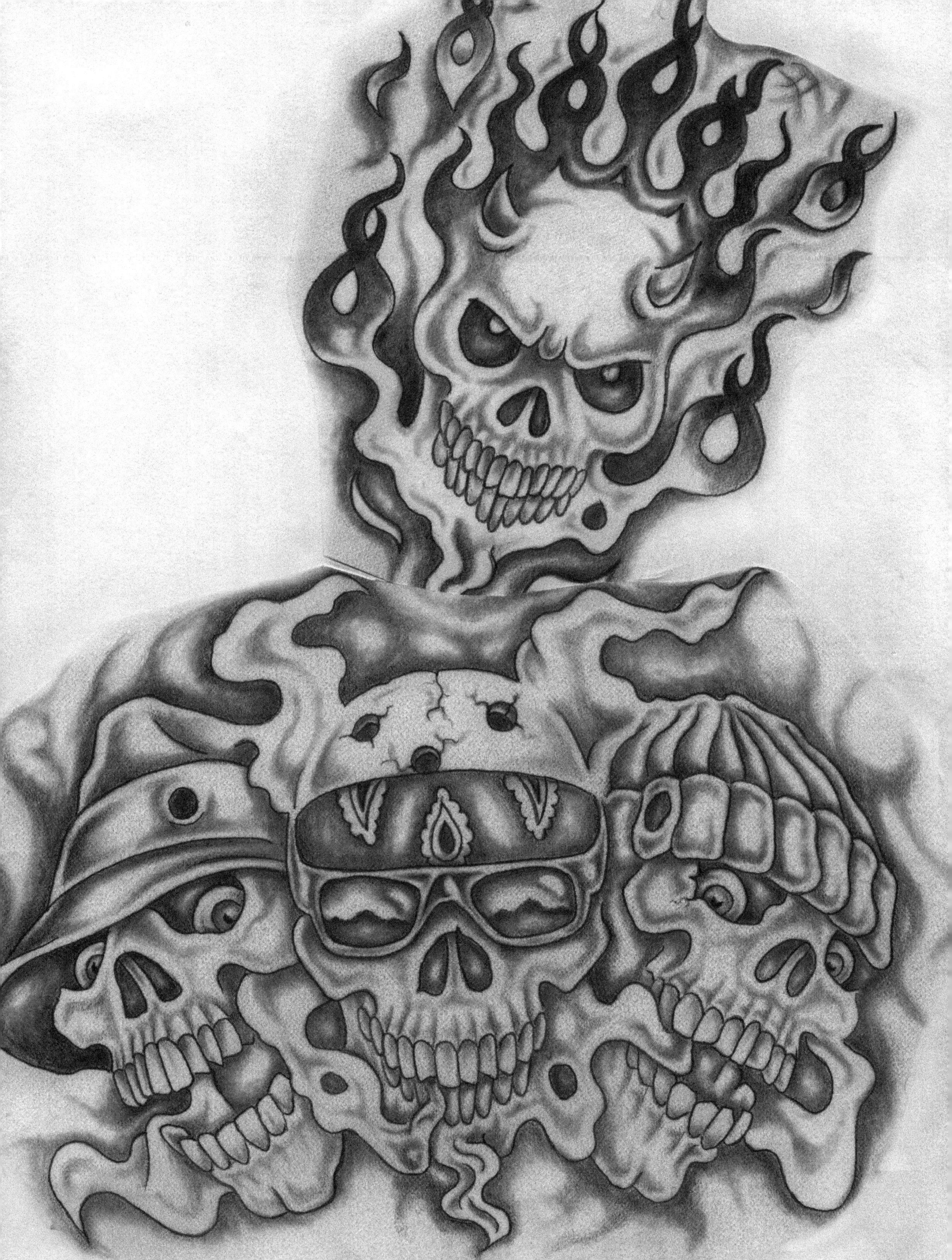

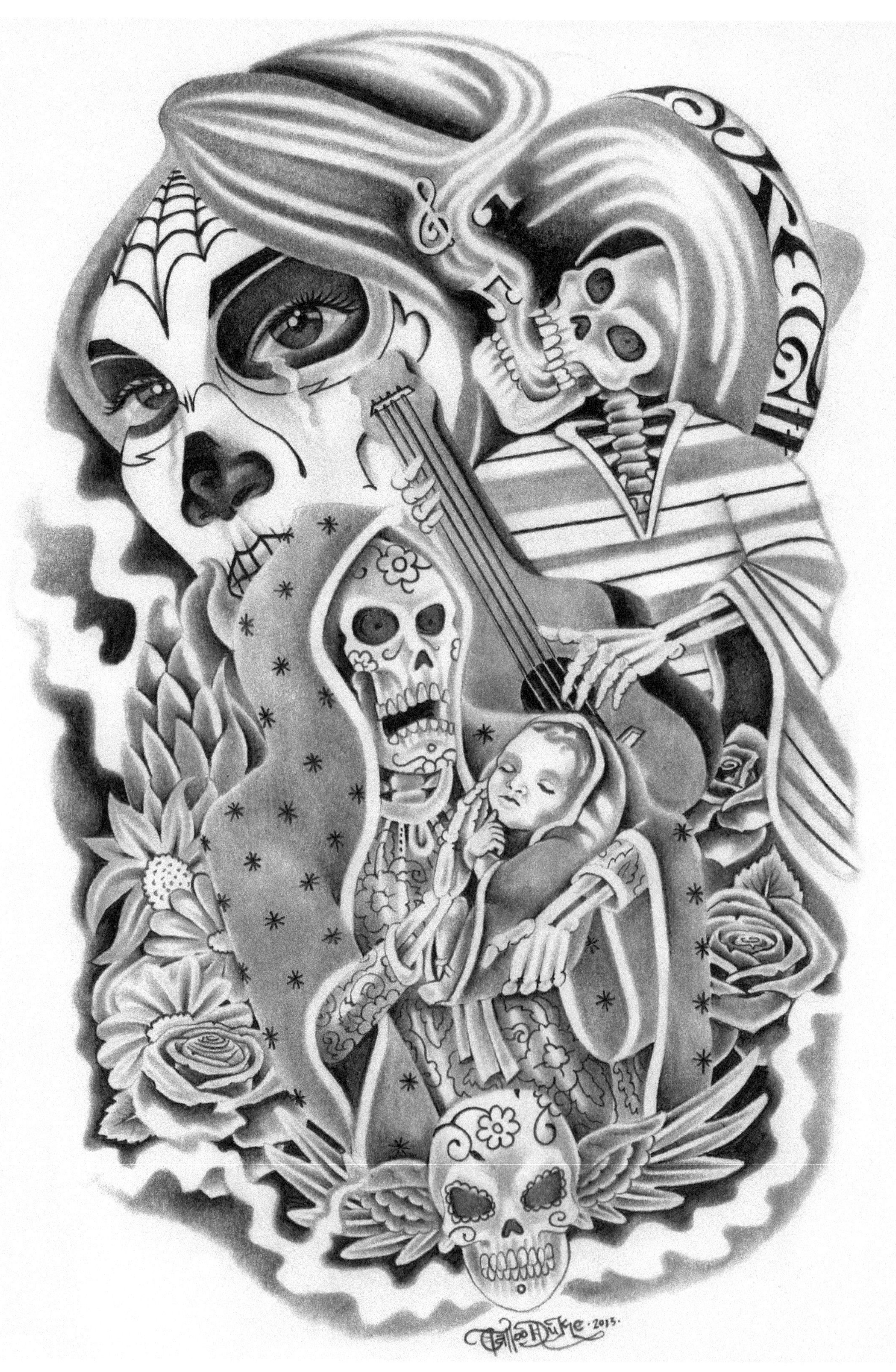

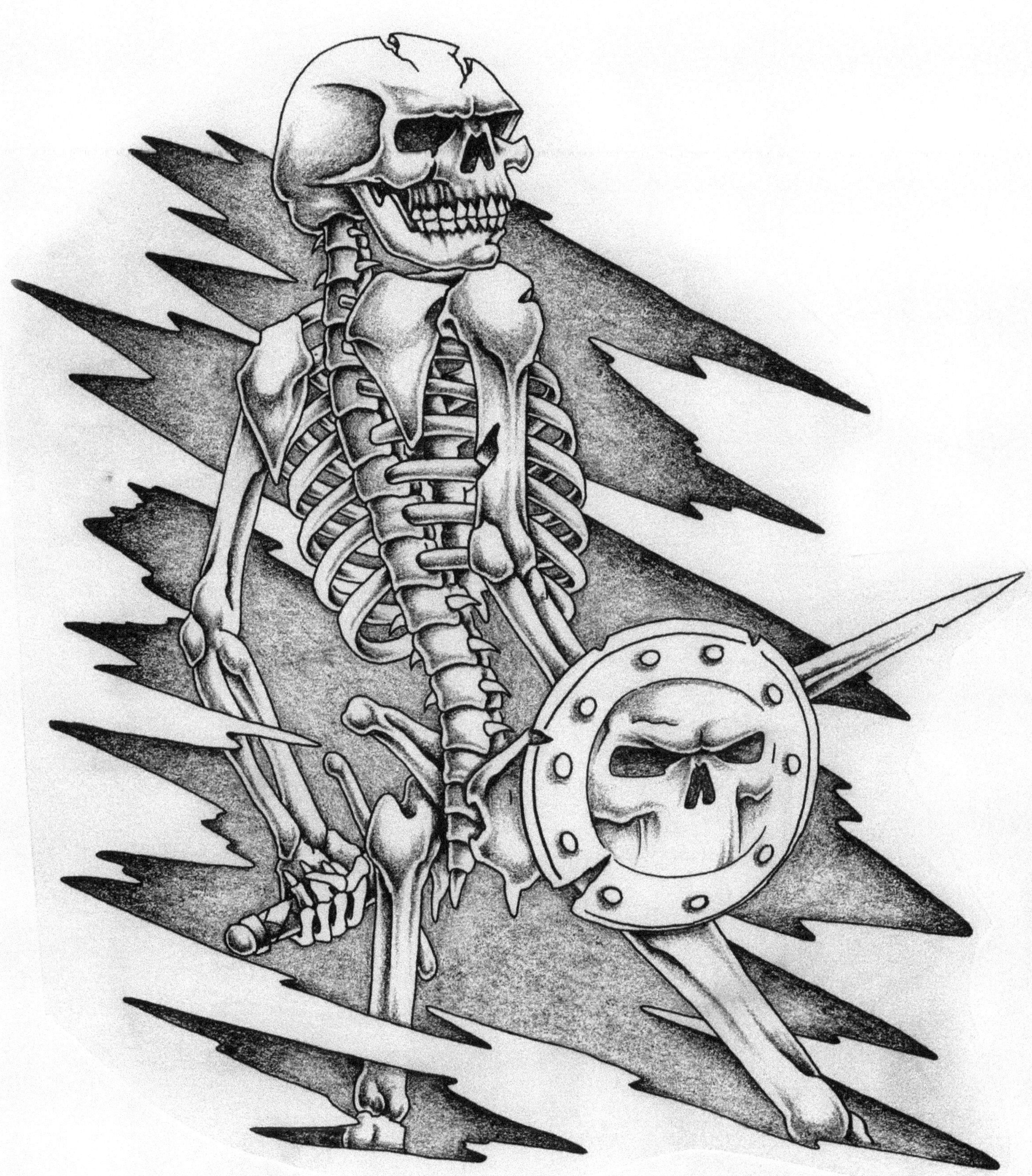

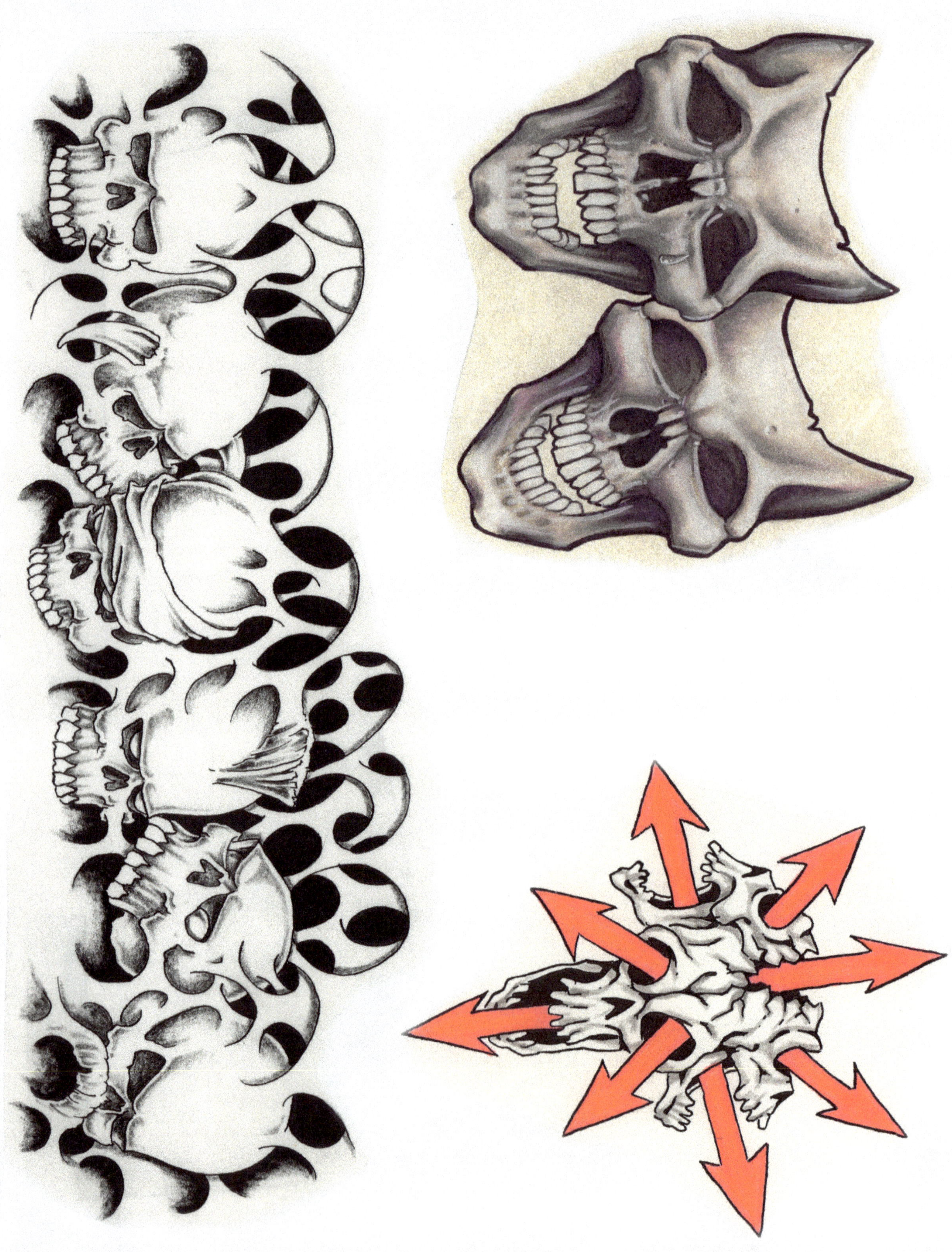

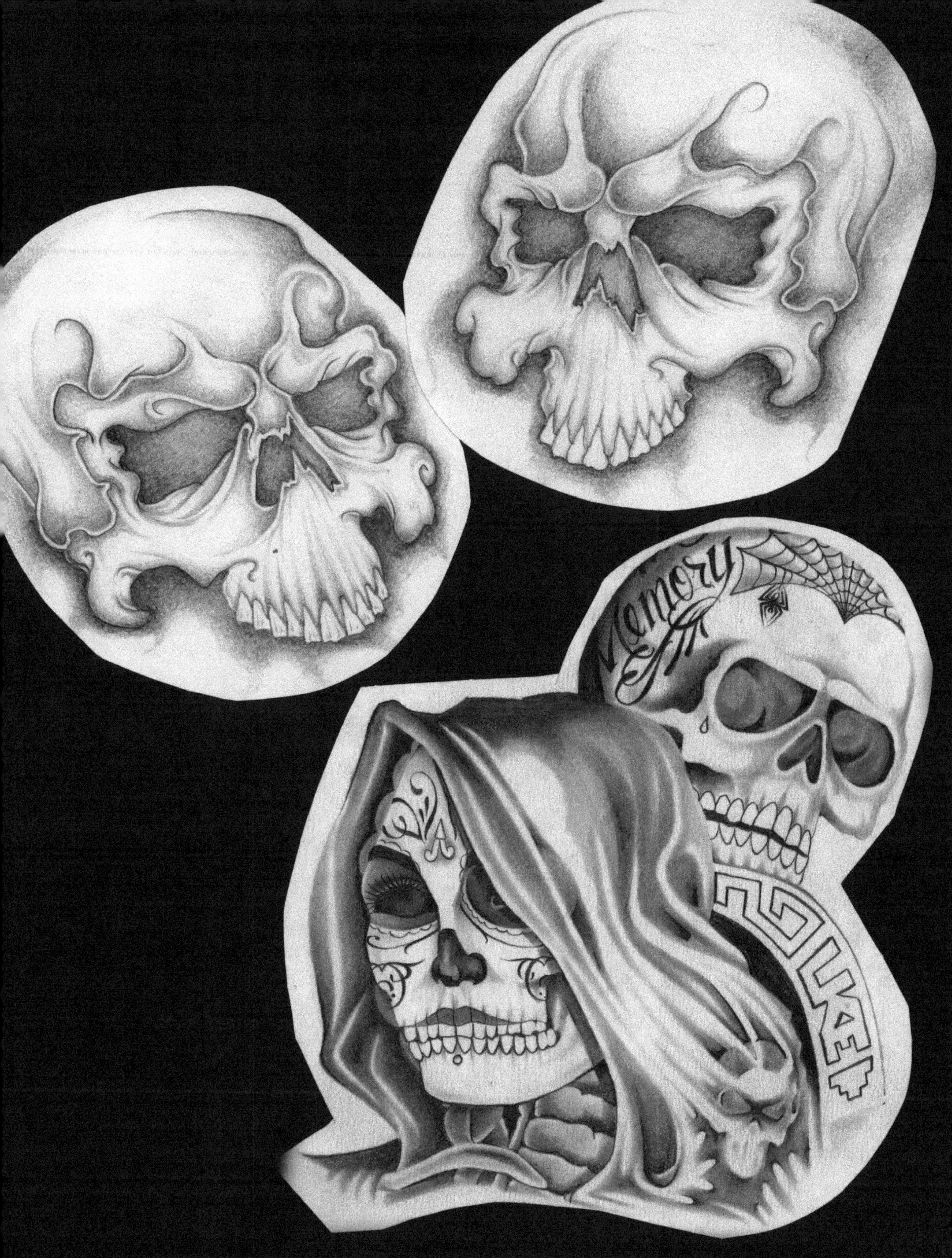
Memory

BUTTERFLIES

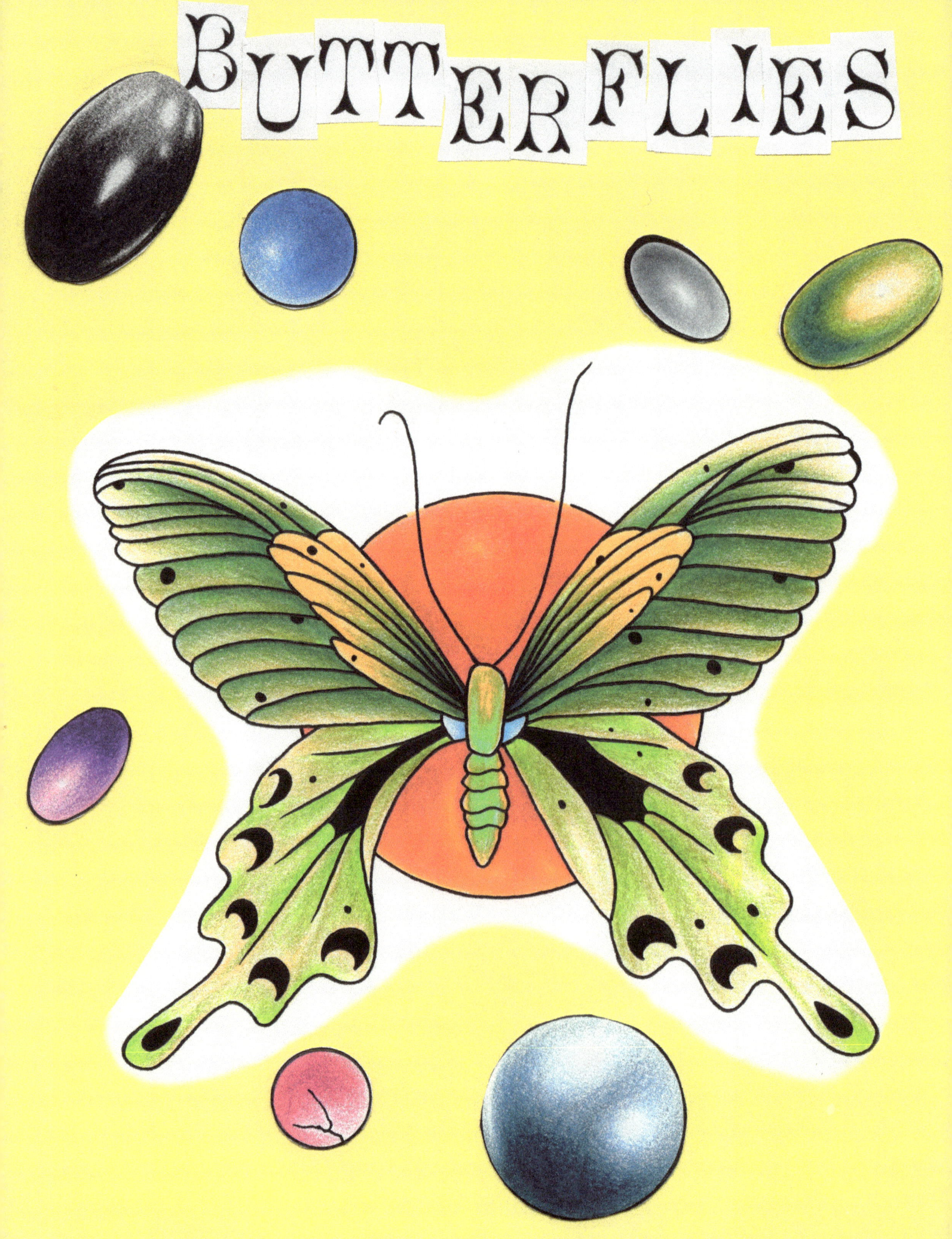

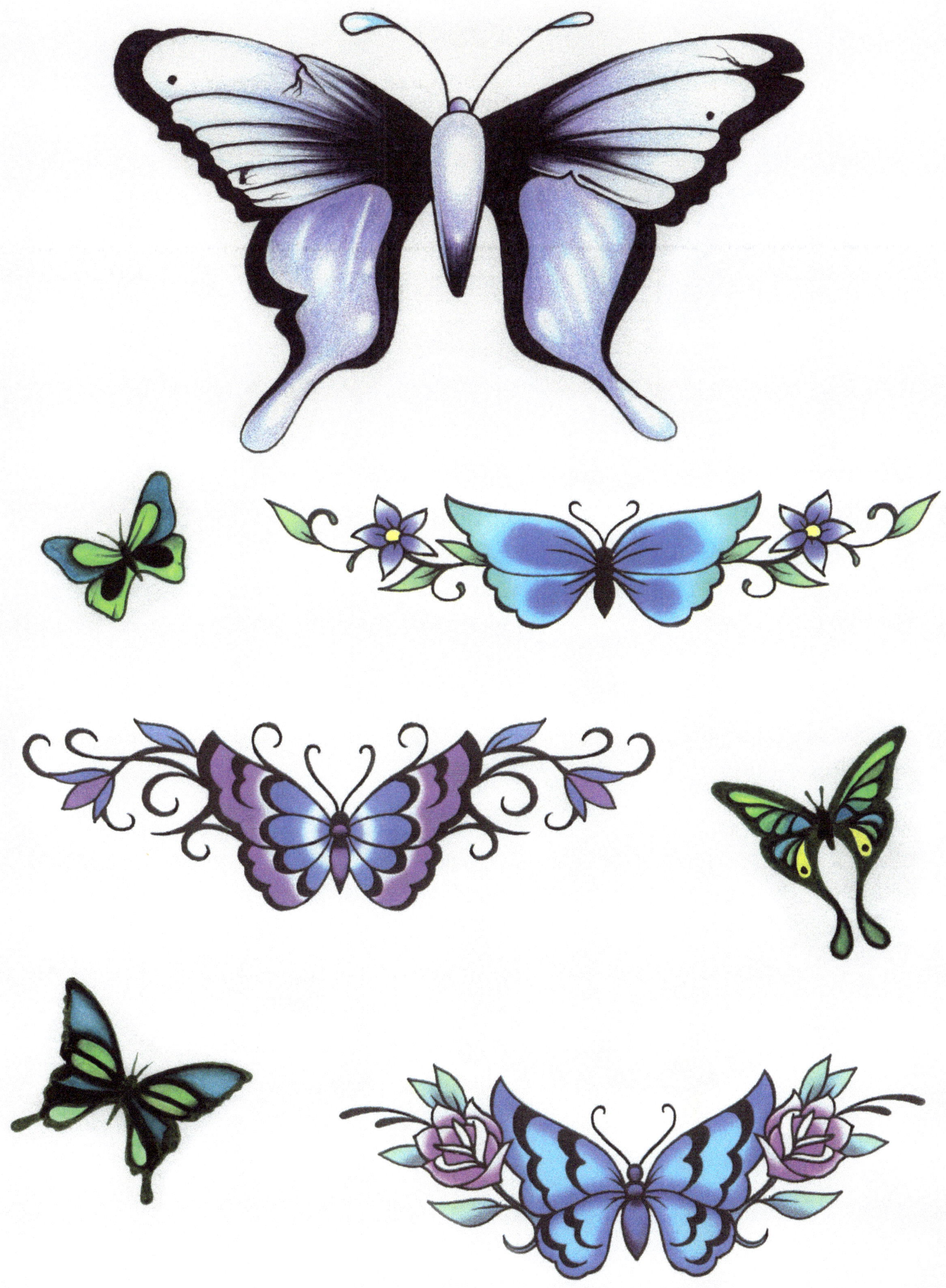

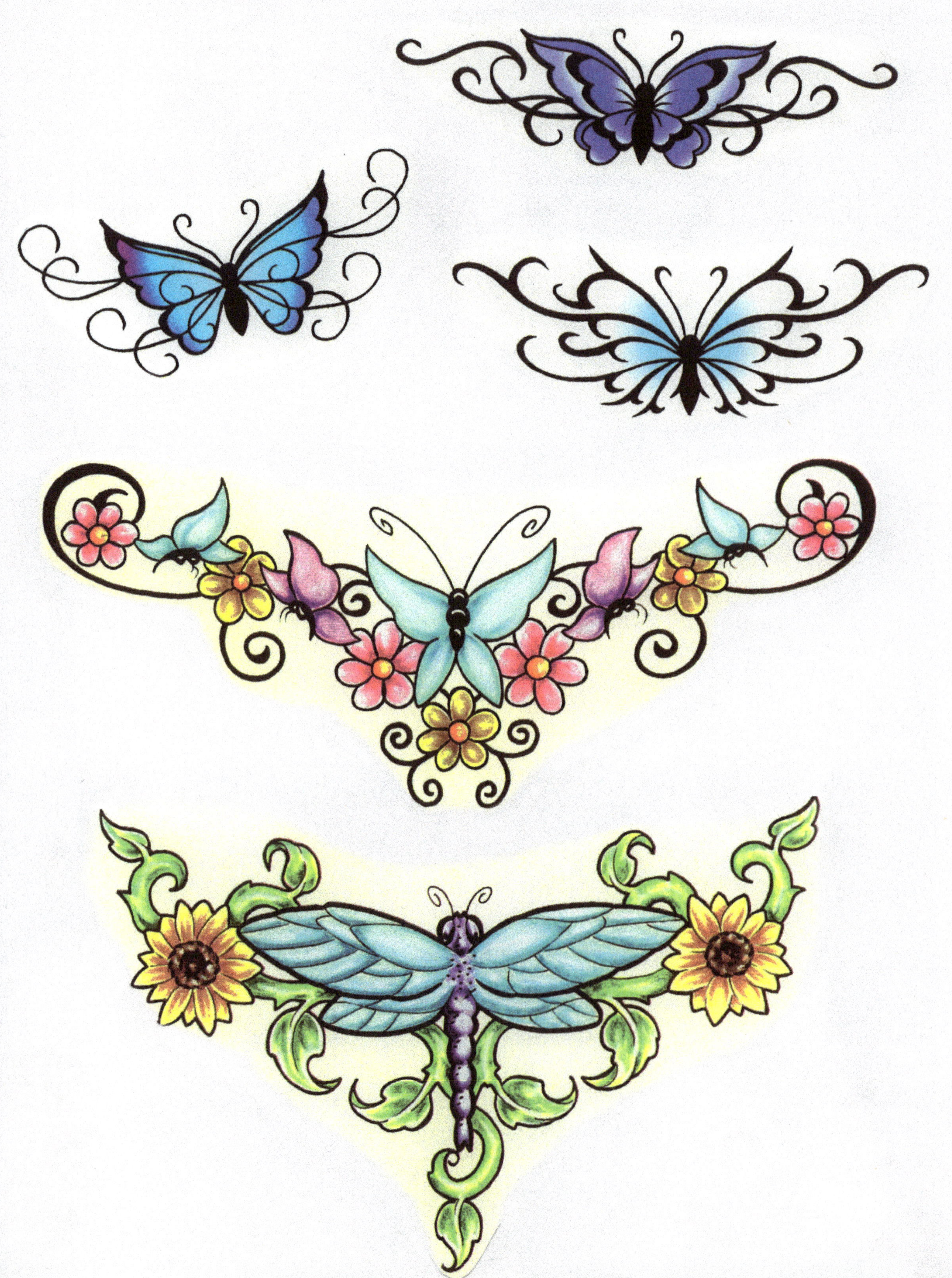

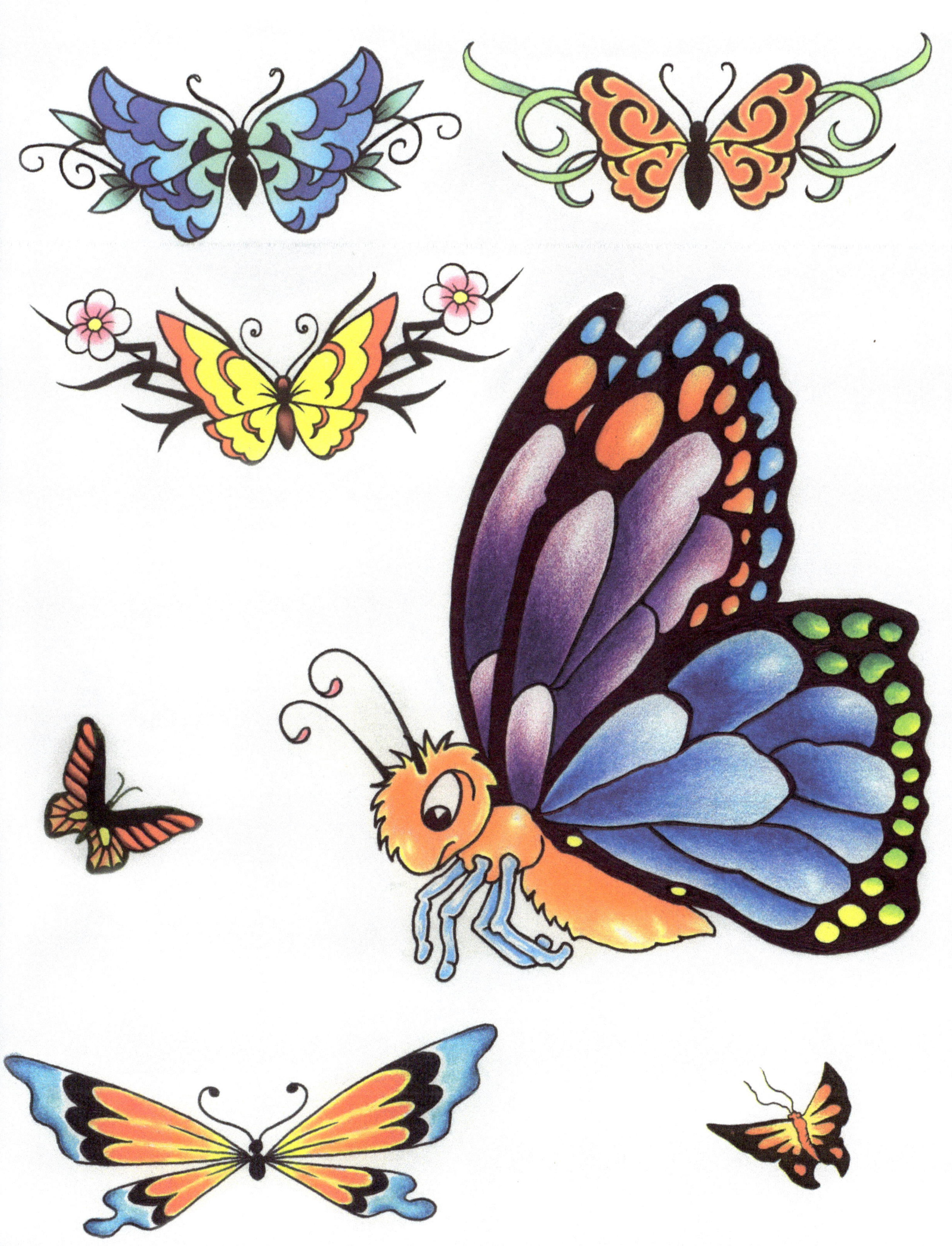

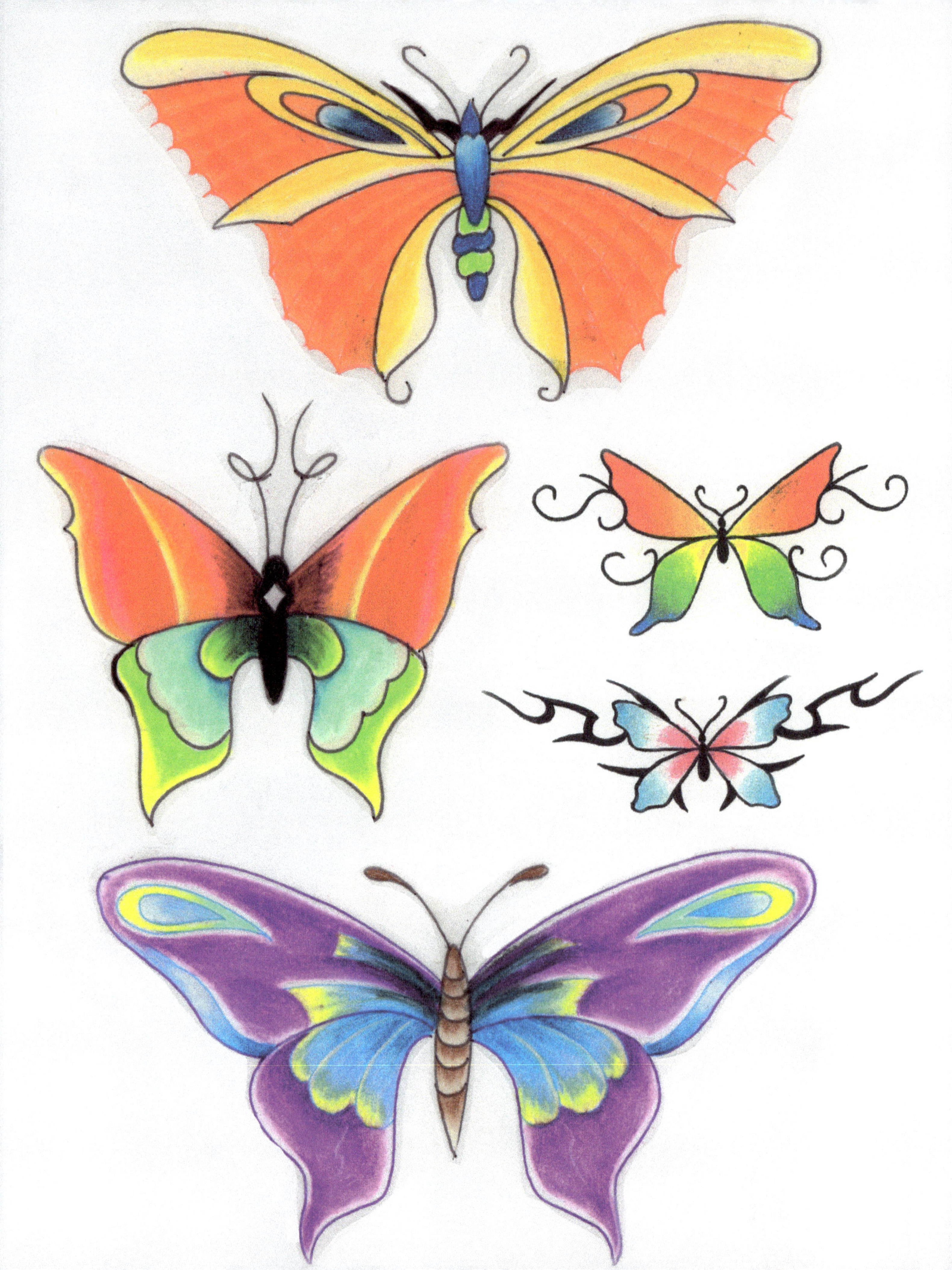

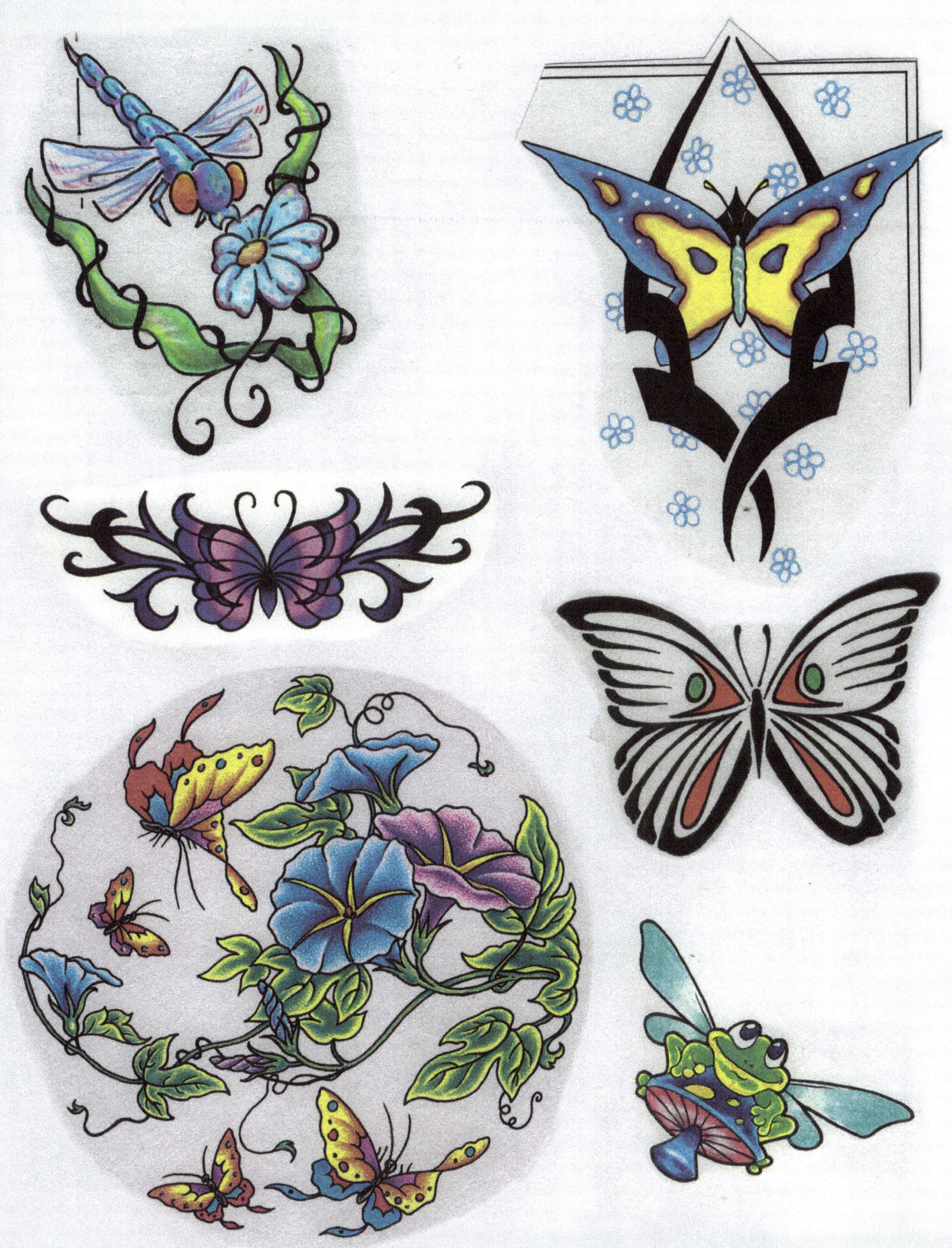

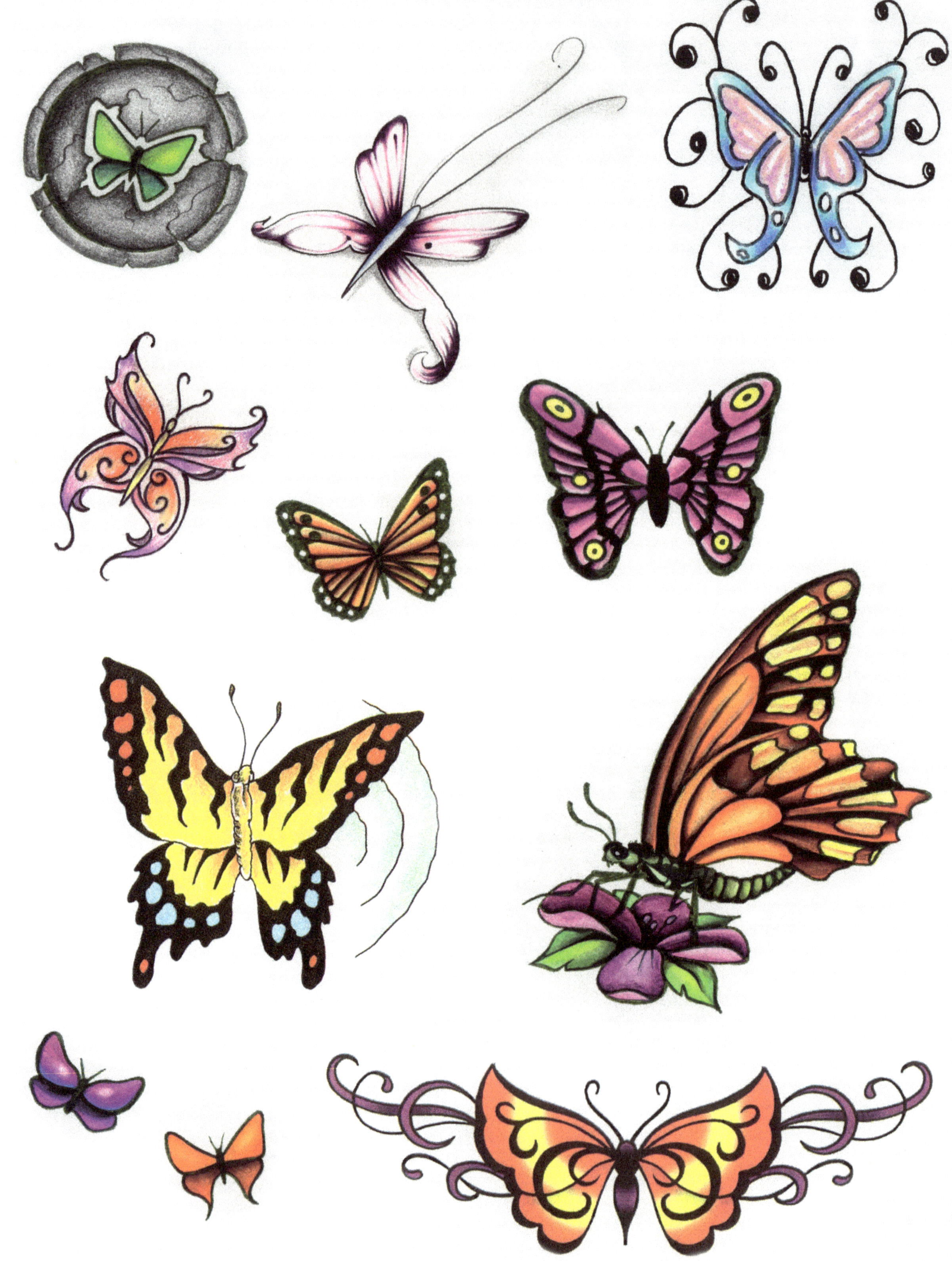

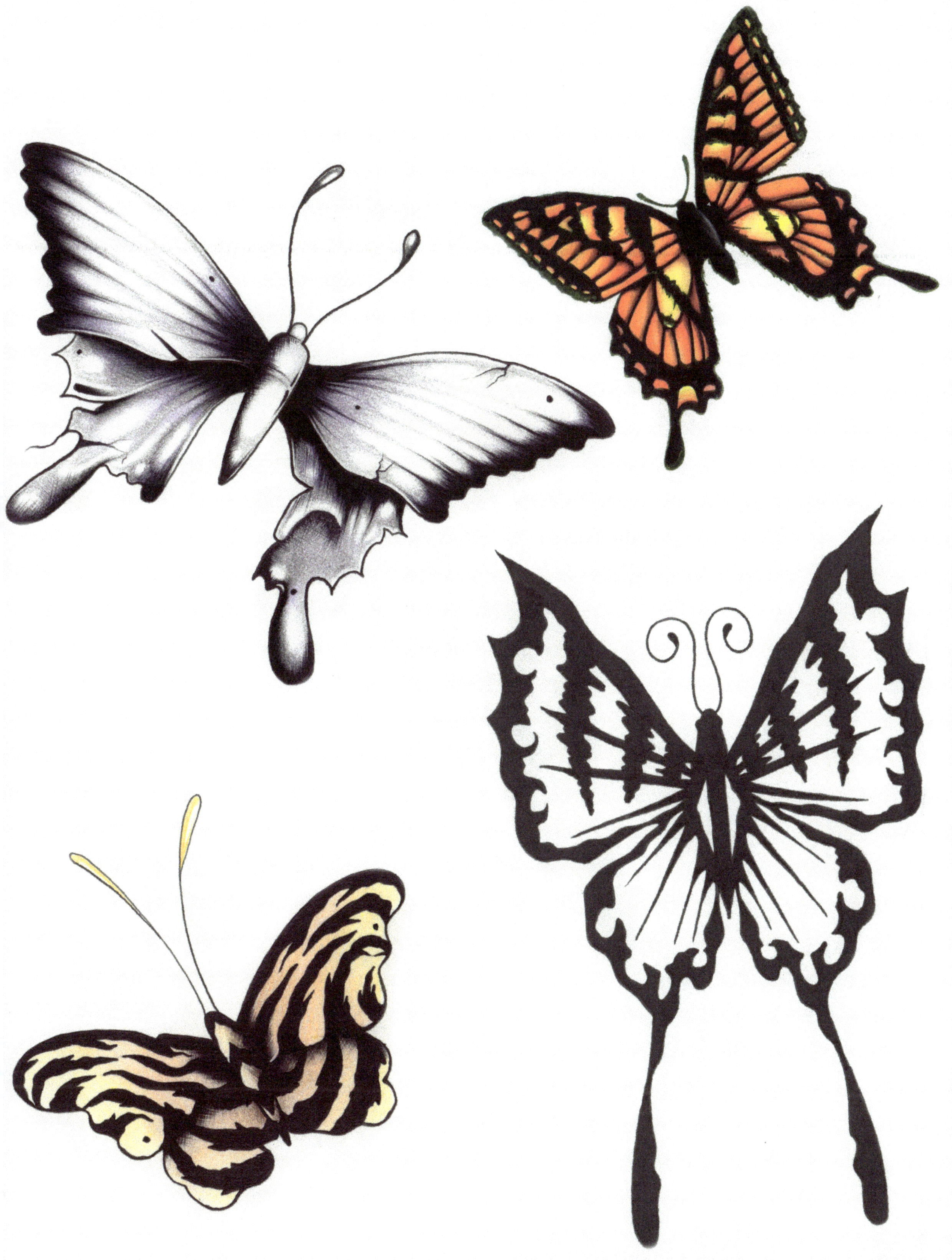

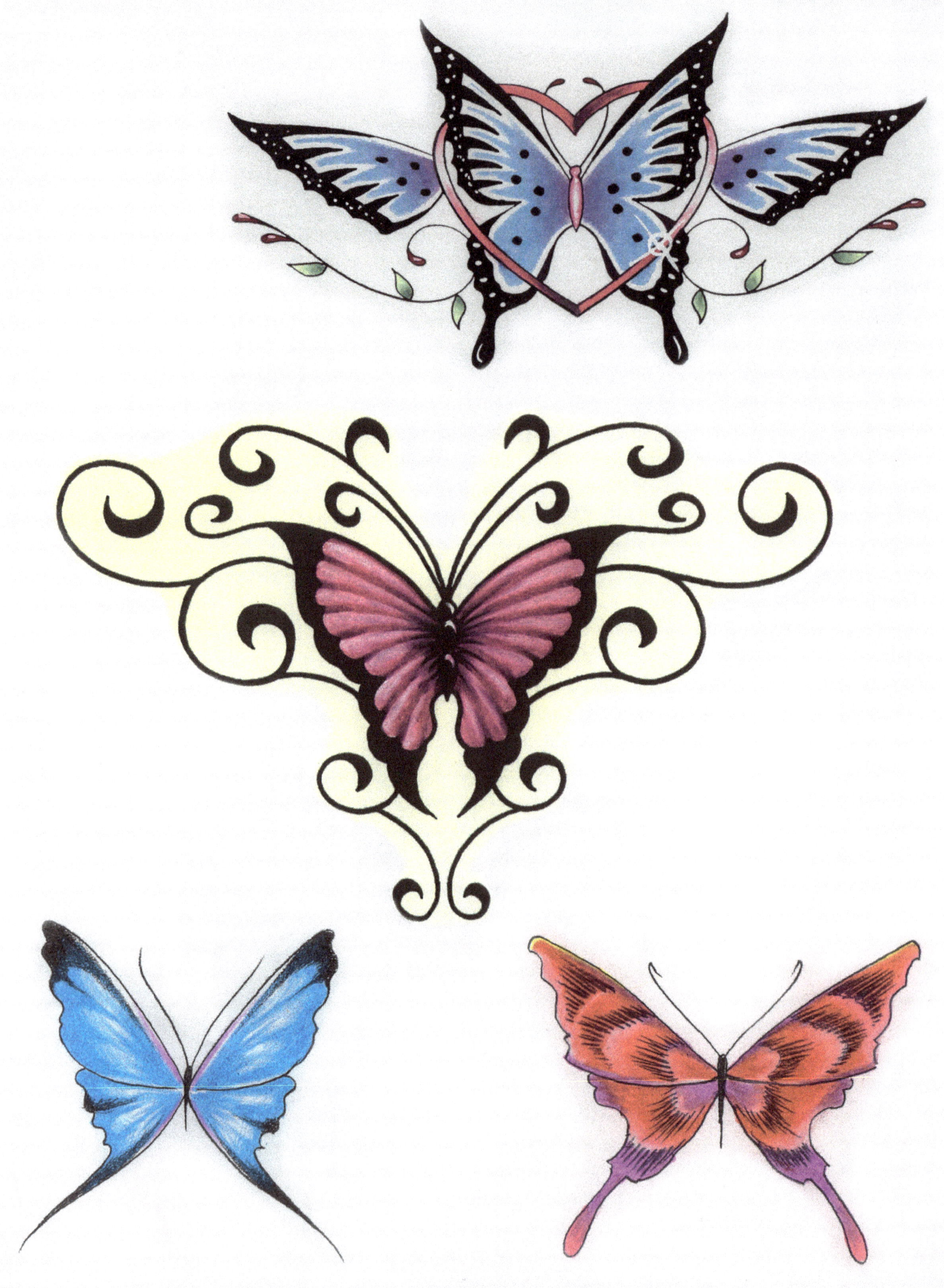

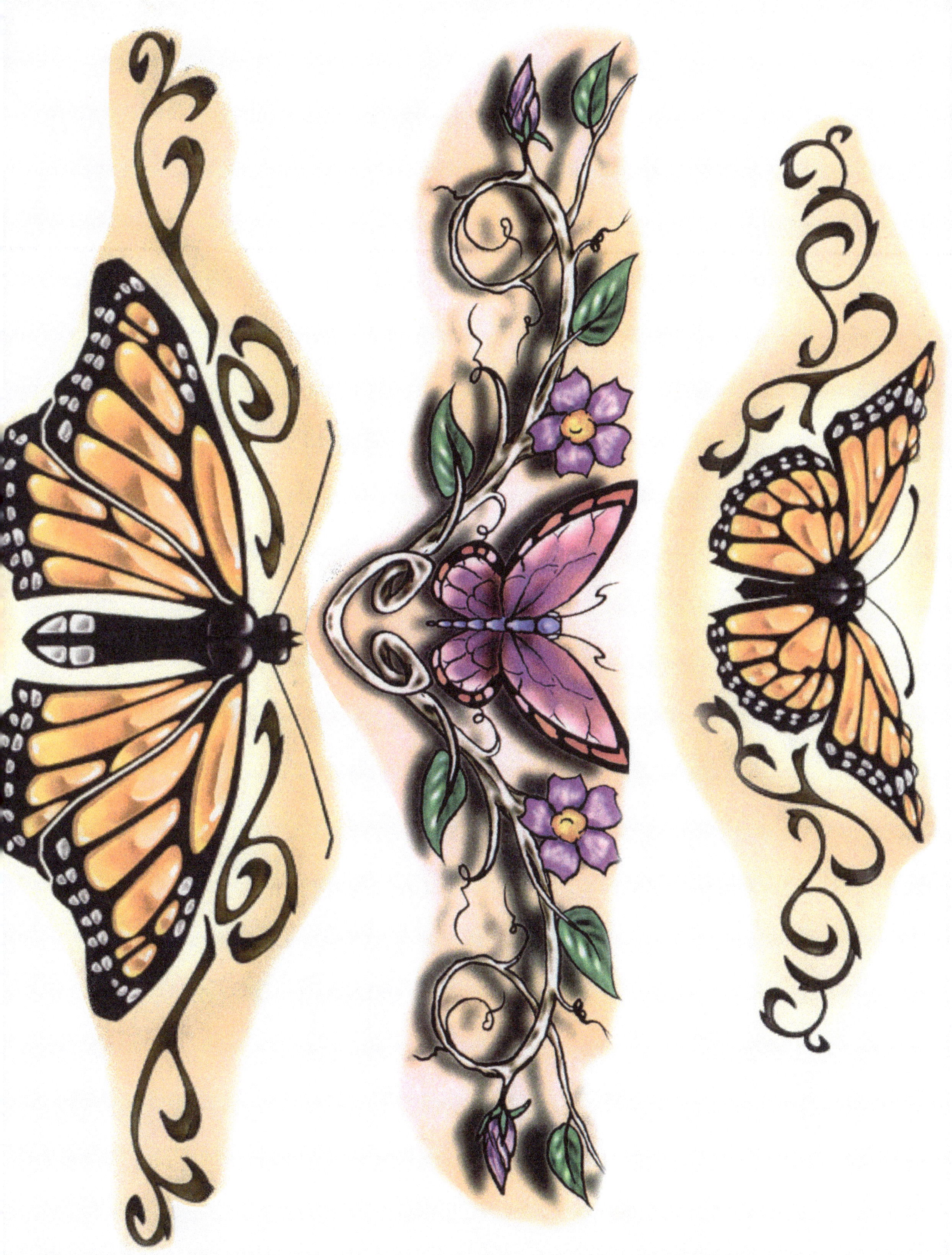

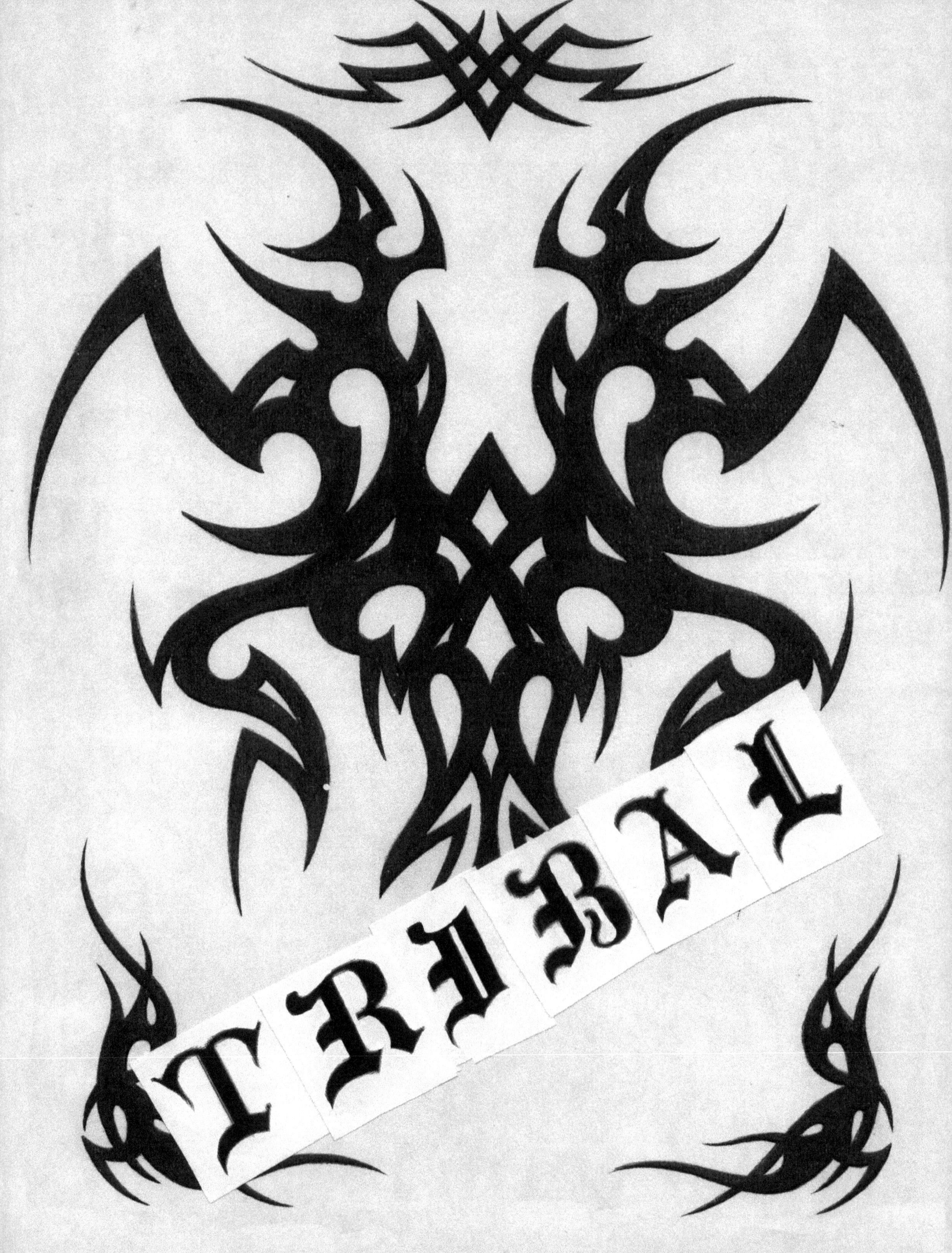

TRIBAL

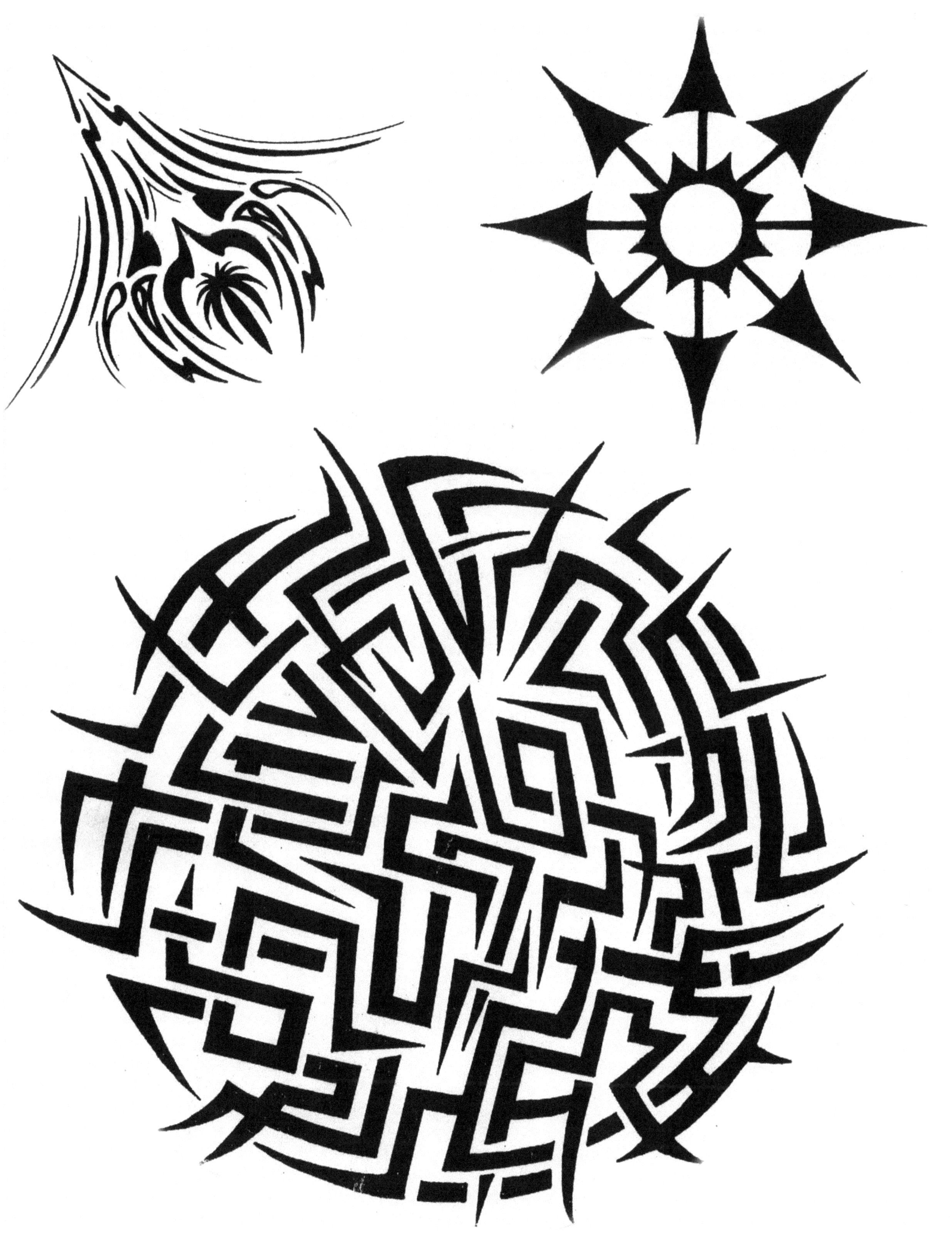

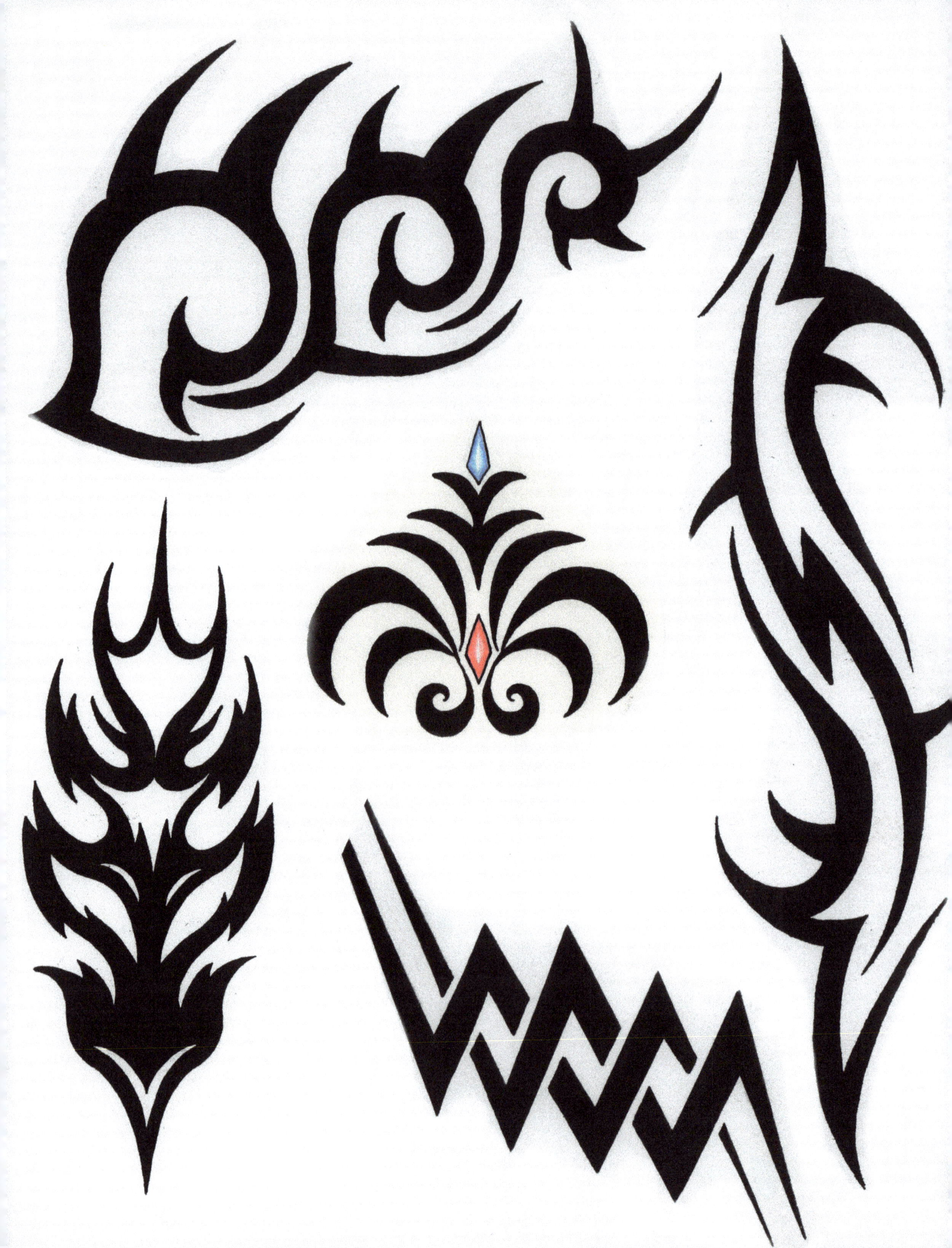

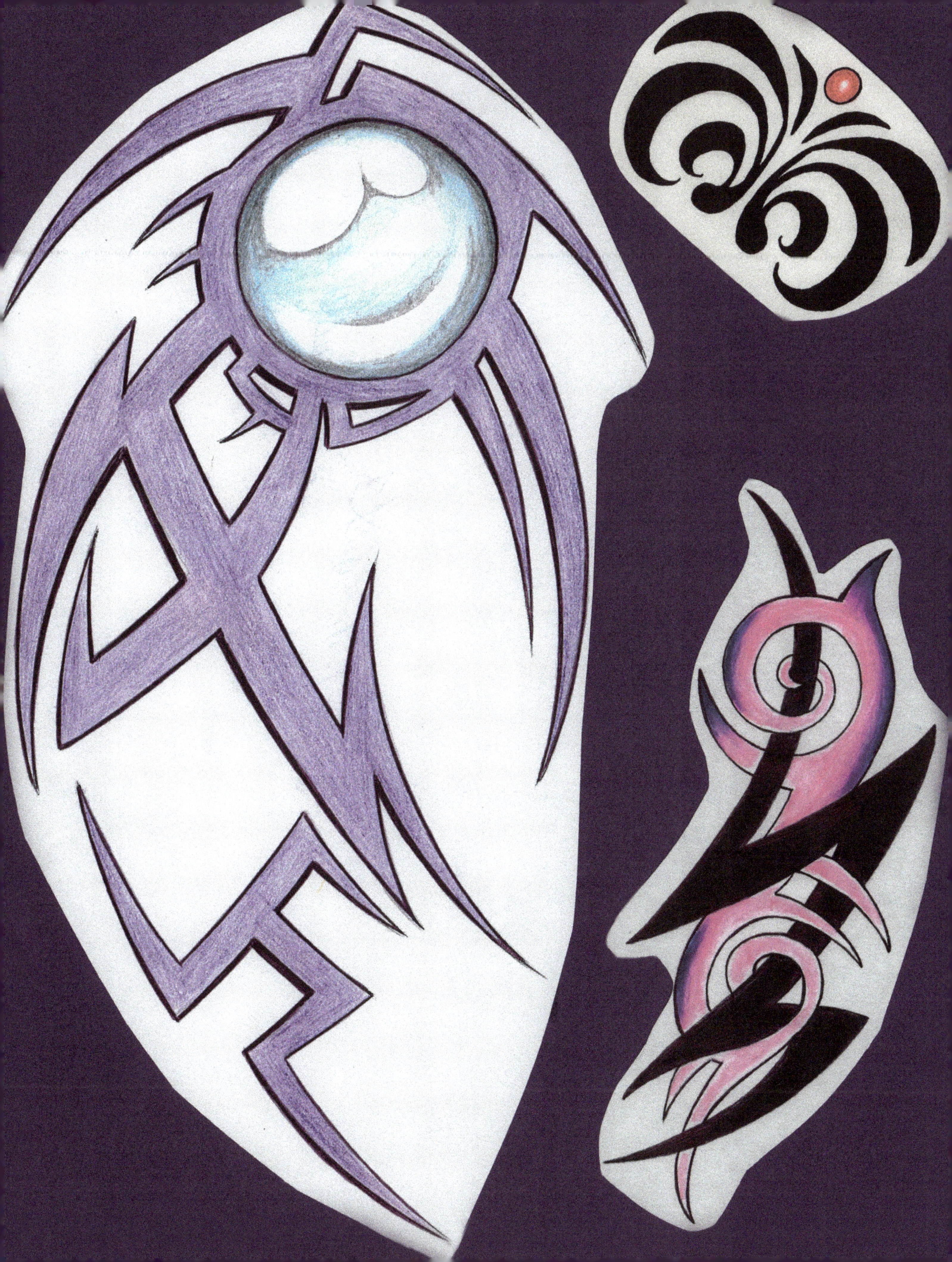

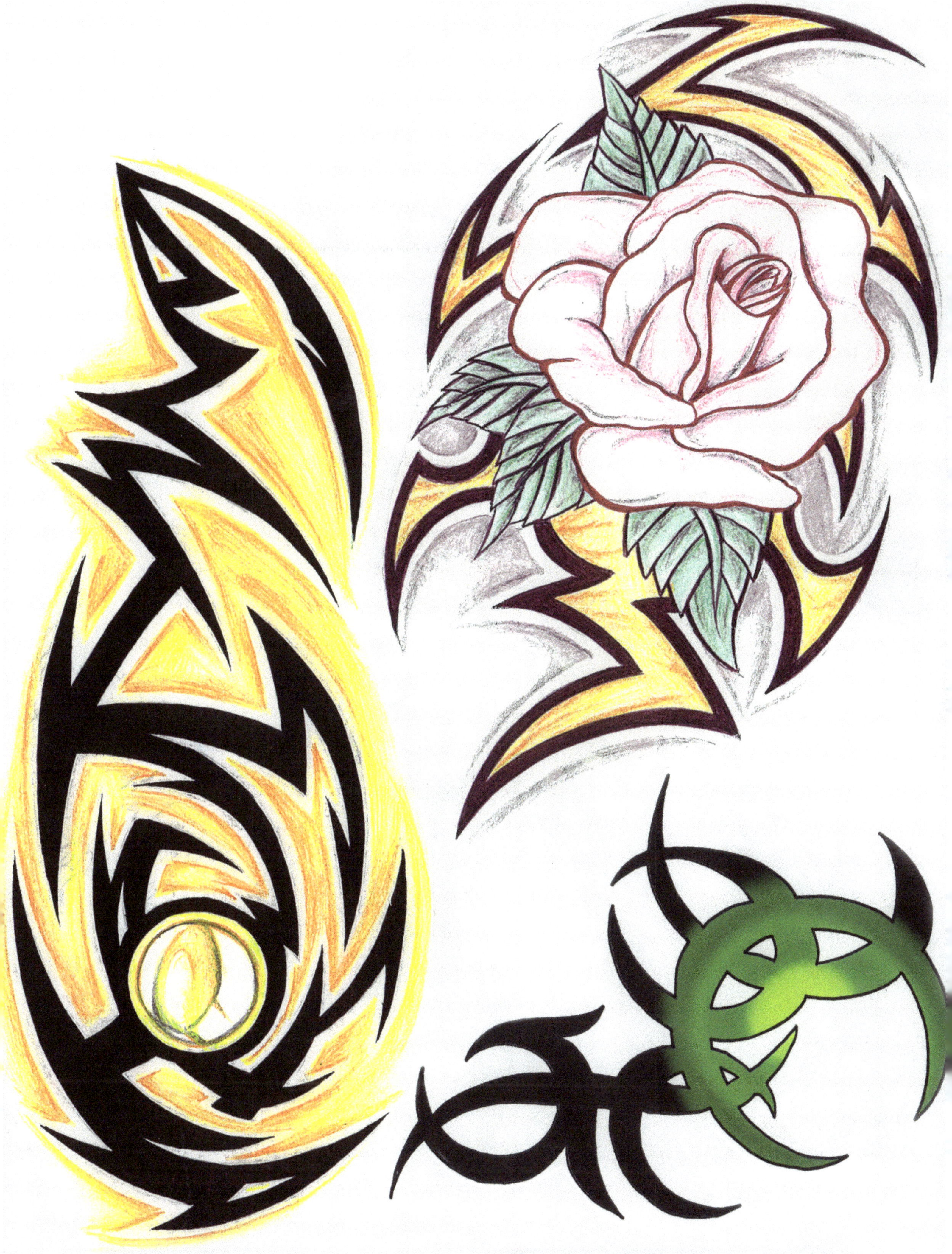

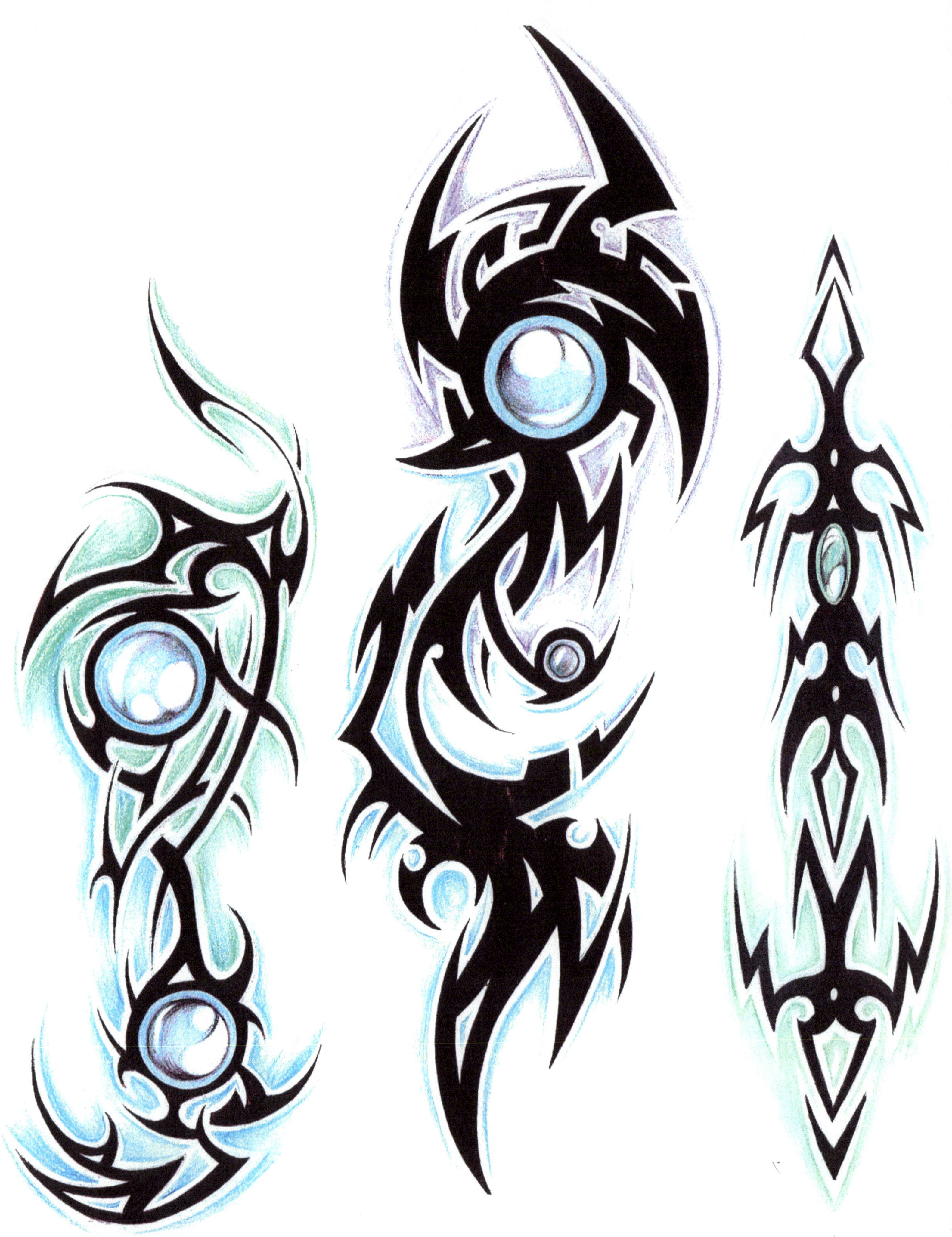

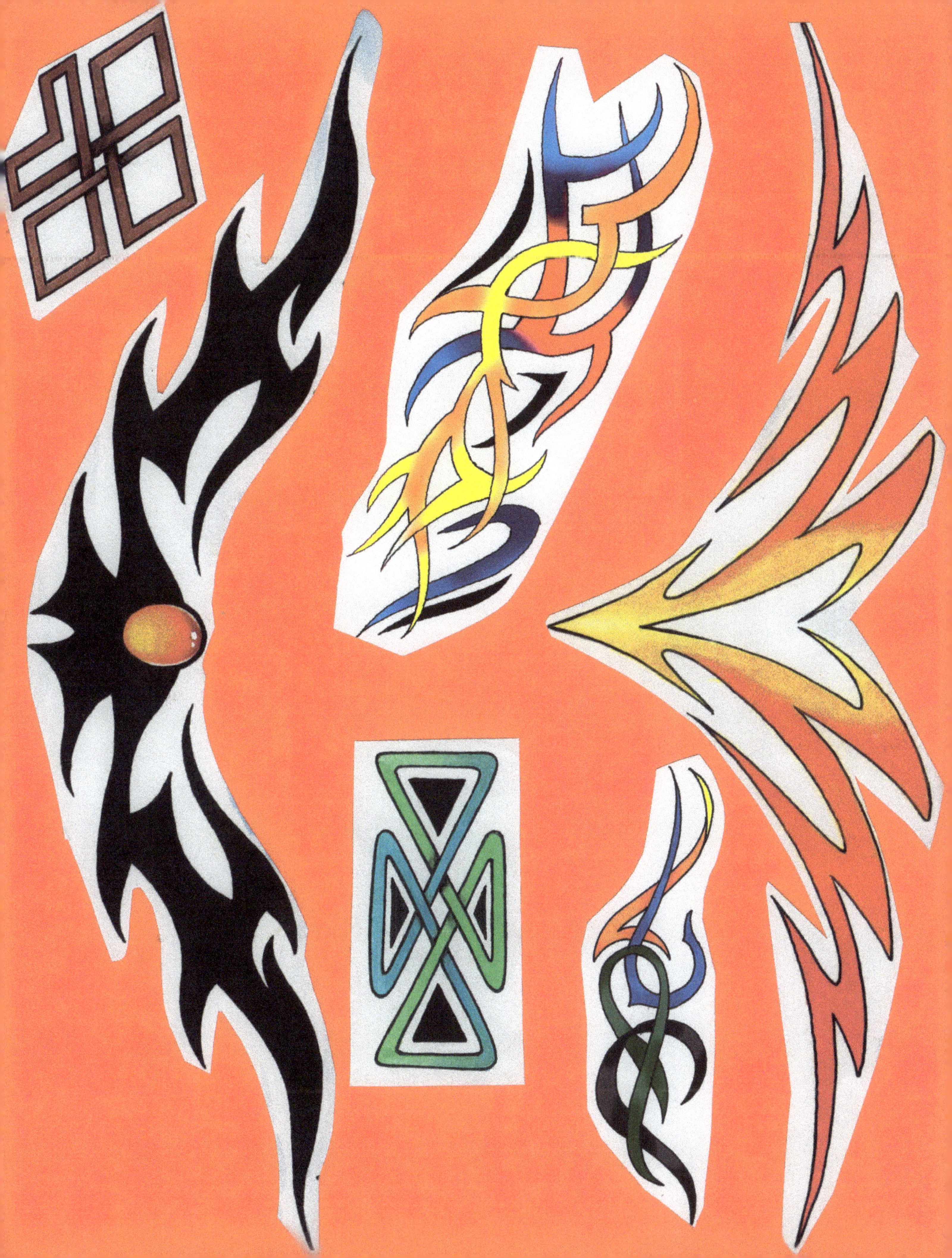

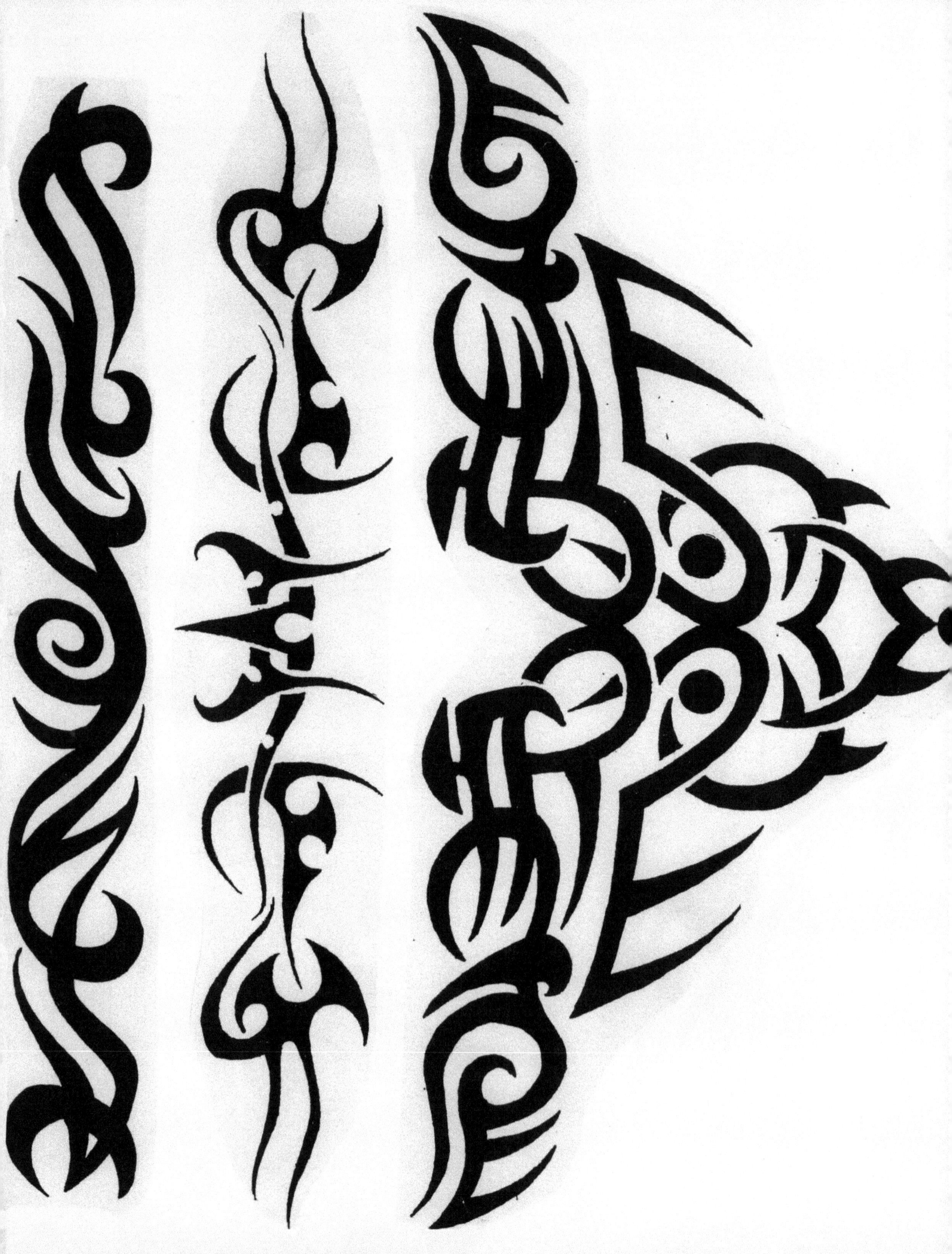

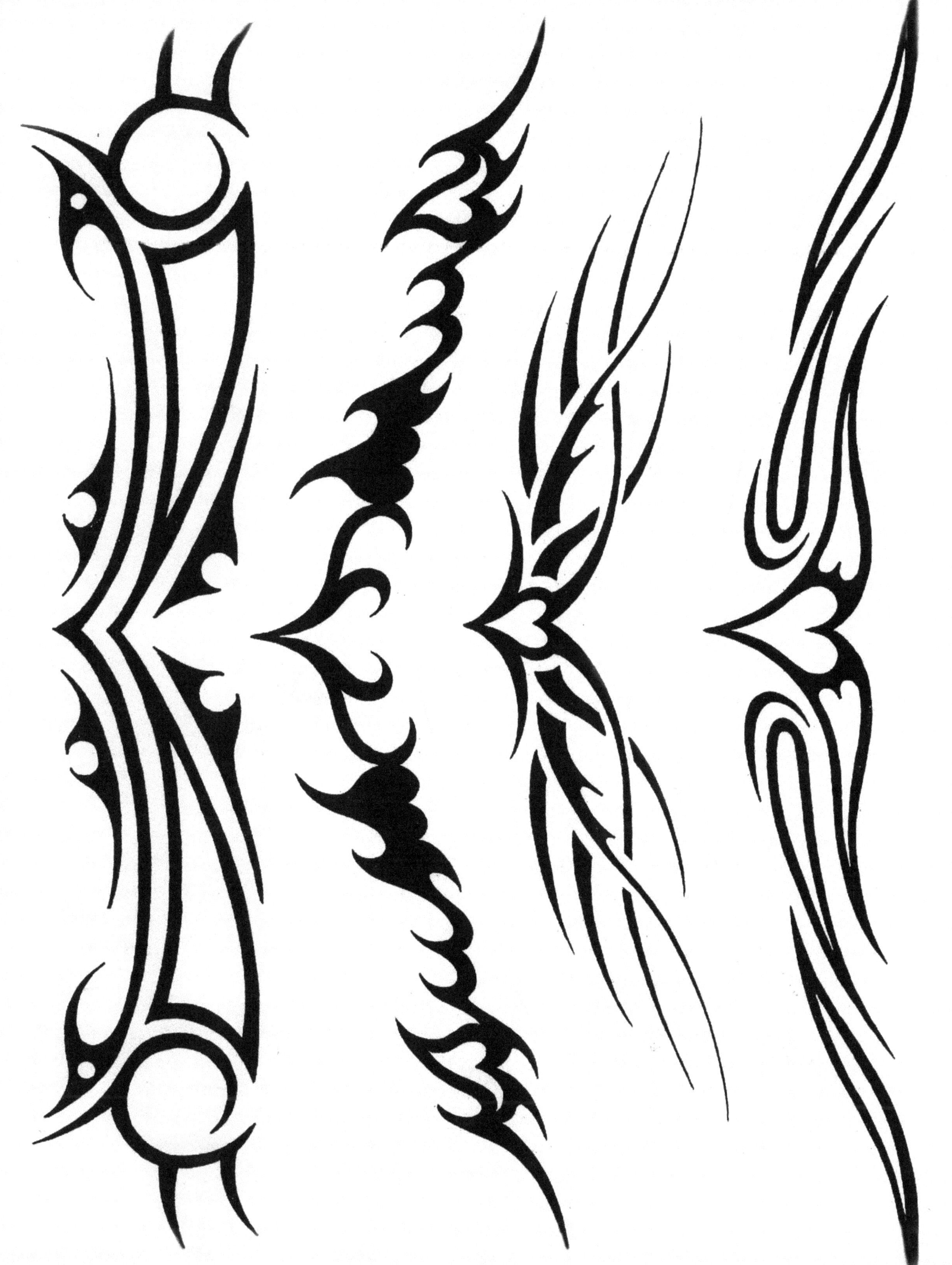

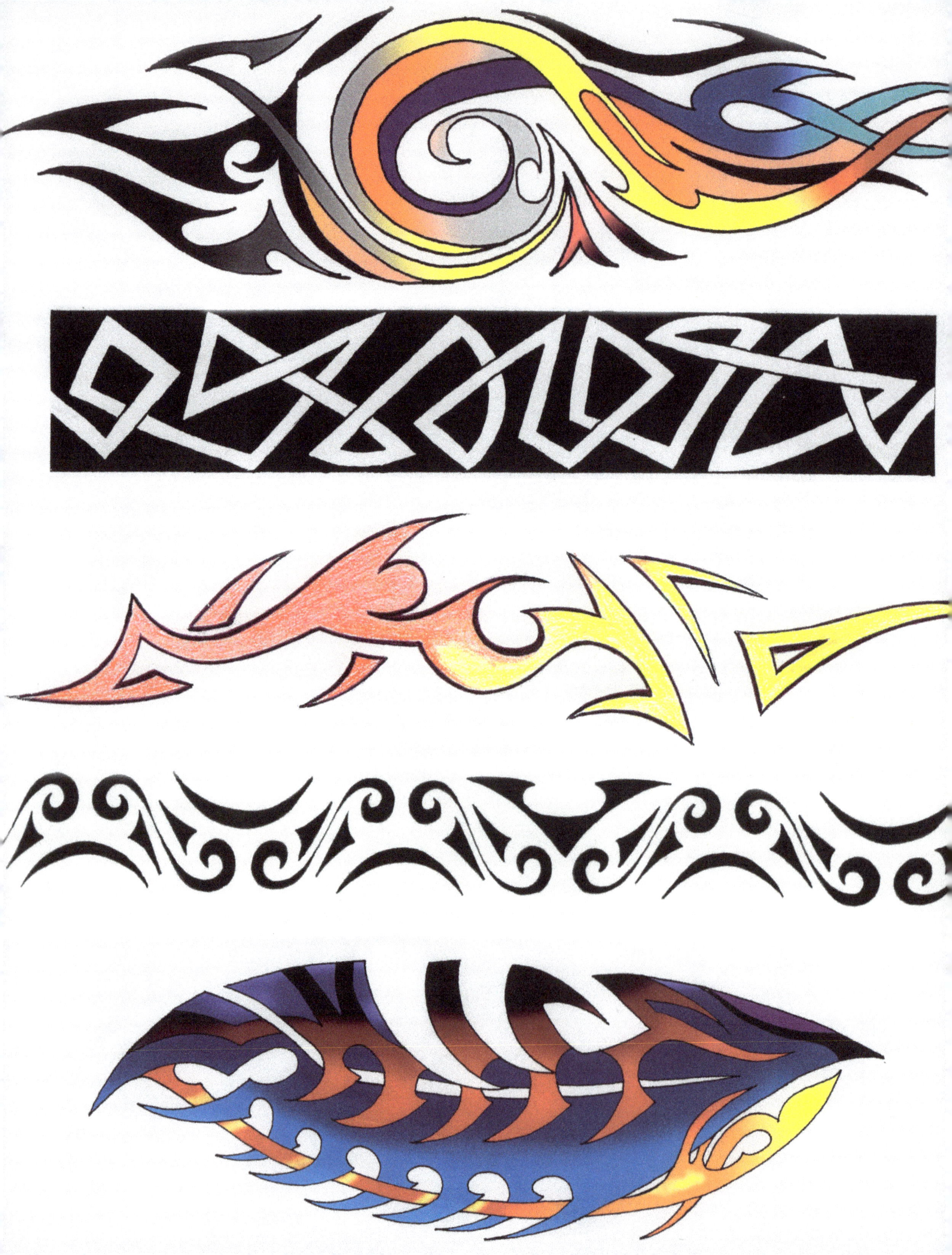

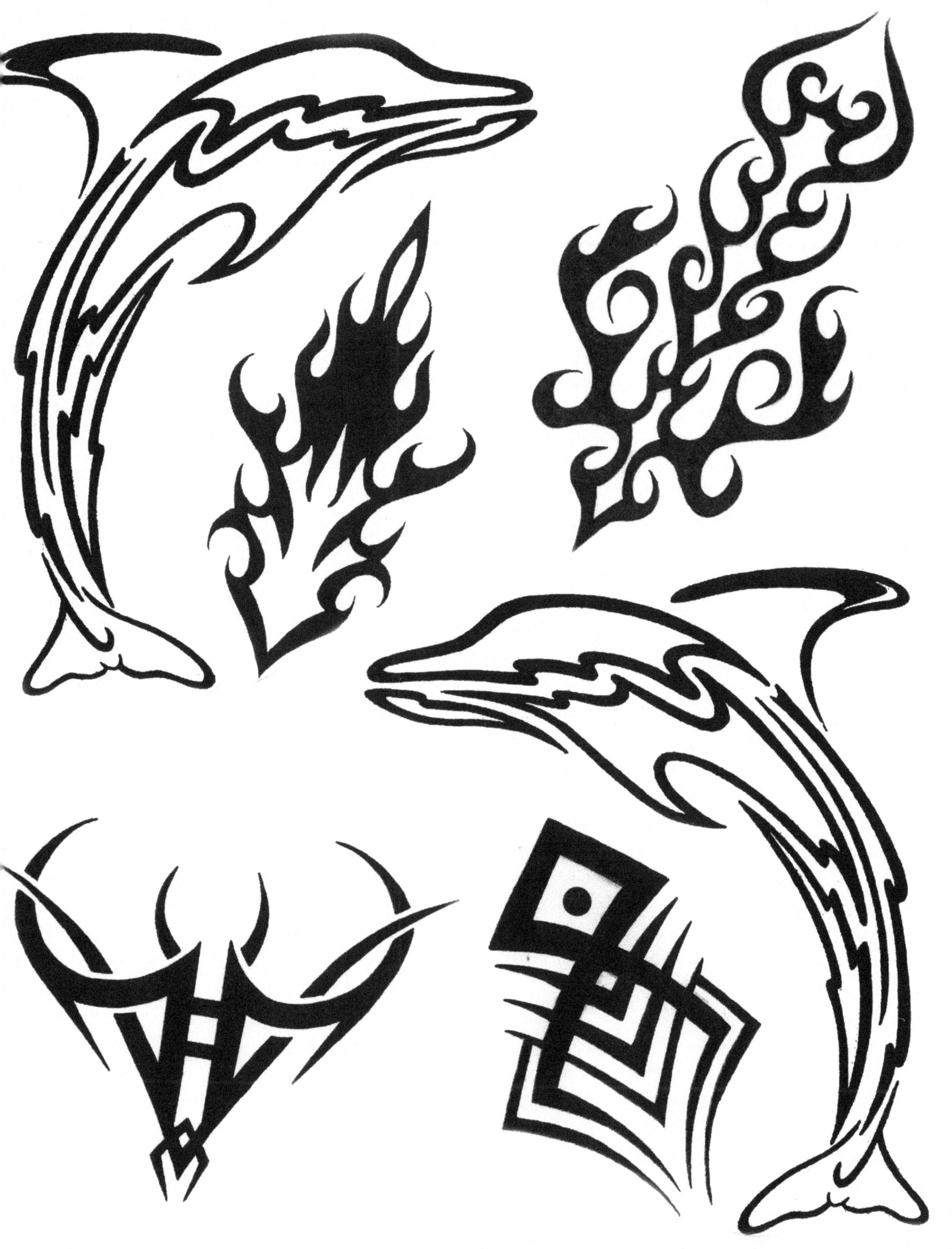

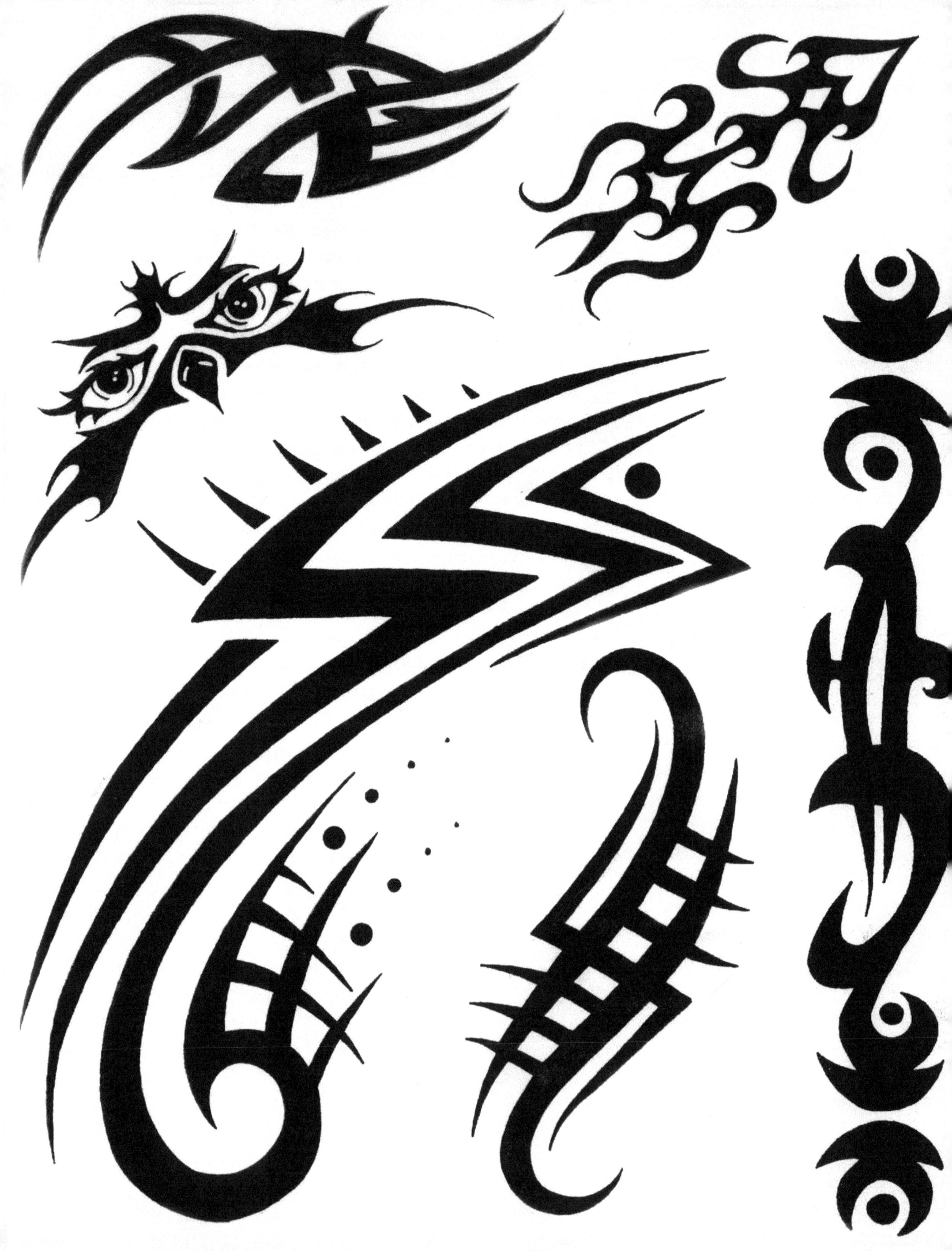

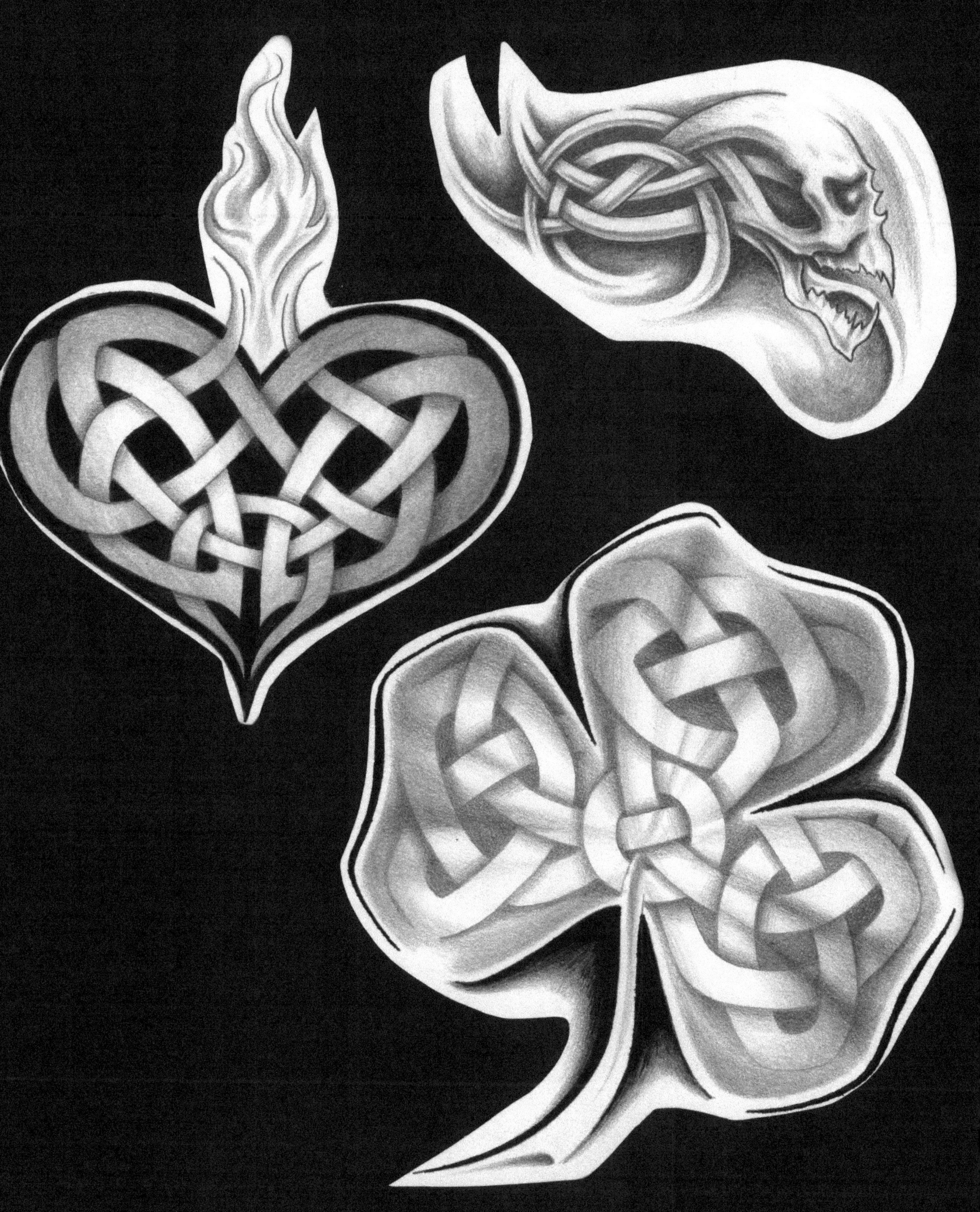

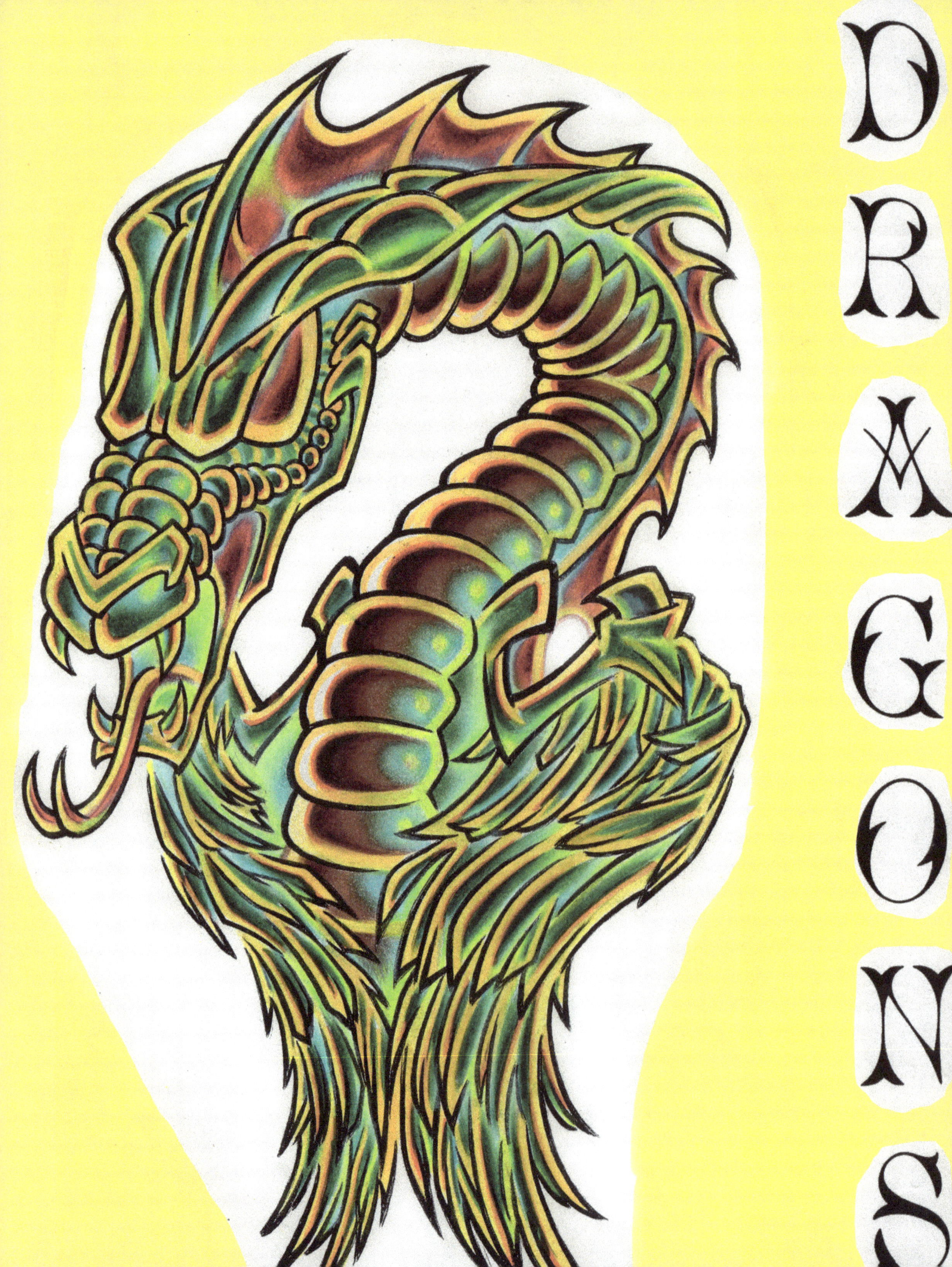

DRAGONS

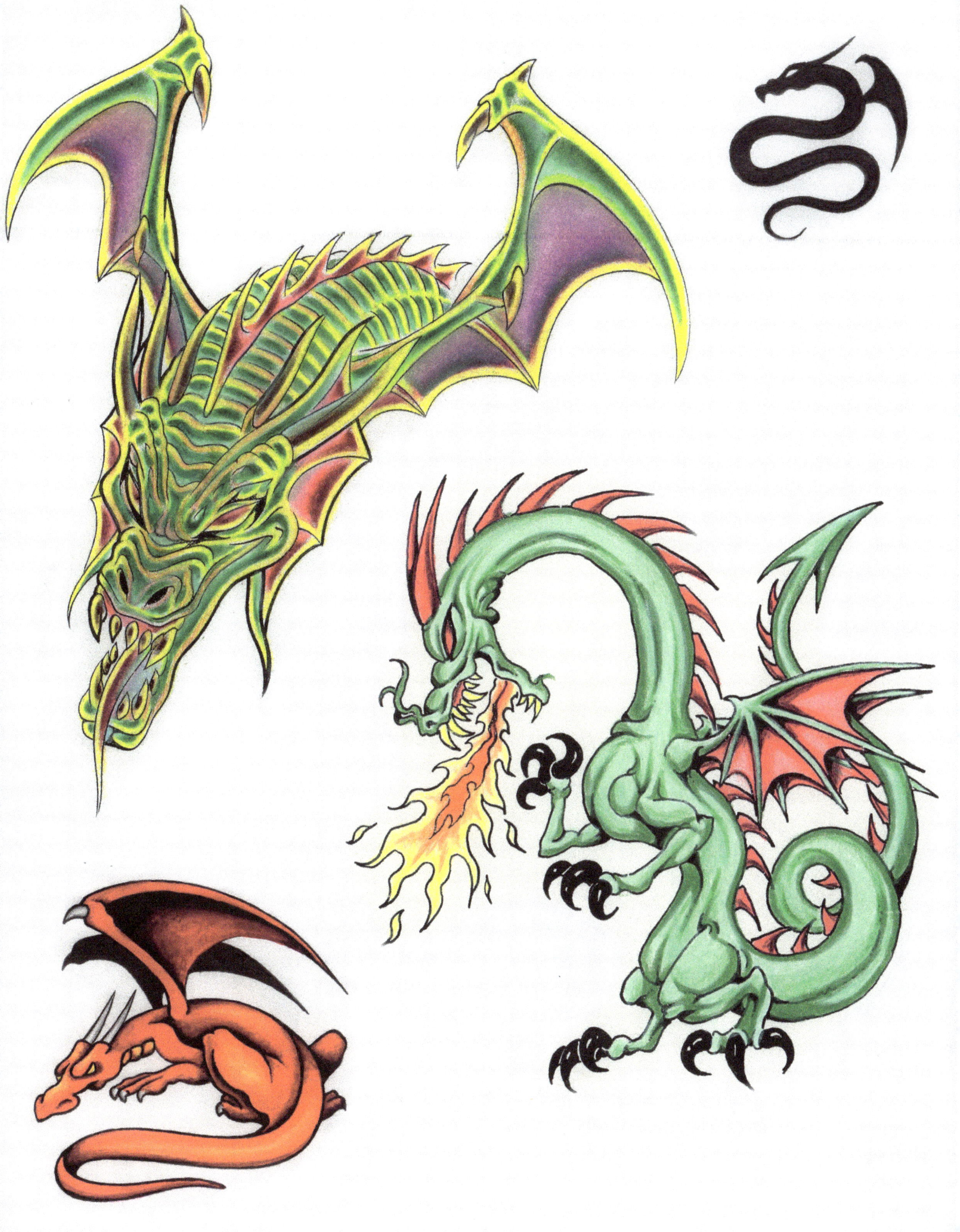

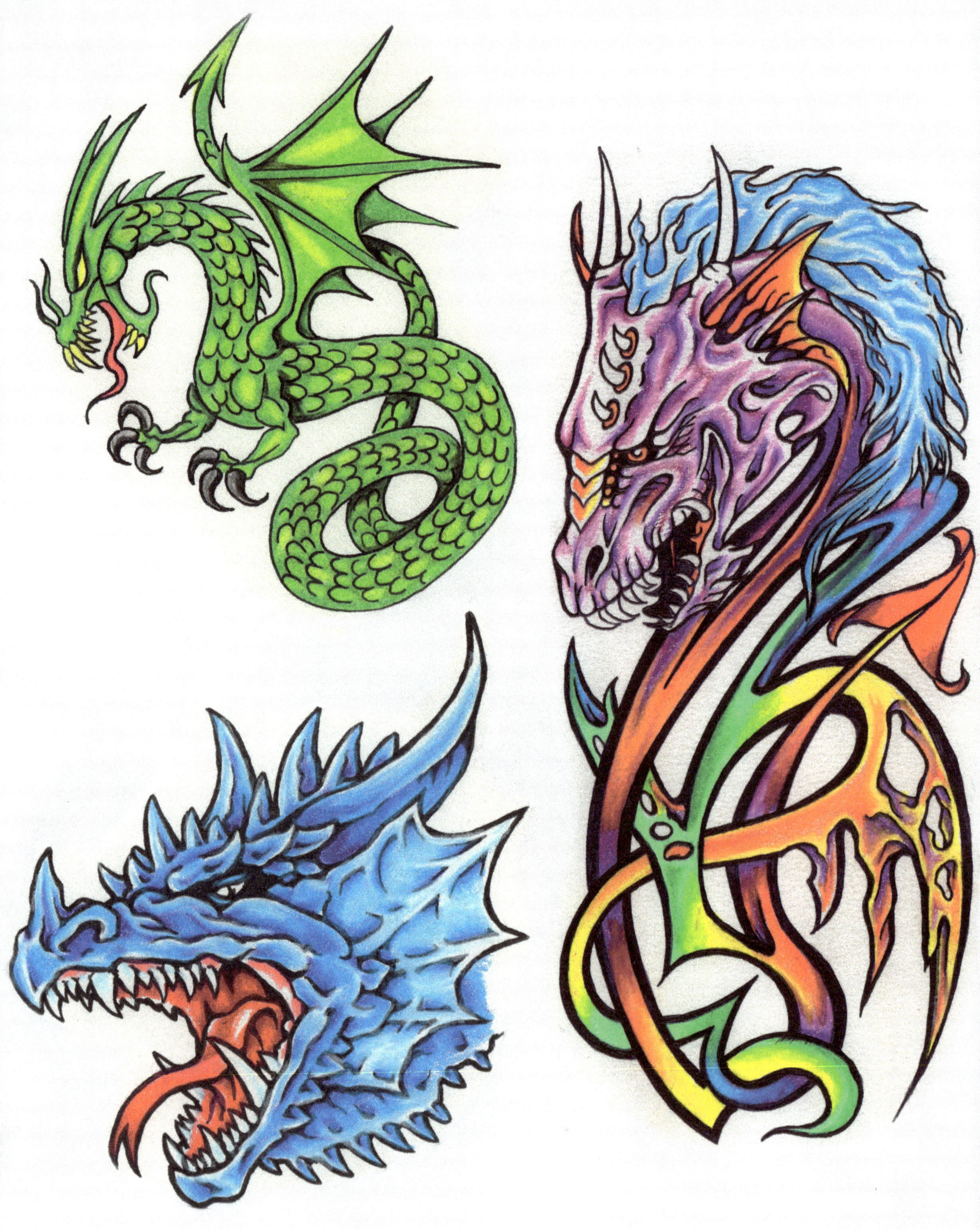

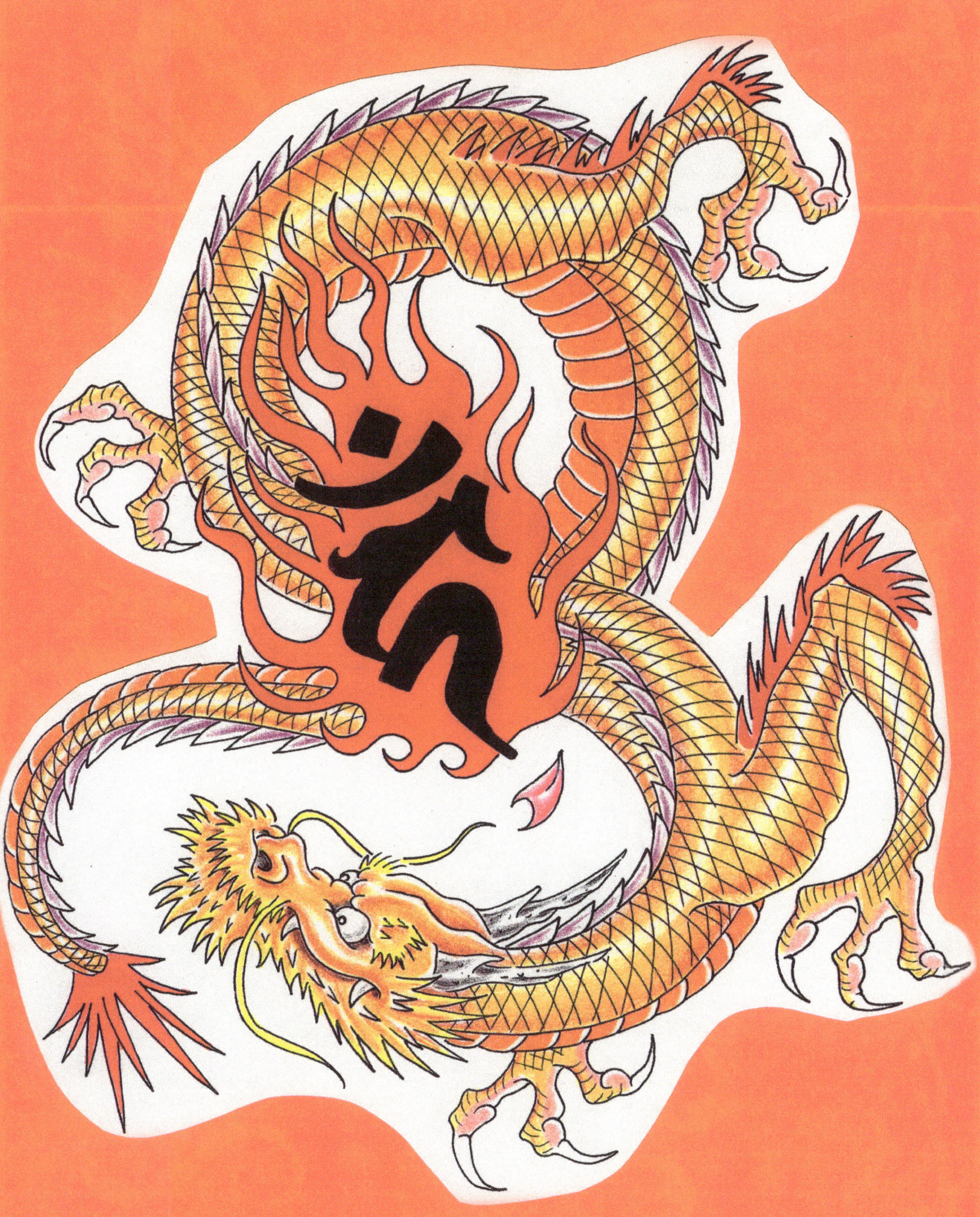

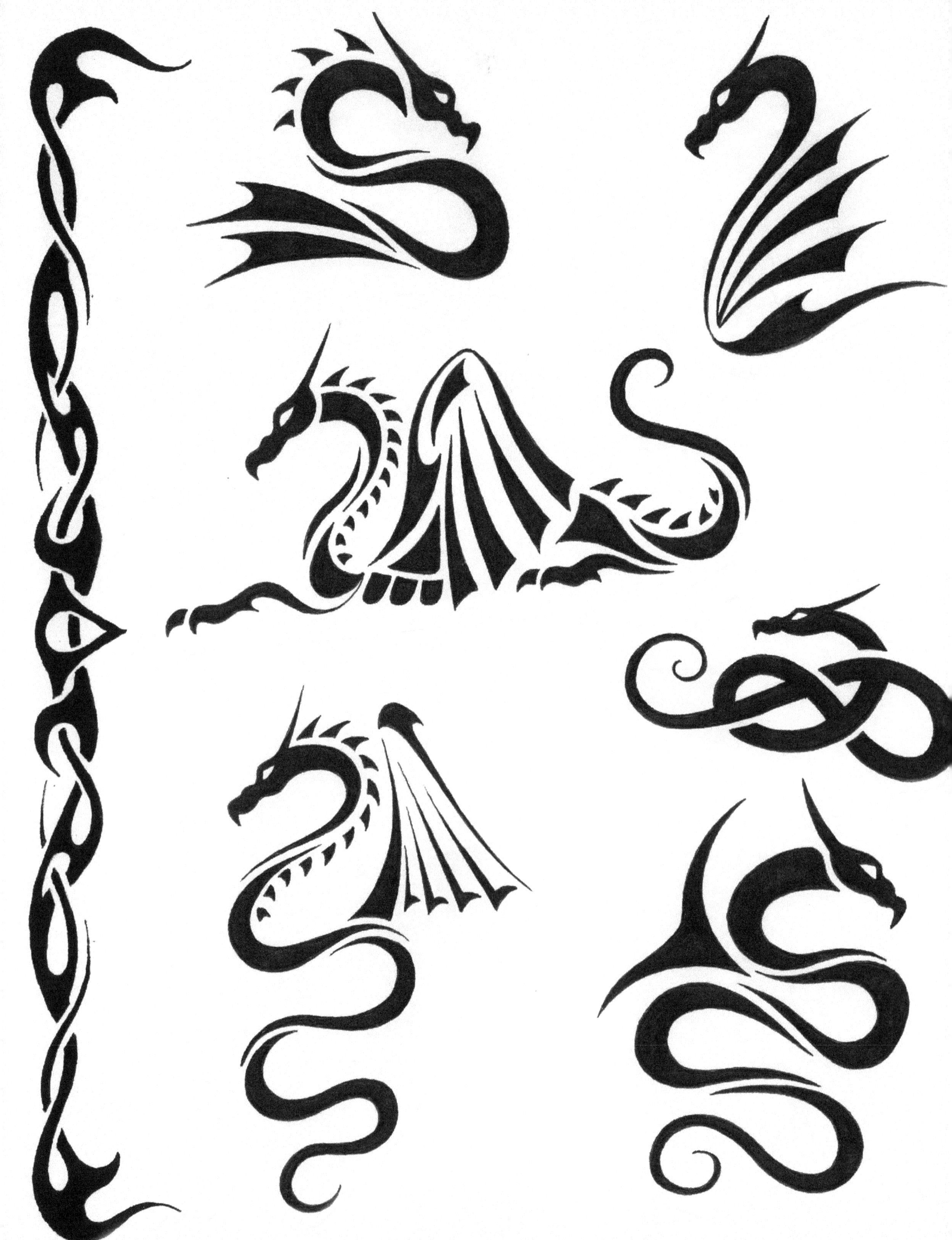

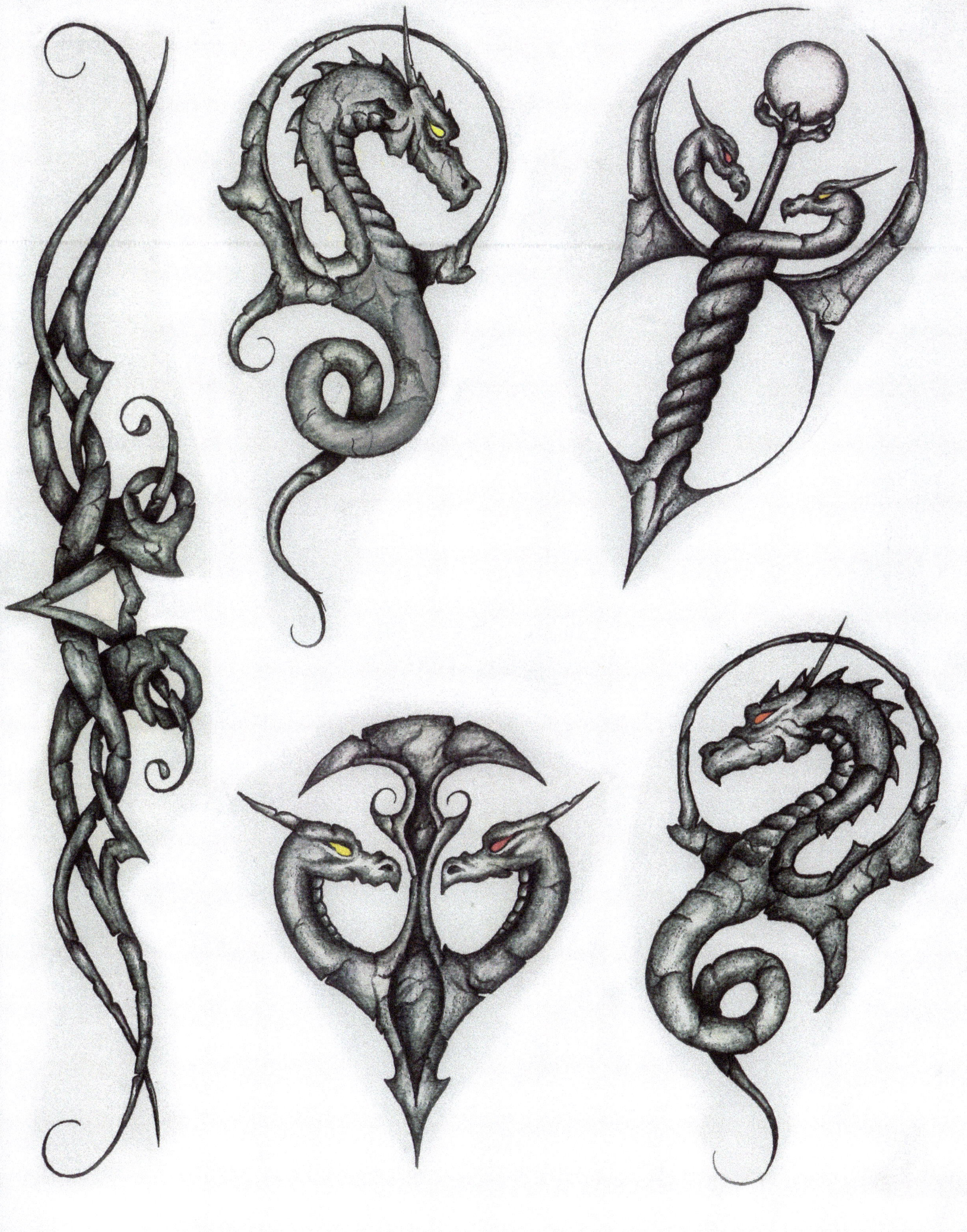

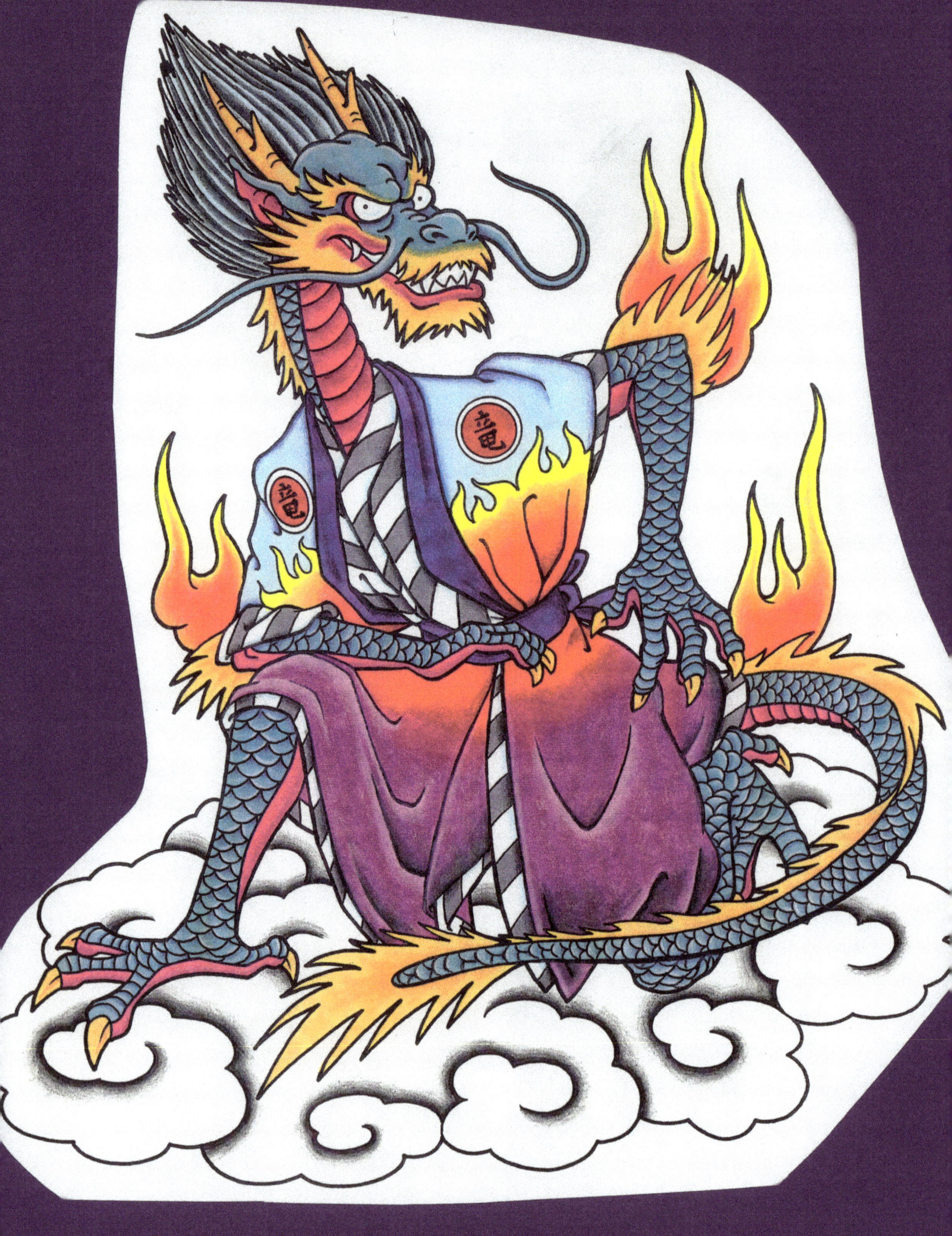

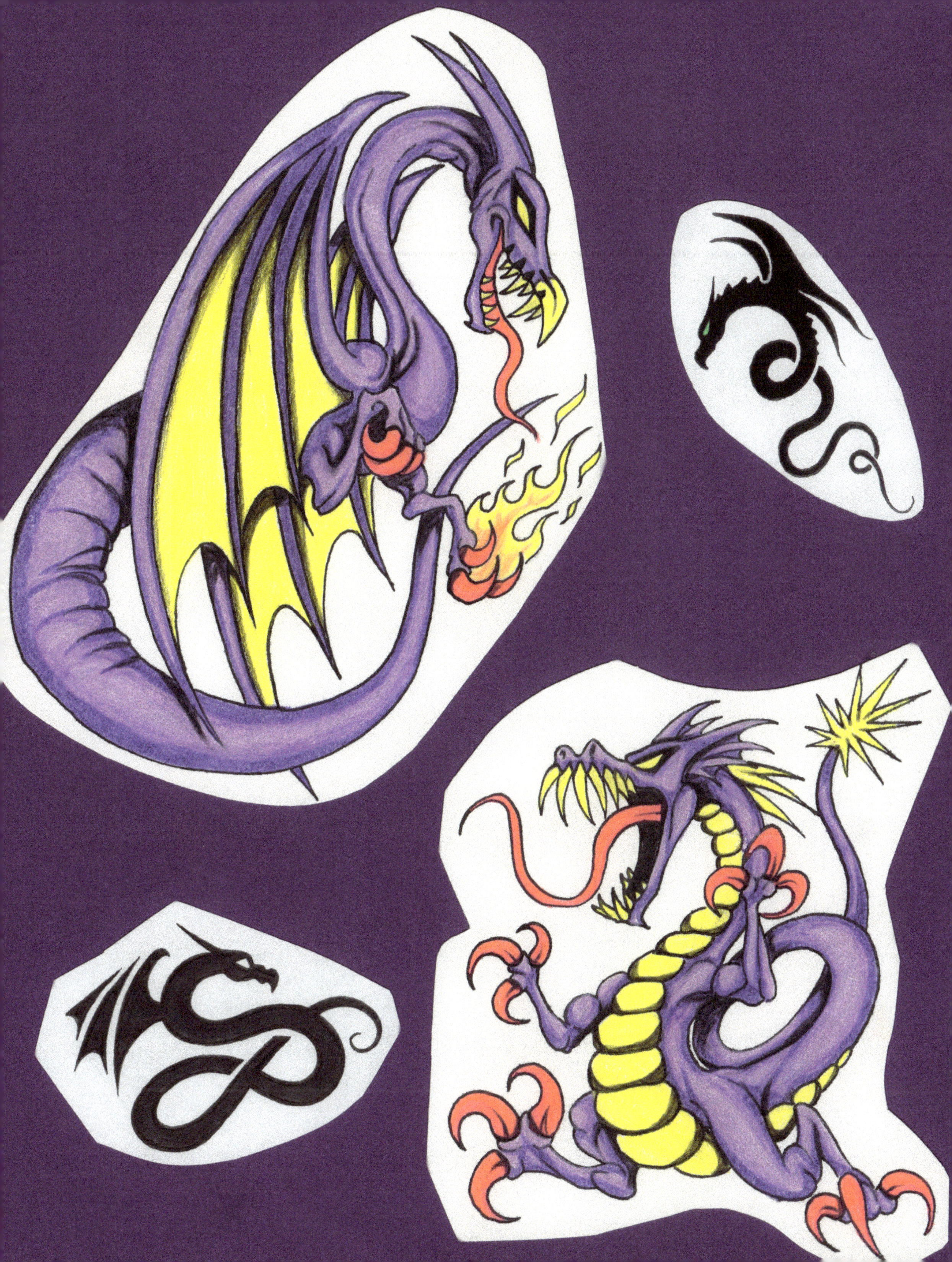

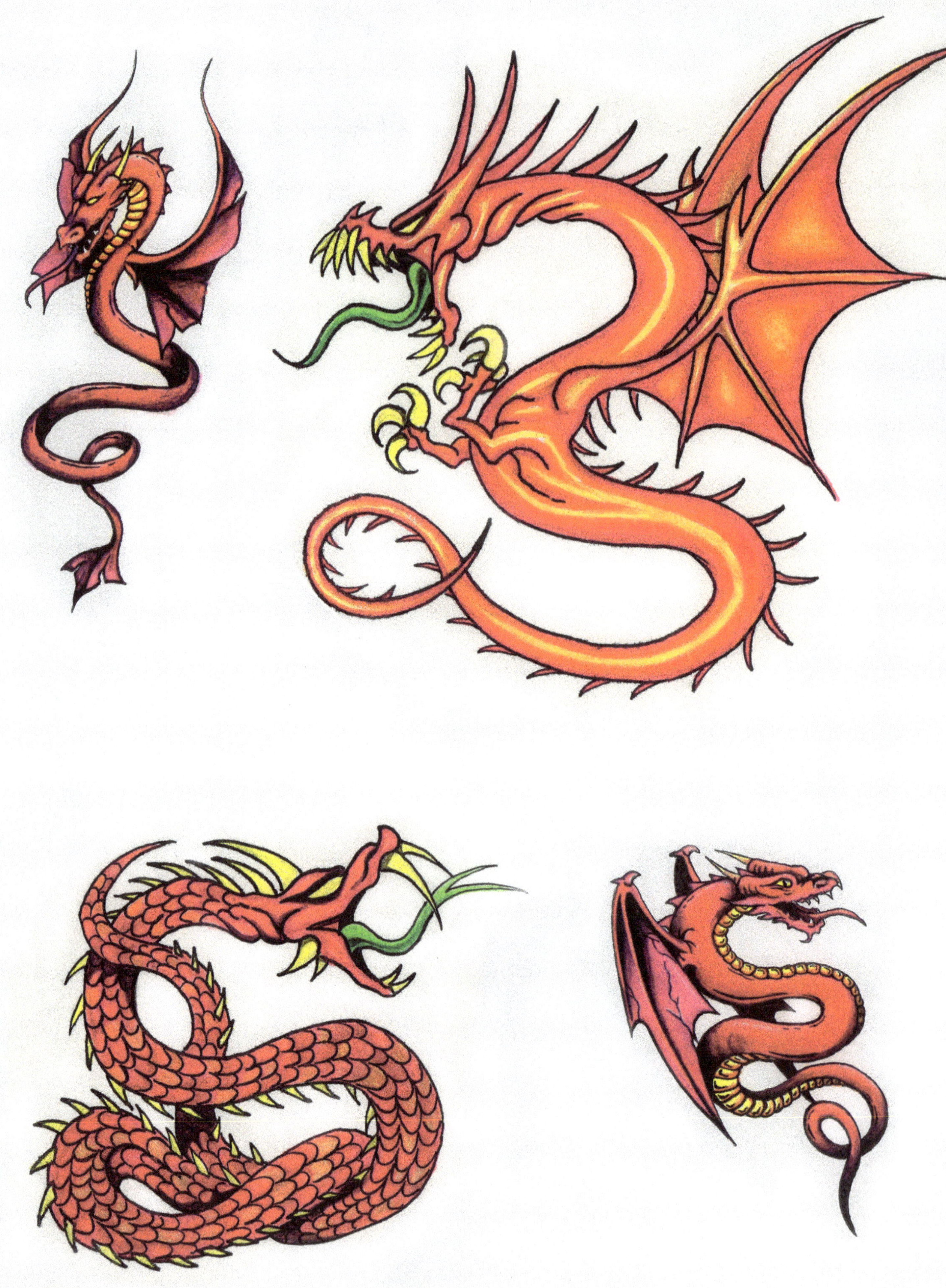

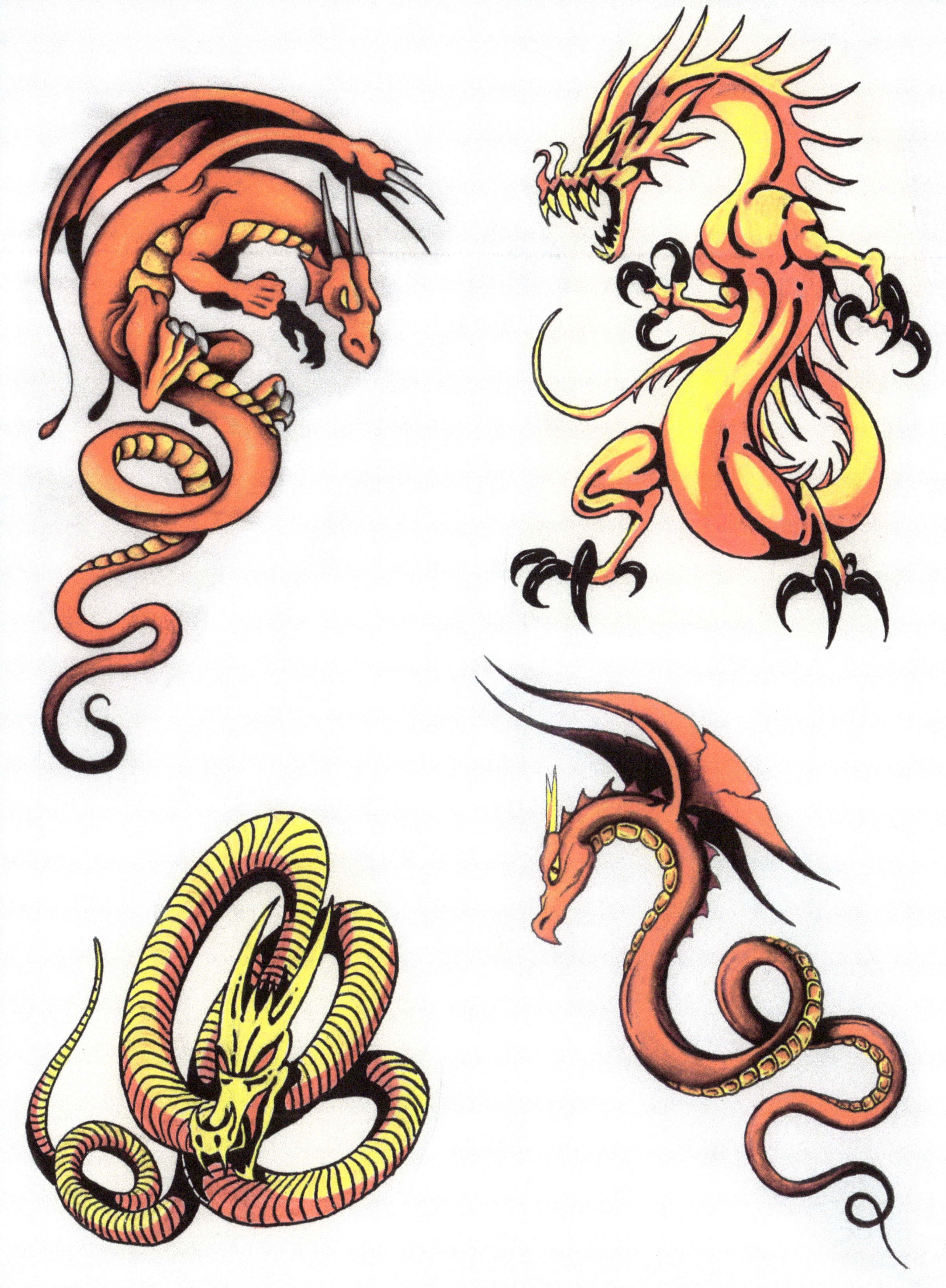

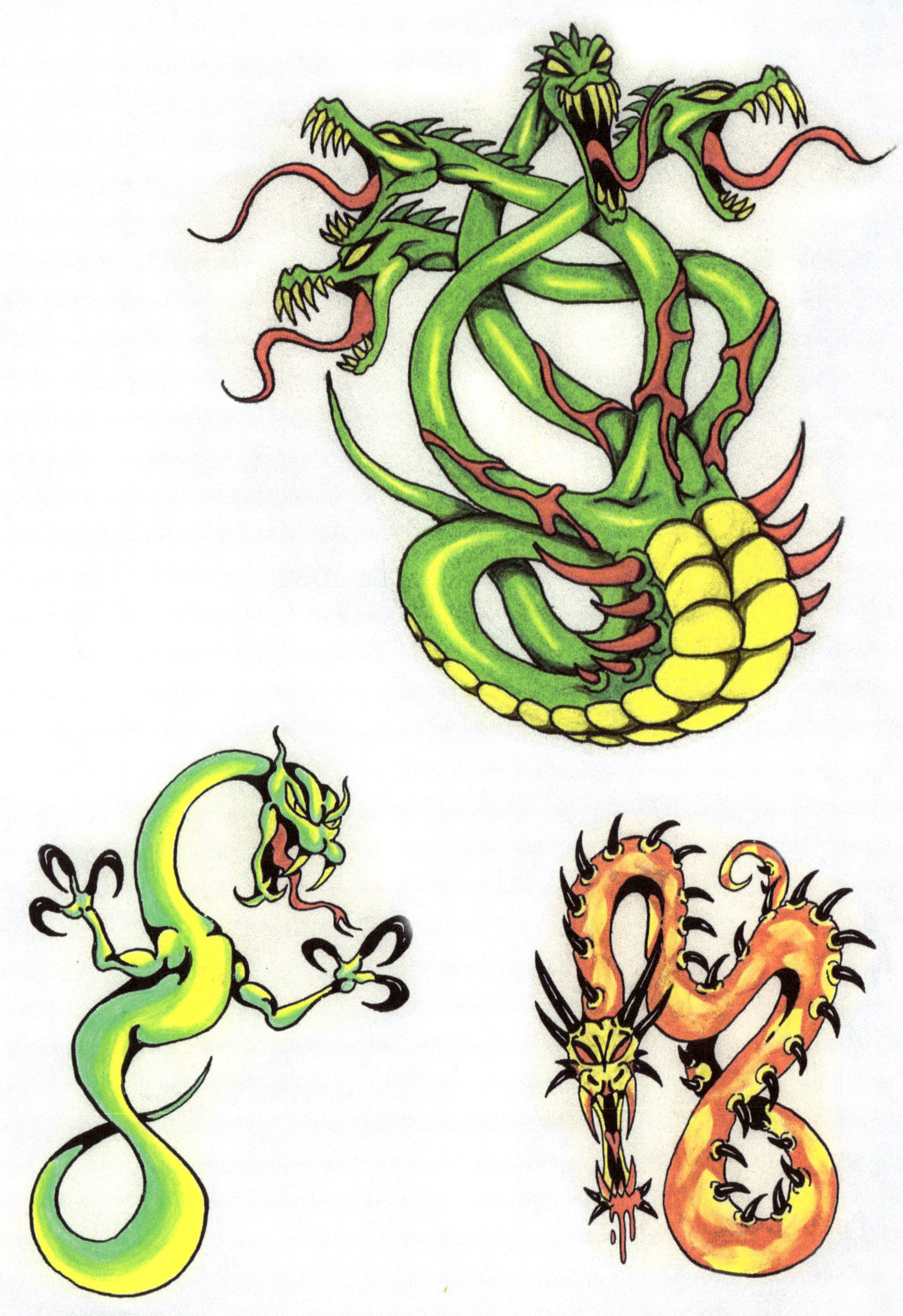

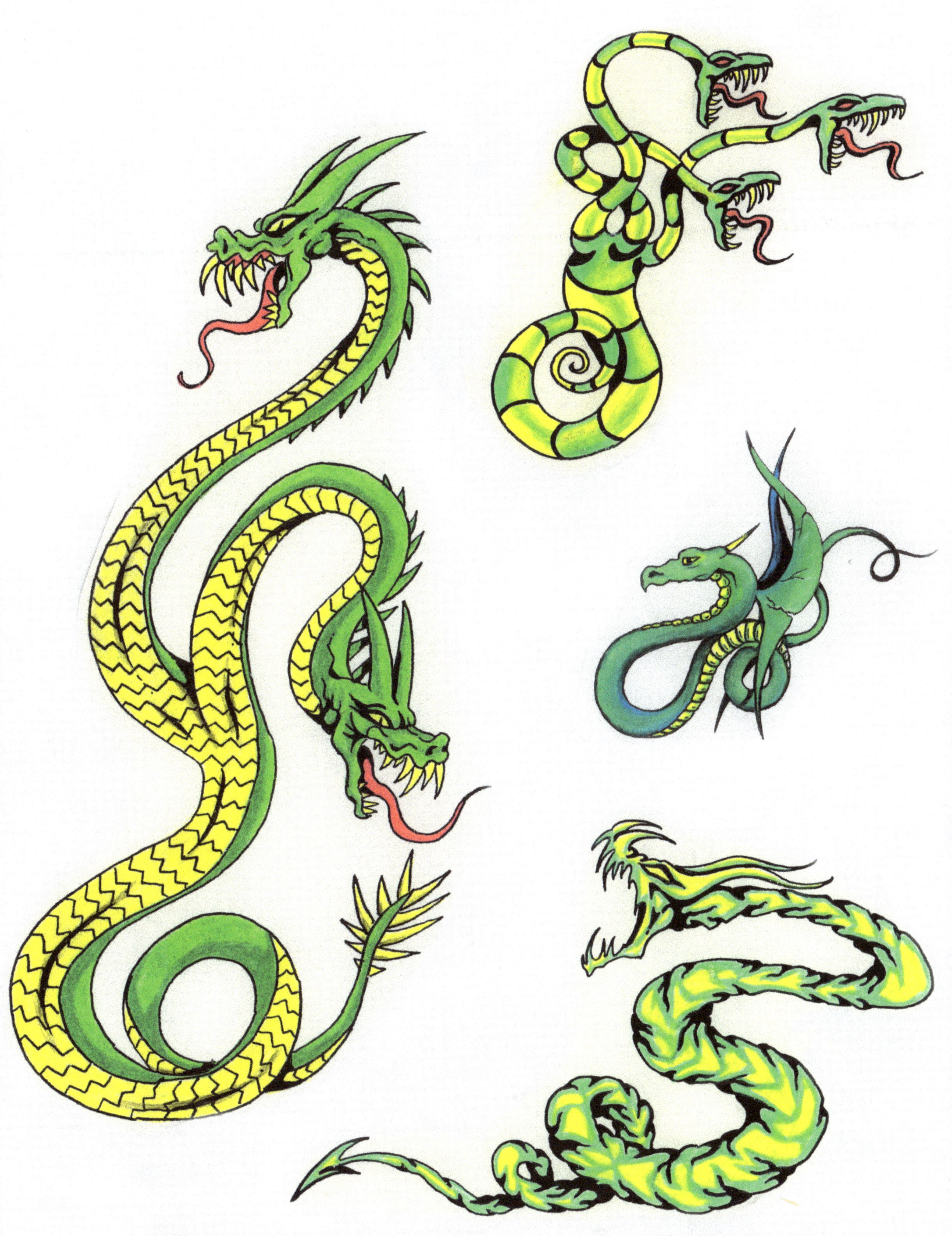

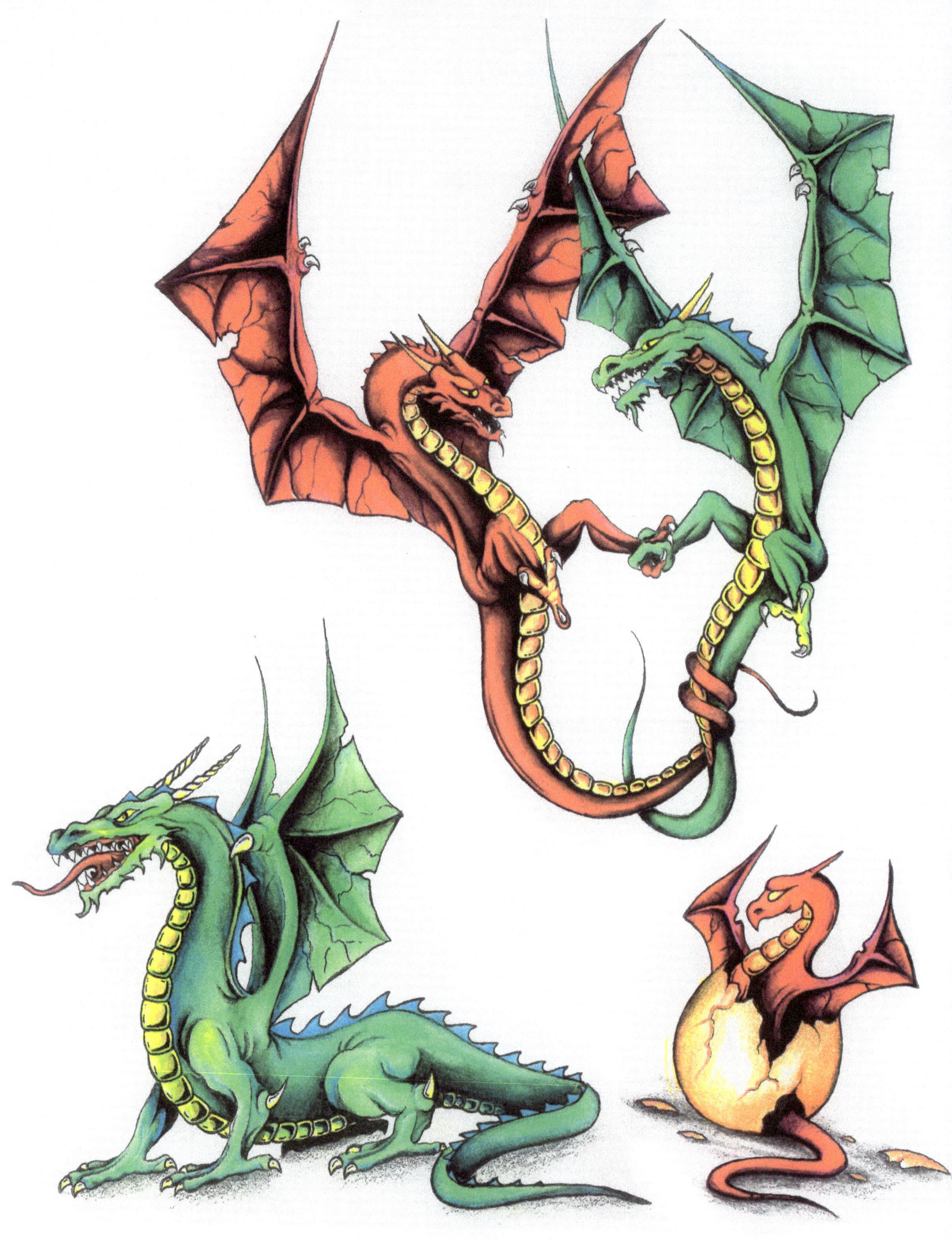

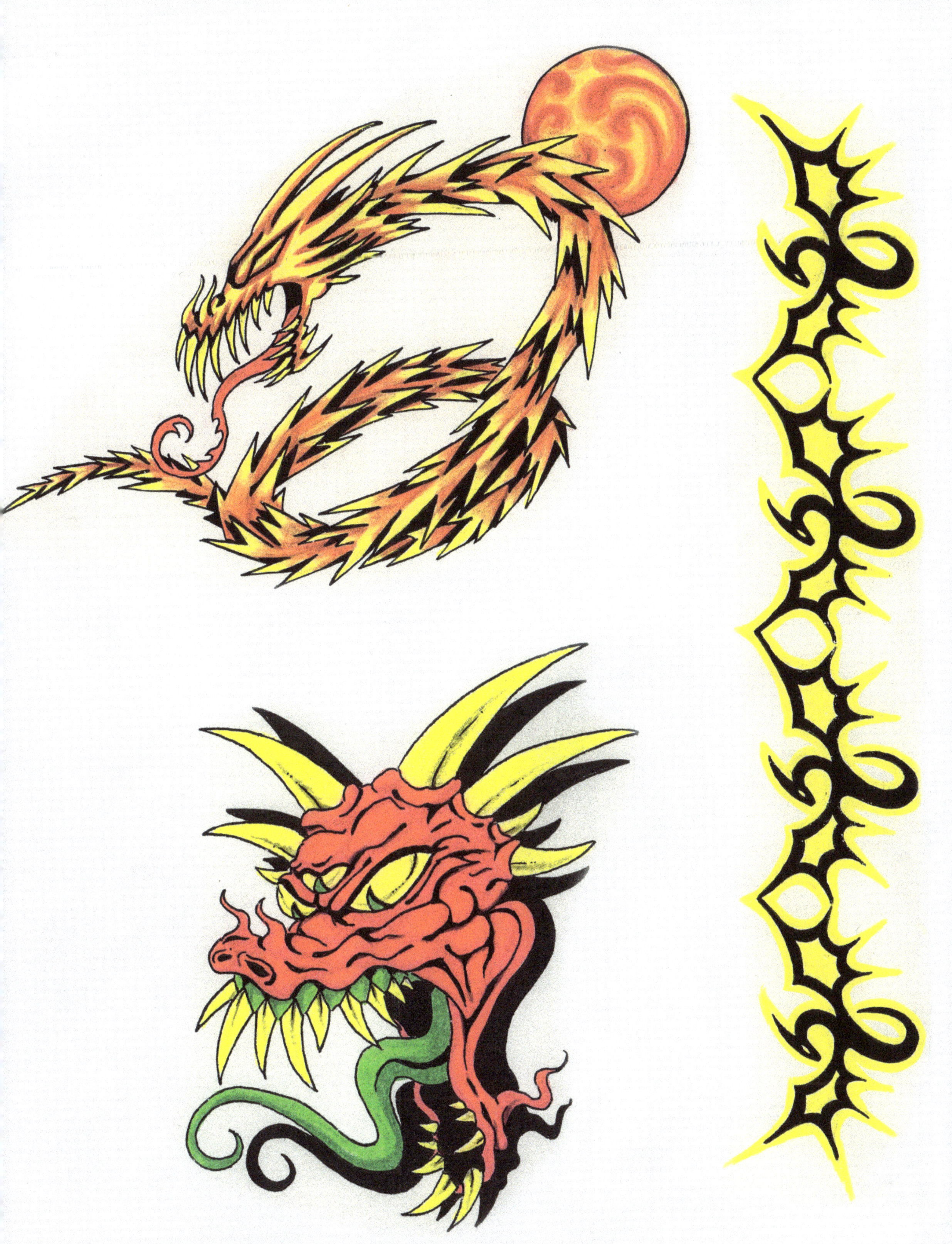

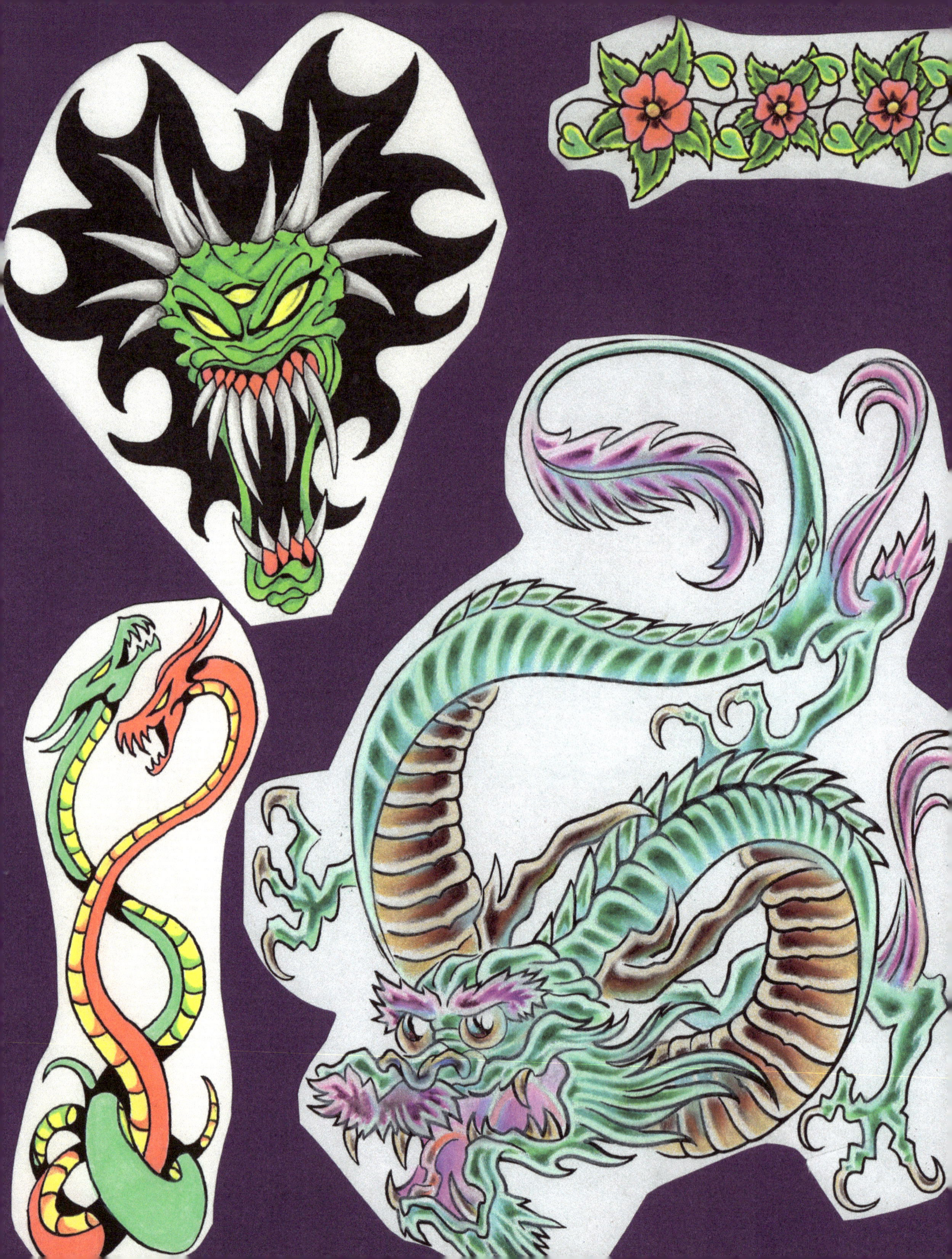

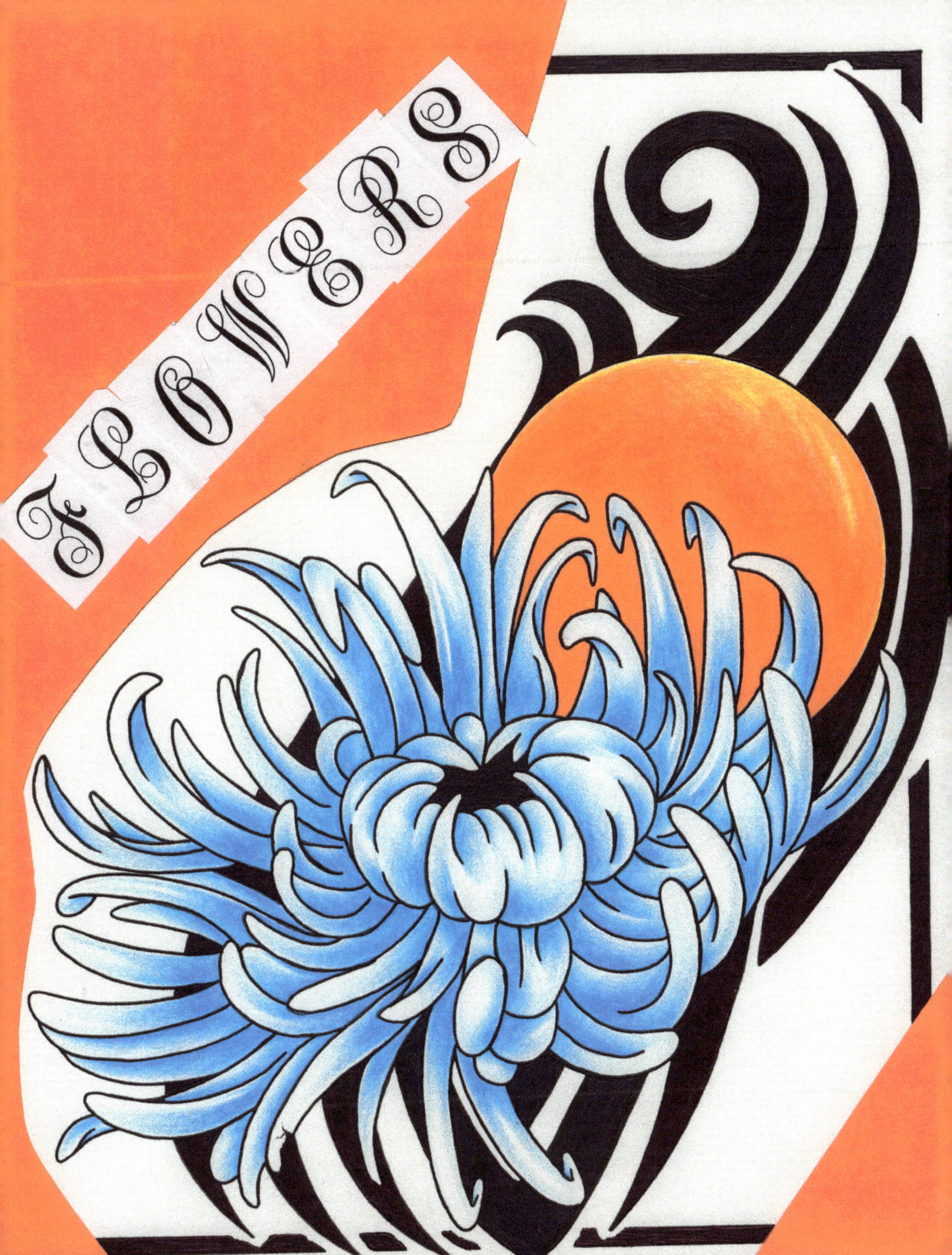

FLOWERS

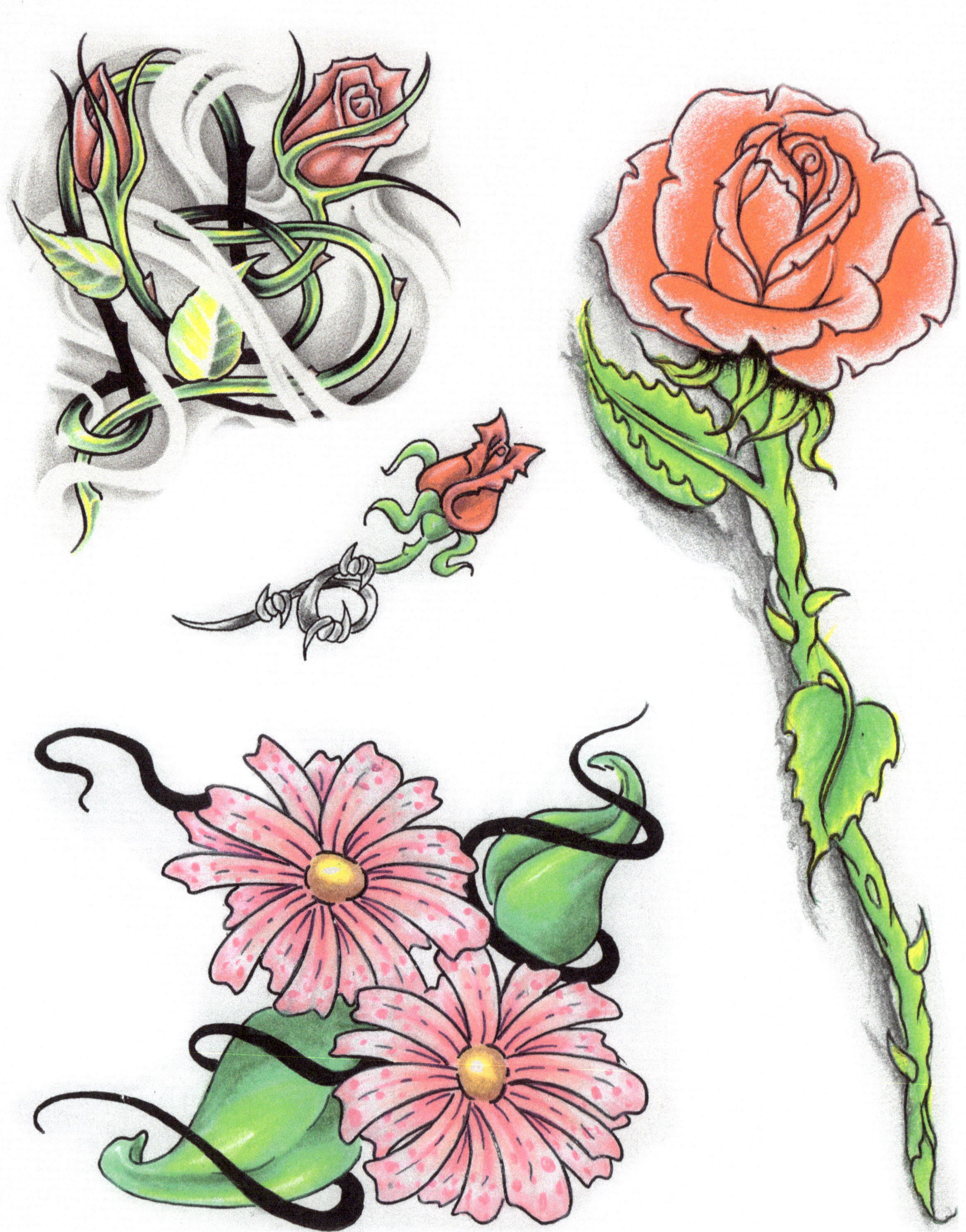

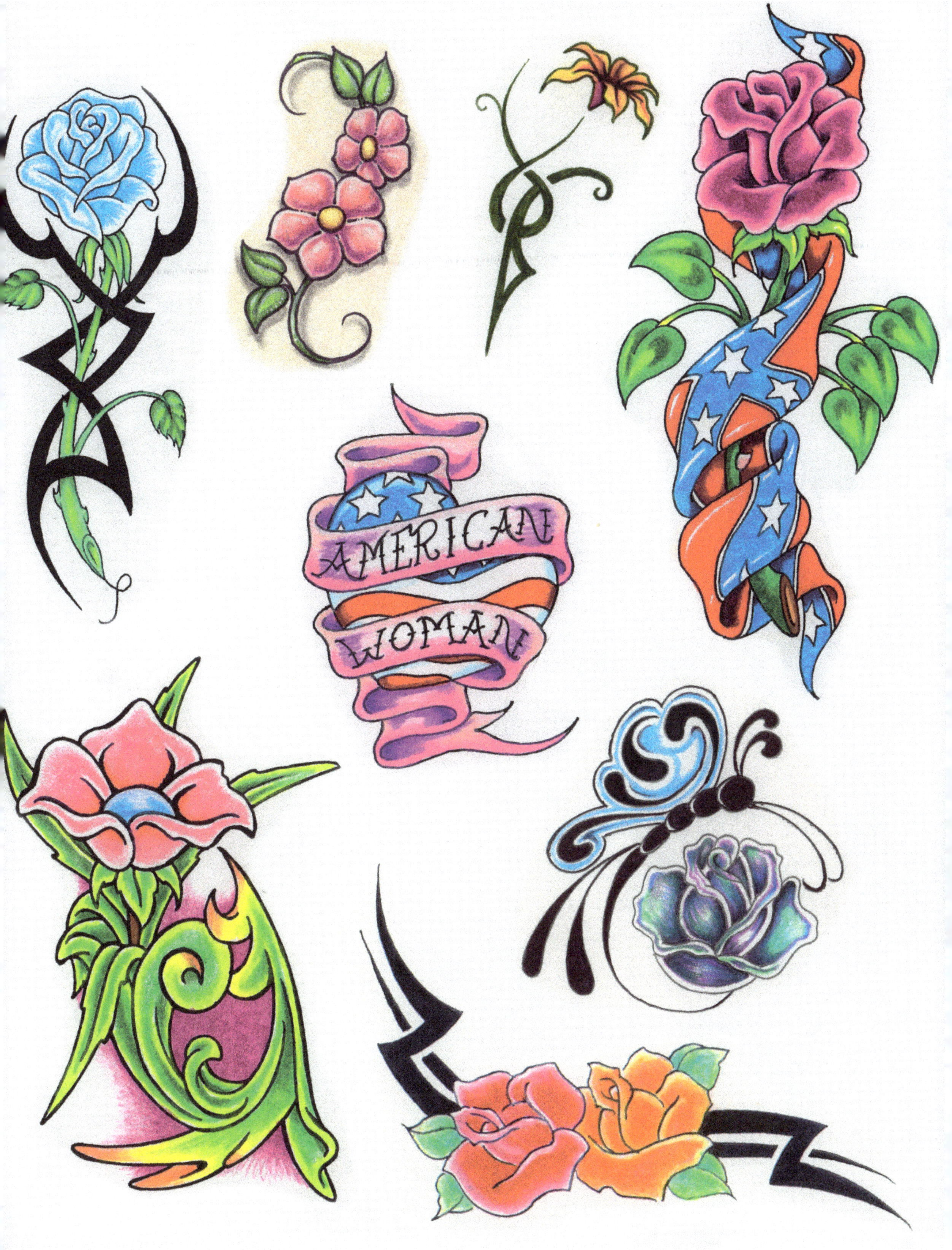

AMERICAN
WOMAN

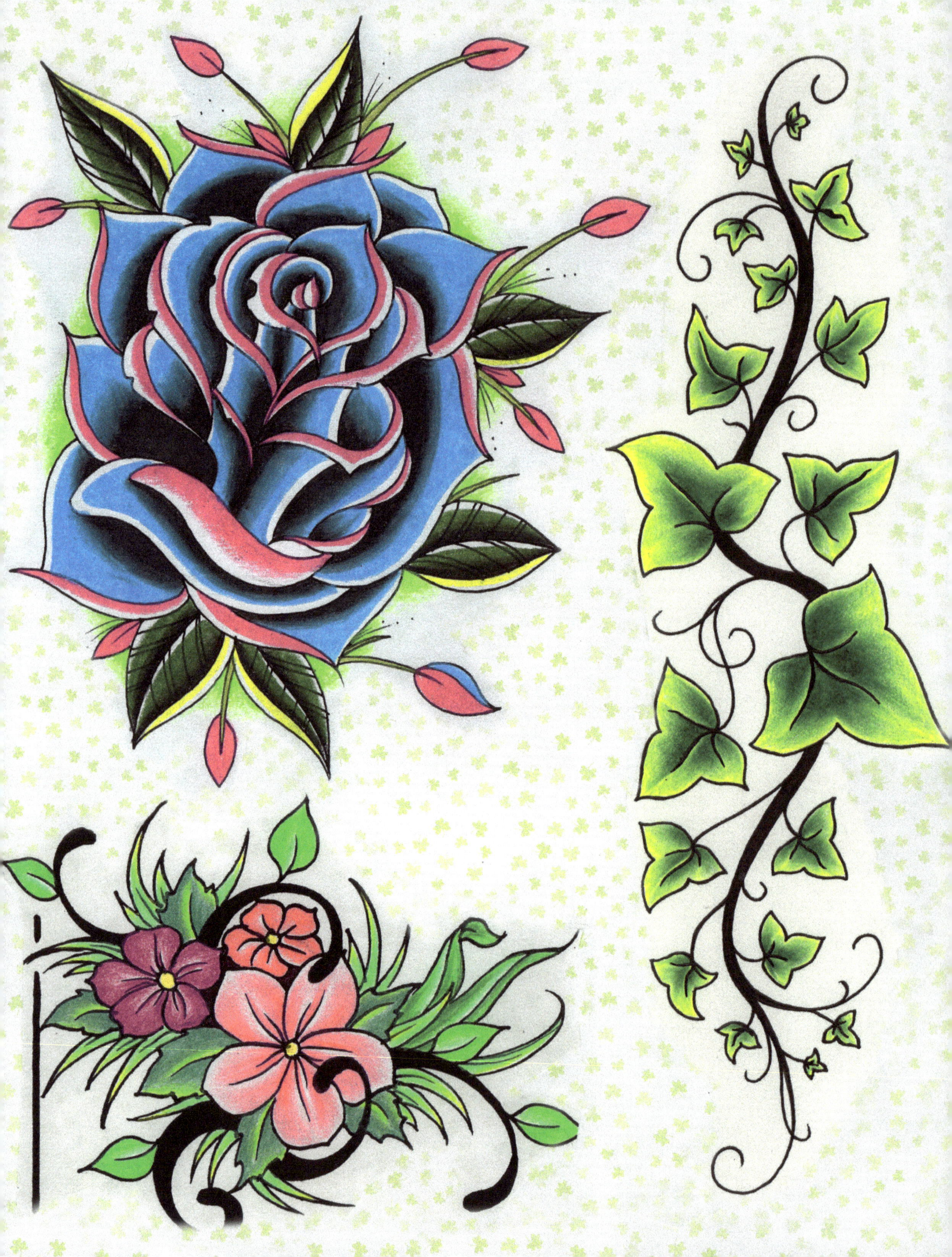

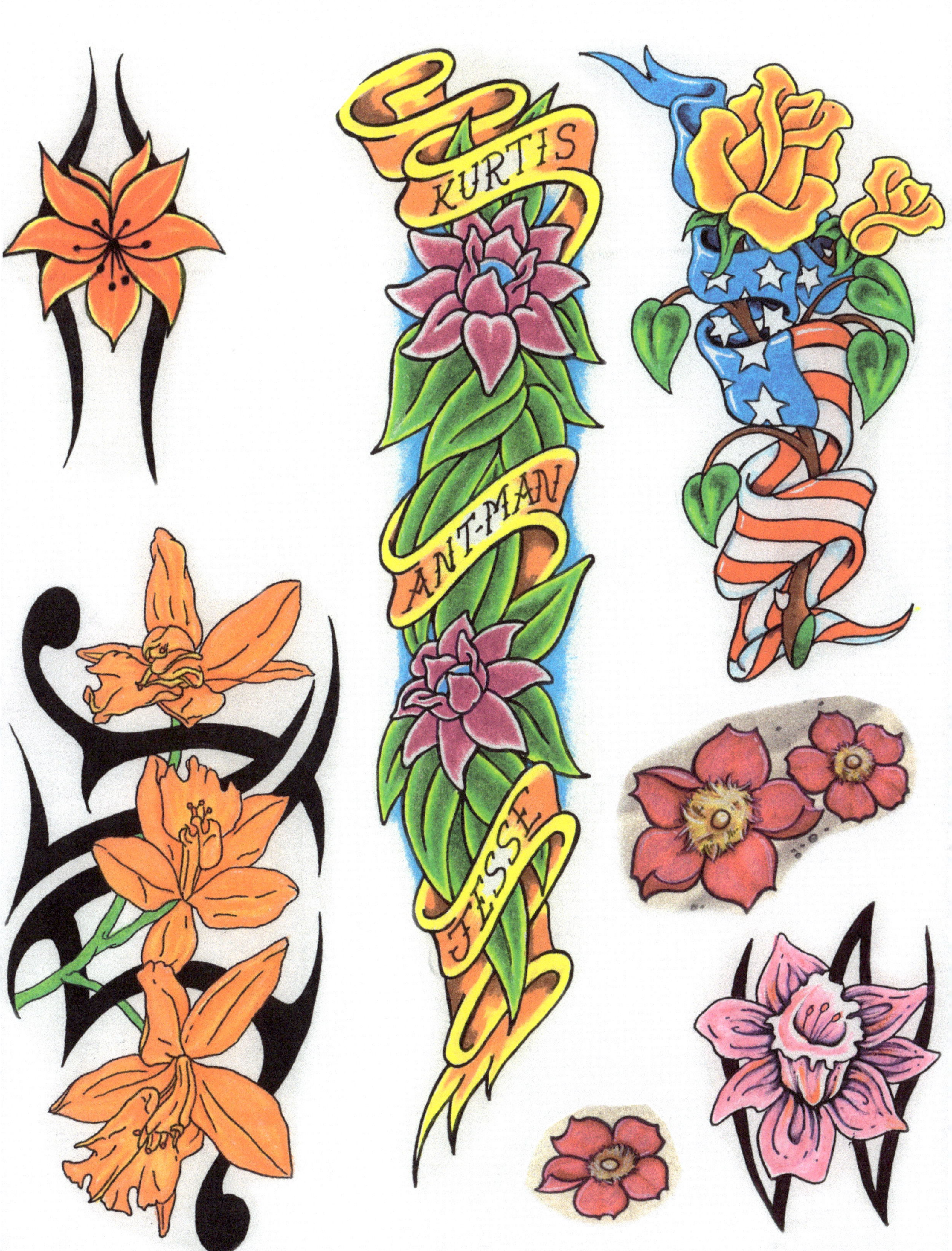
KURTIS
ANT-MAN
JESSE

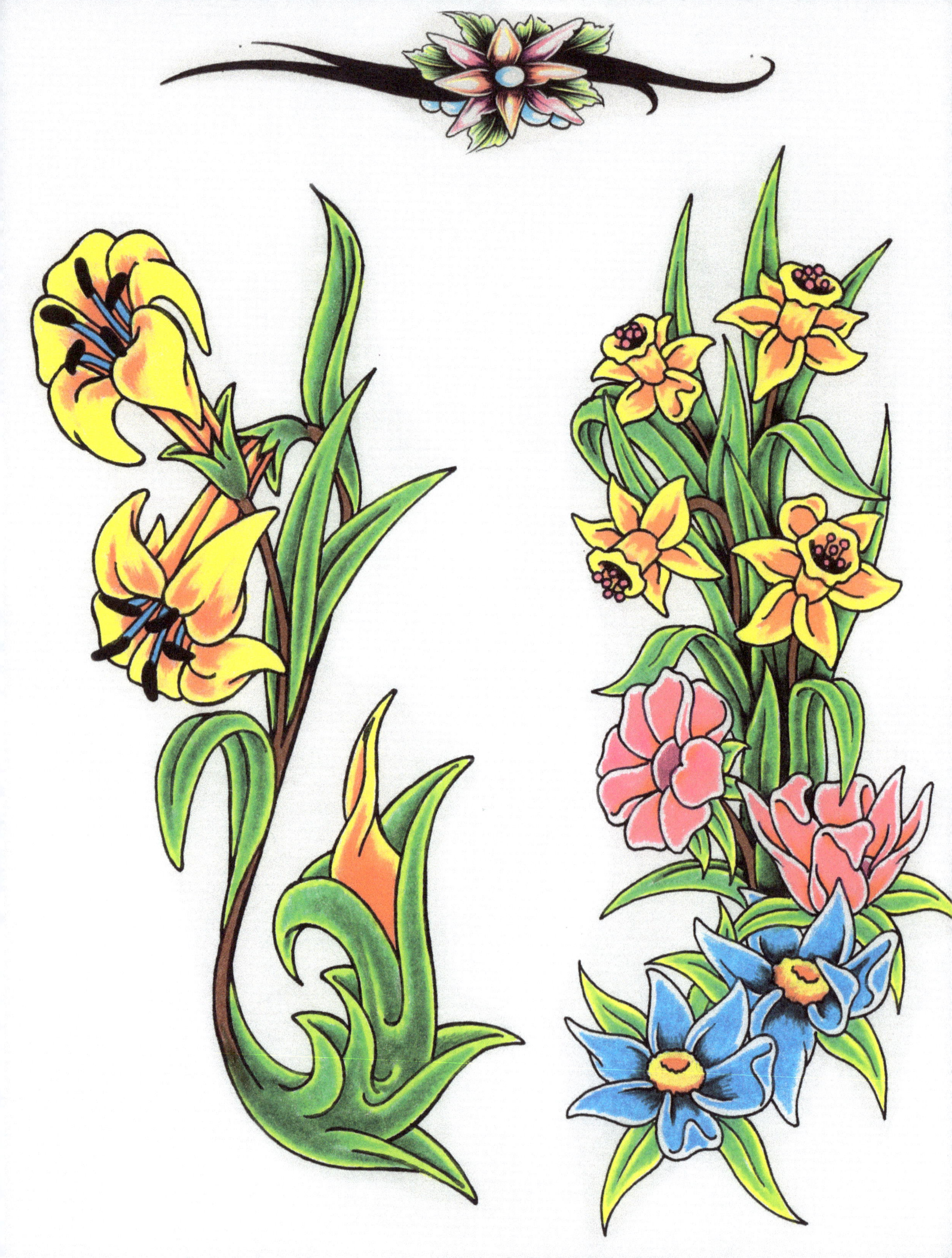

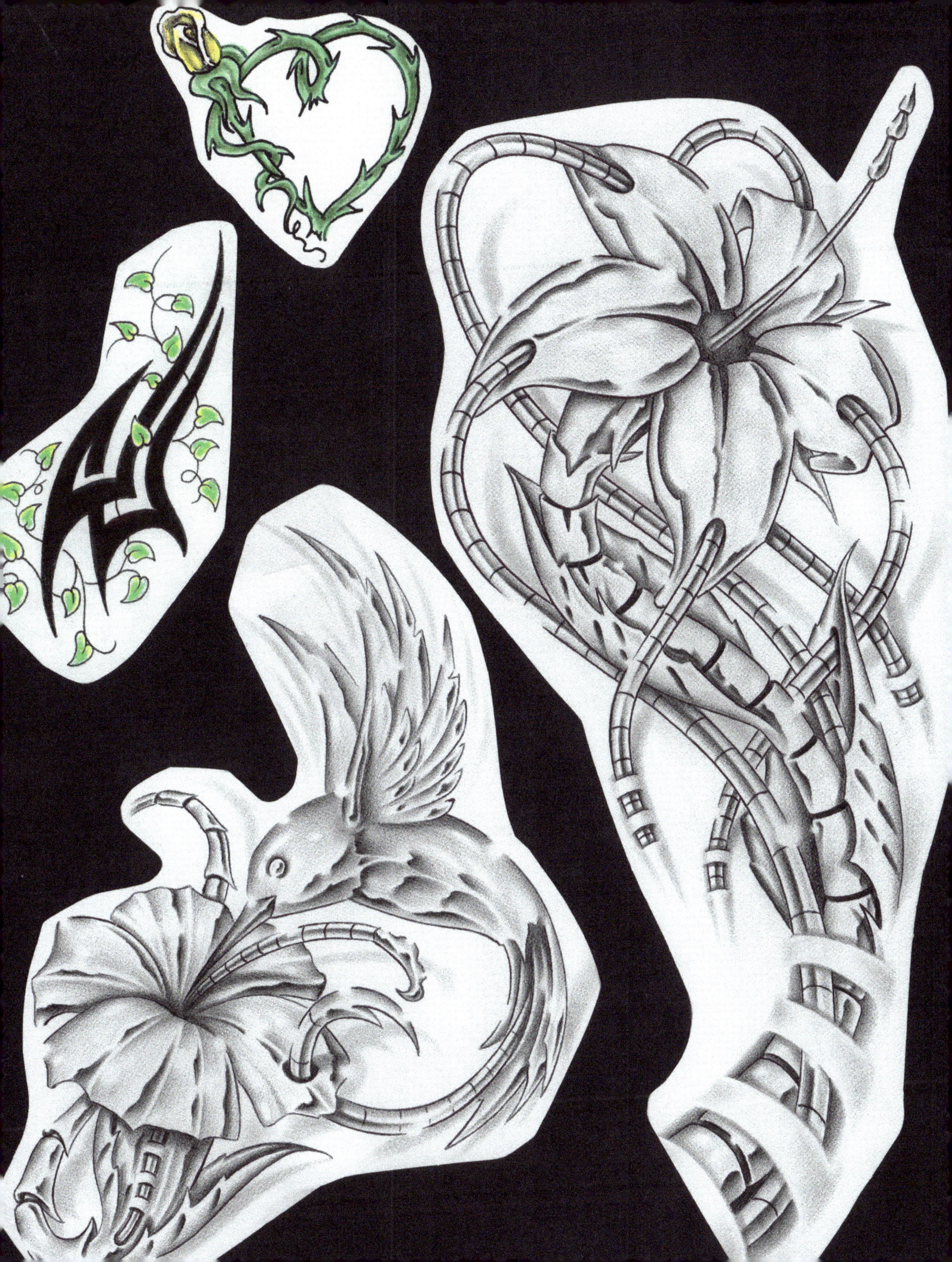

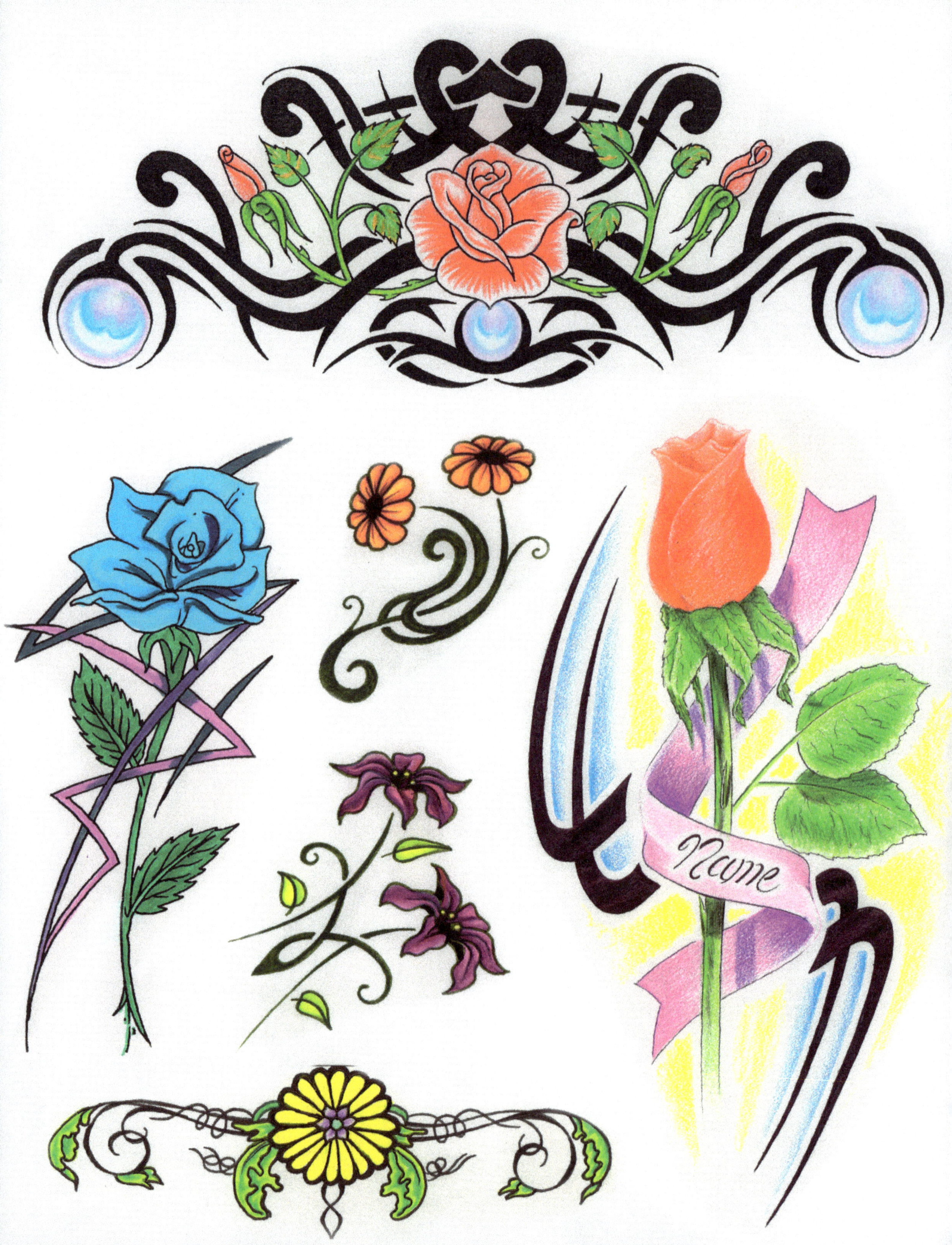

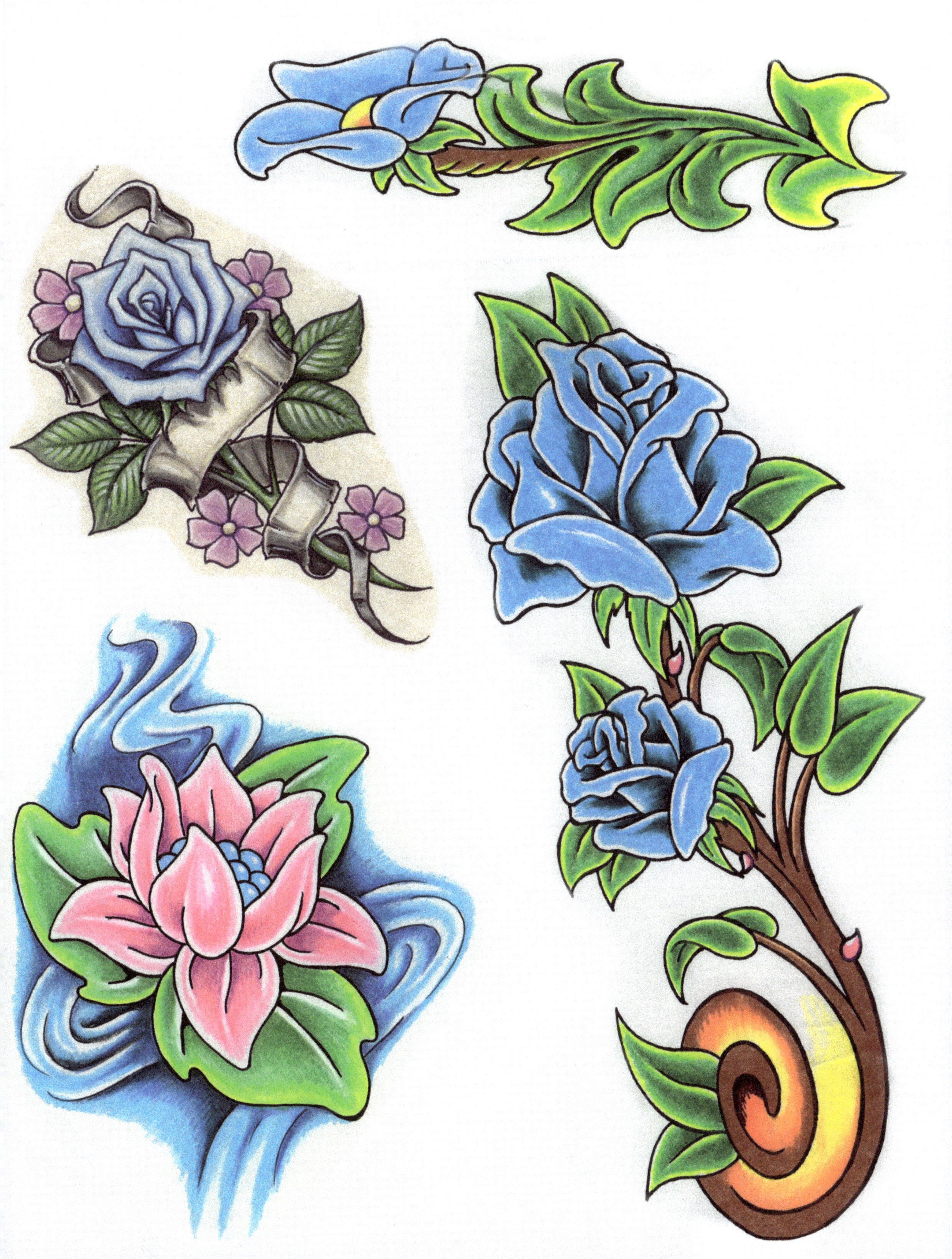

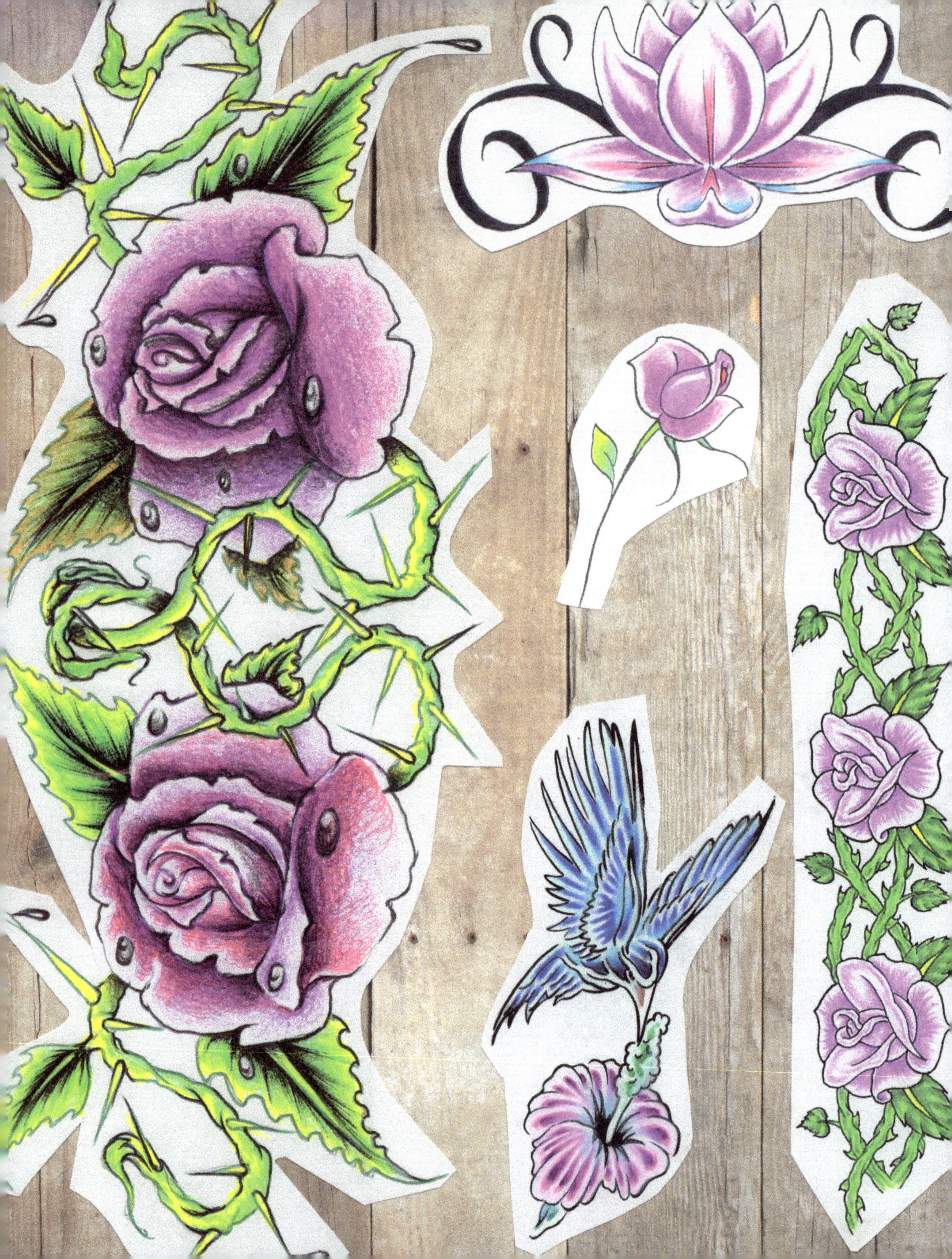

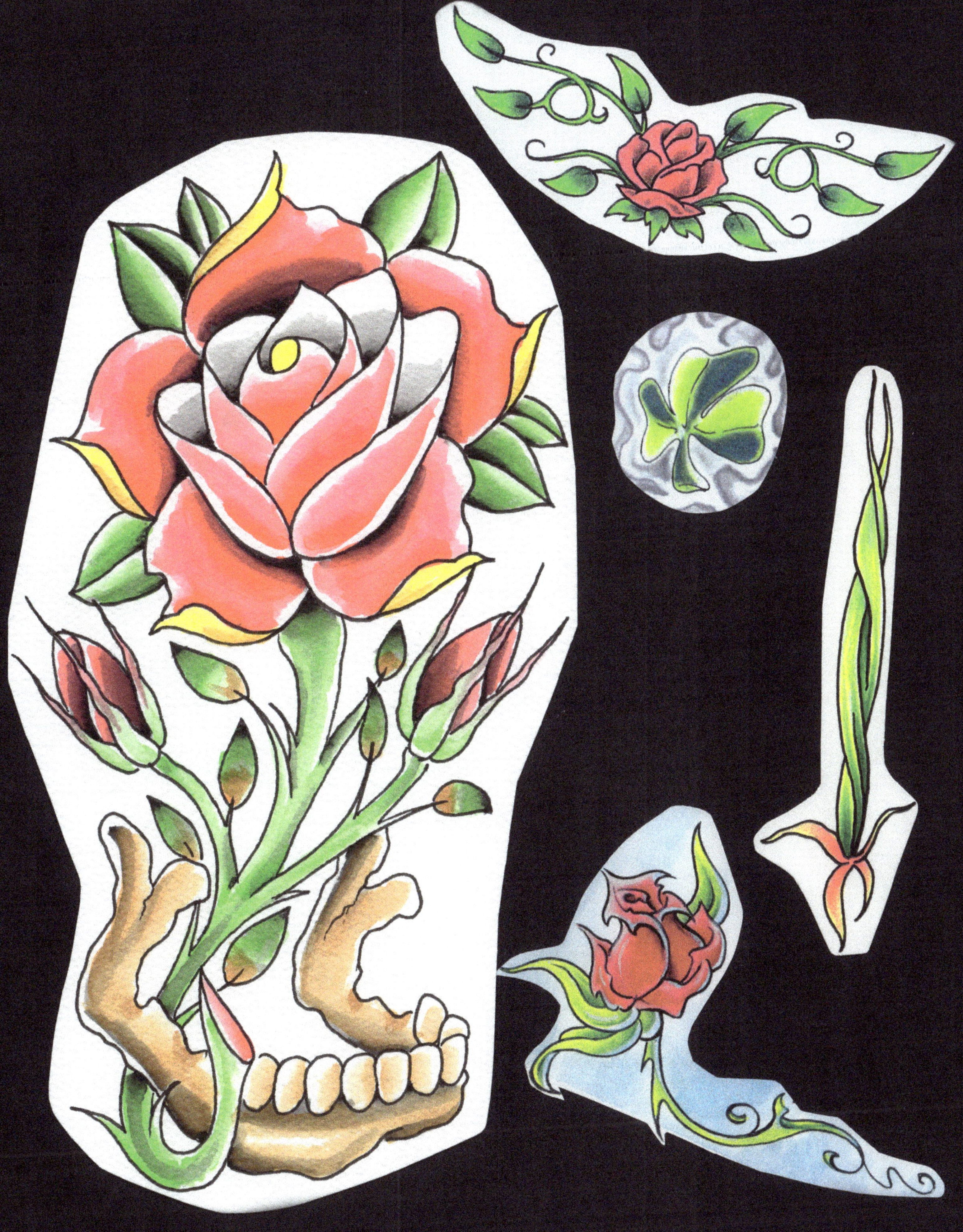

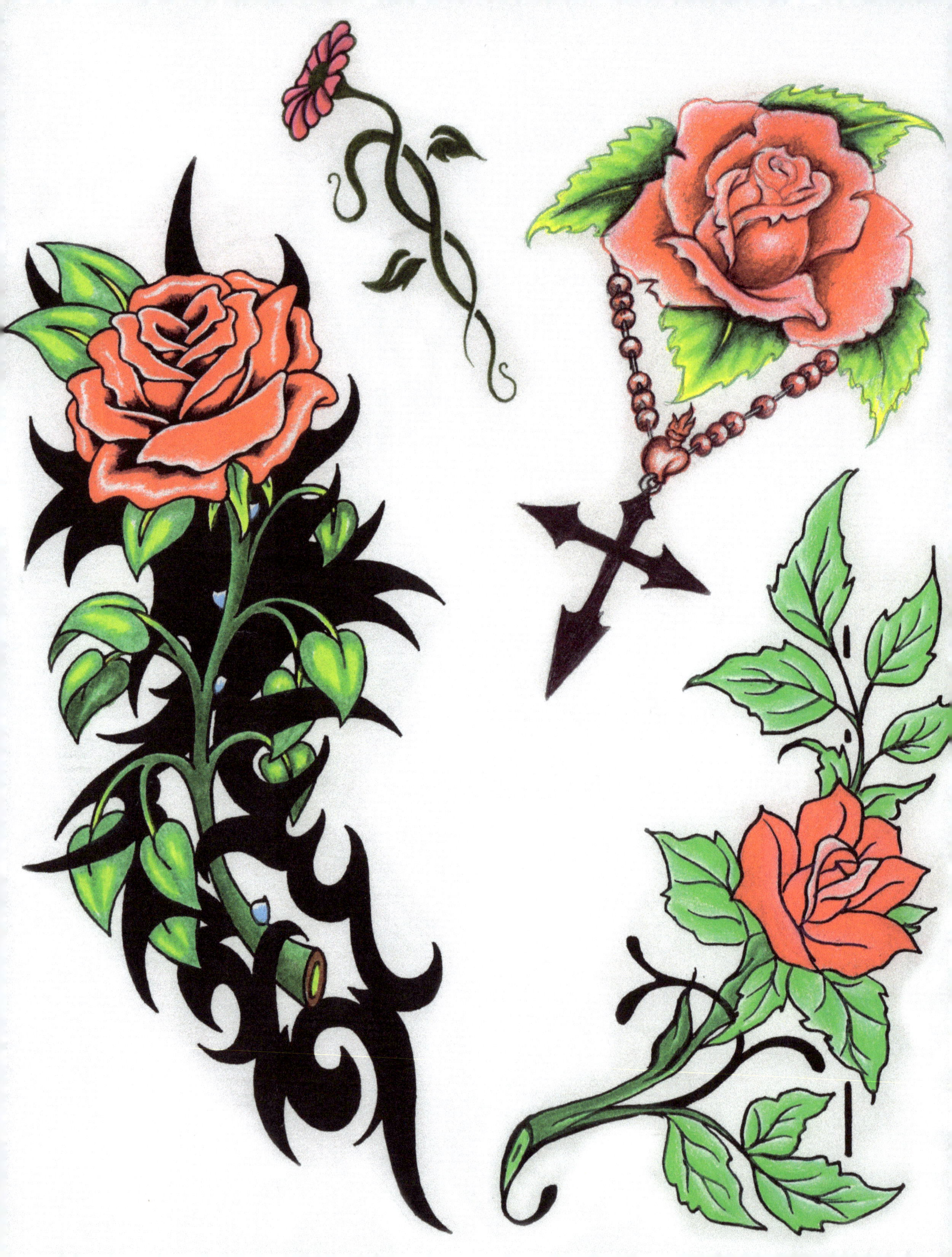

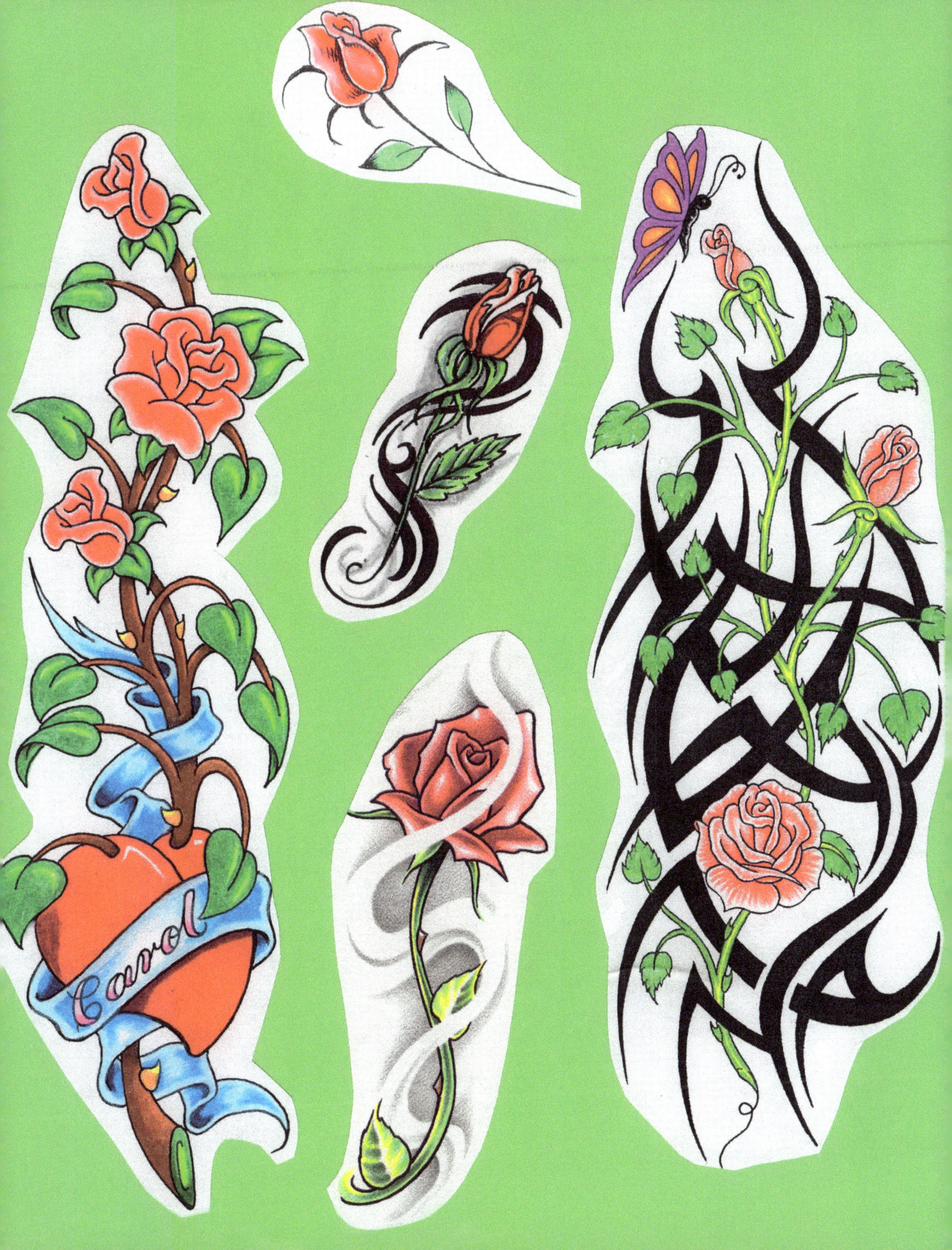

Carol

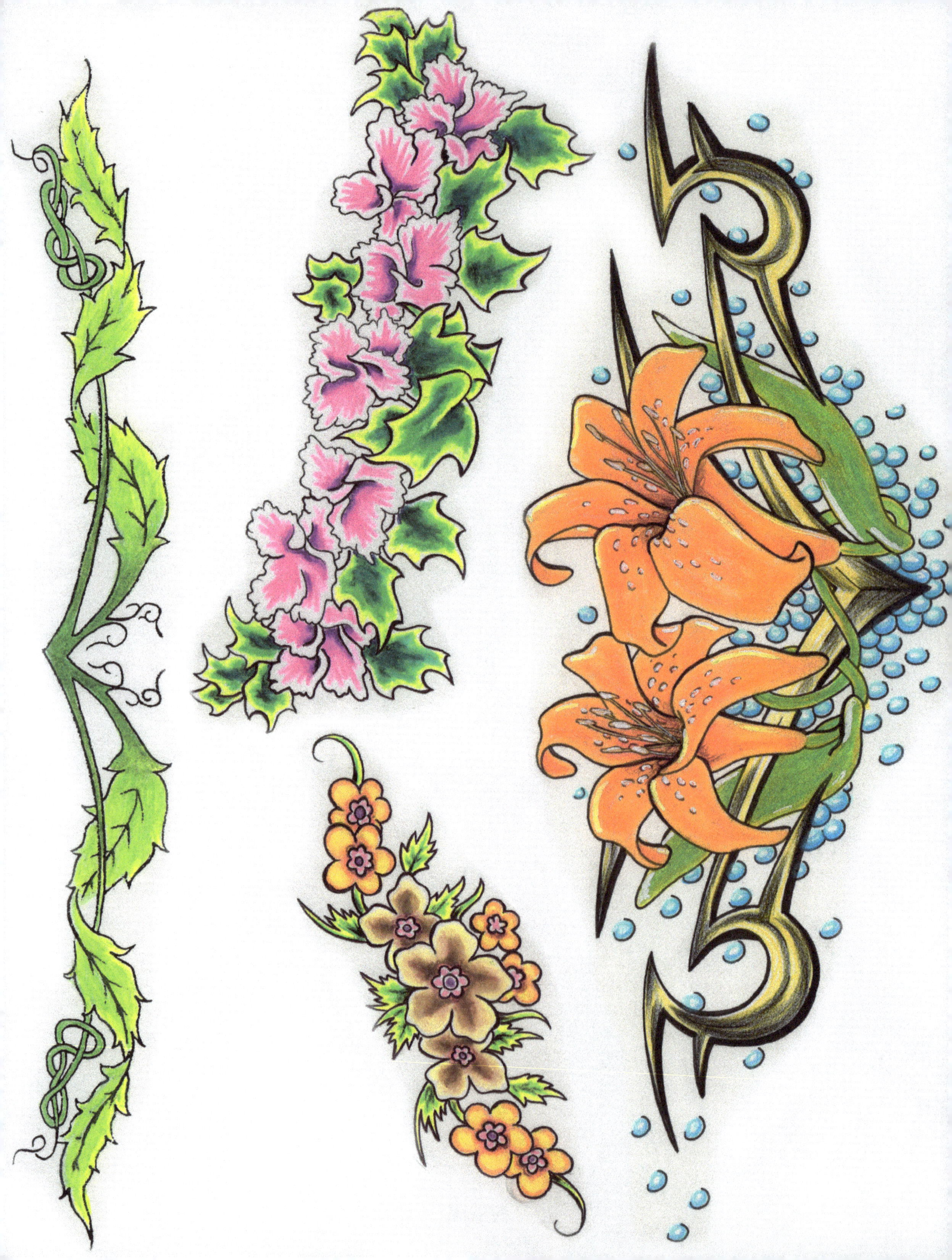

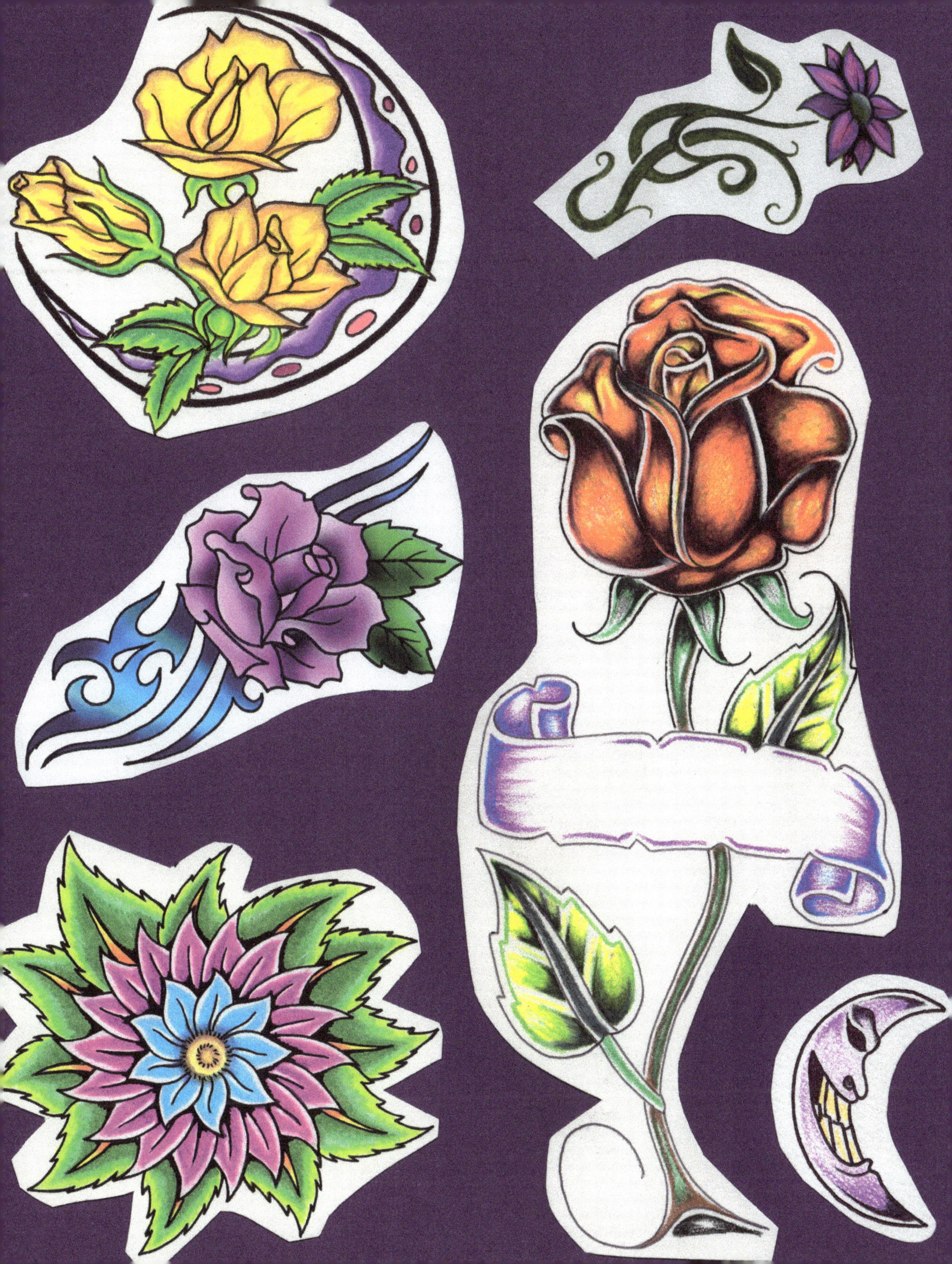

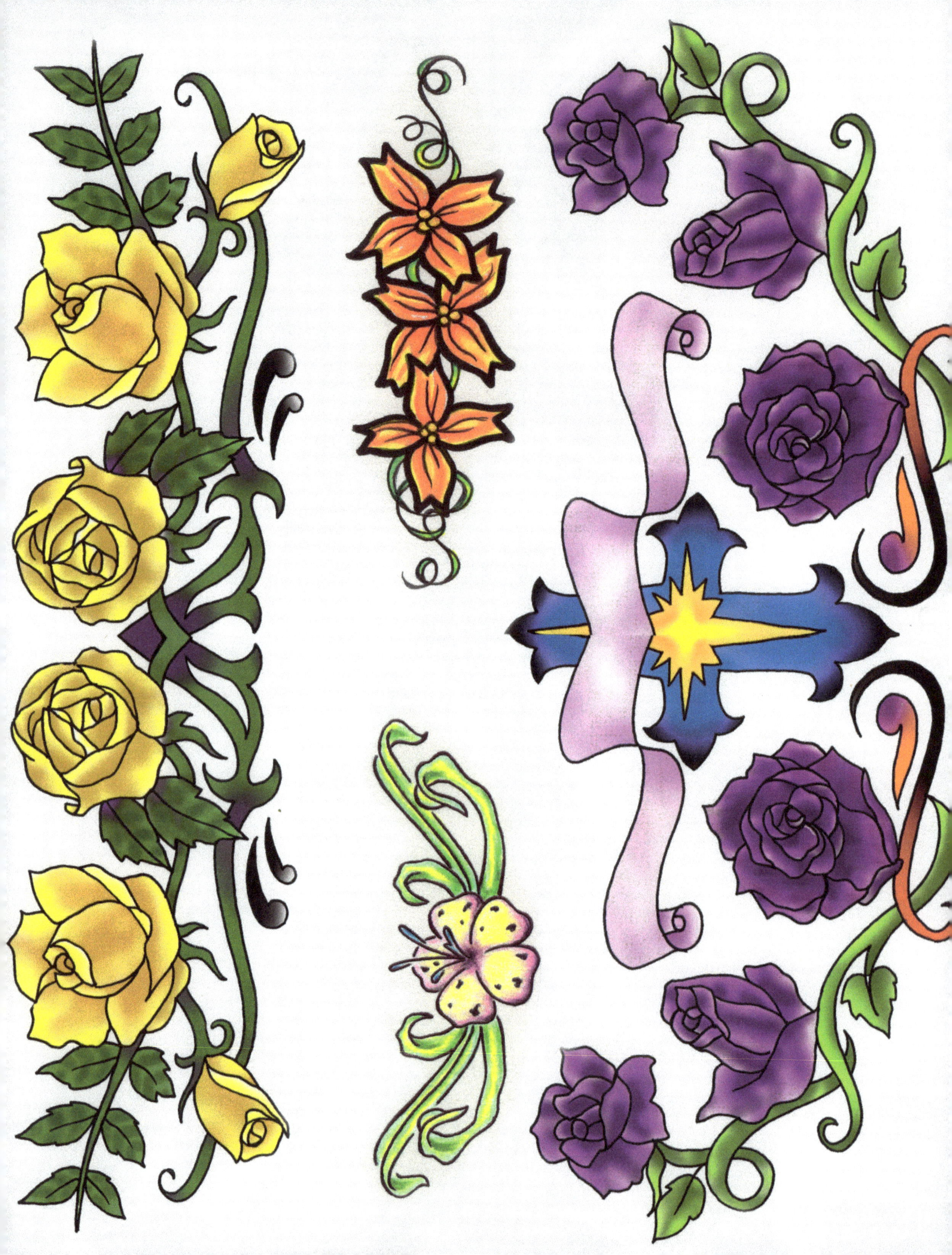

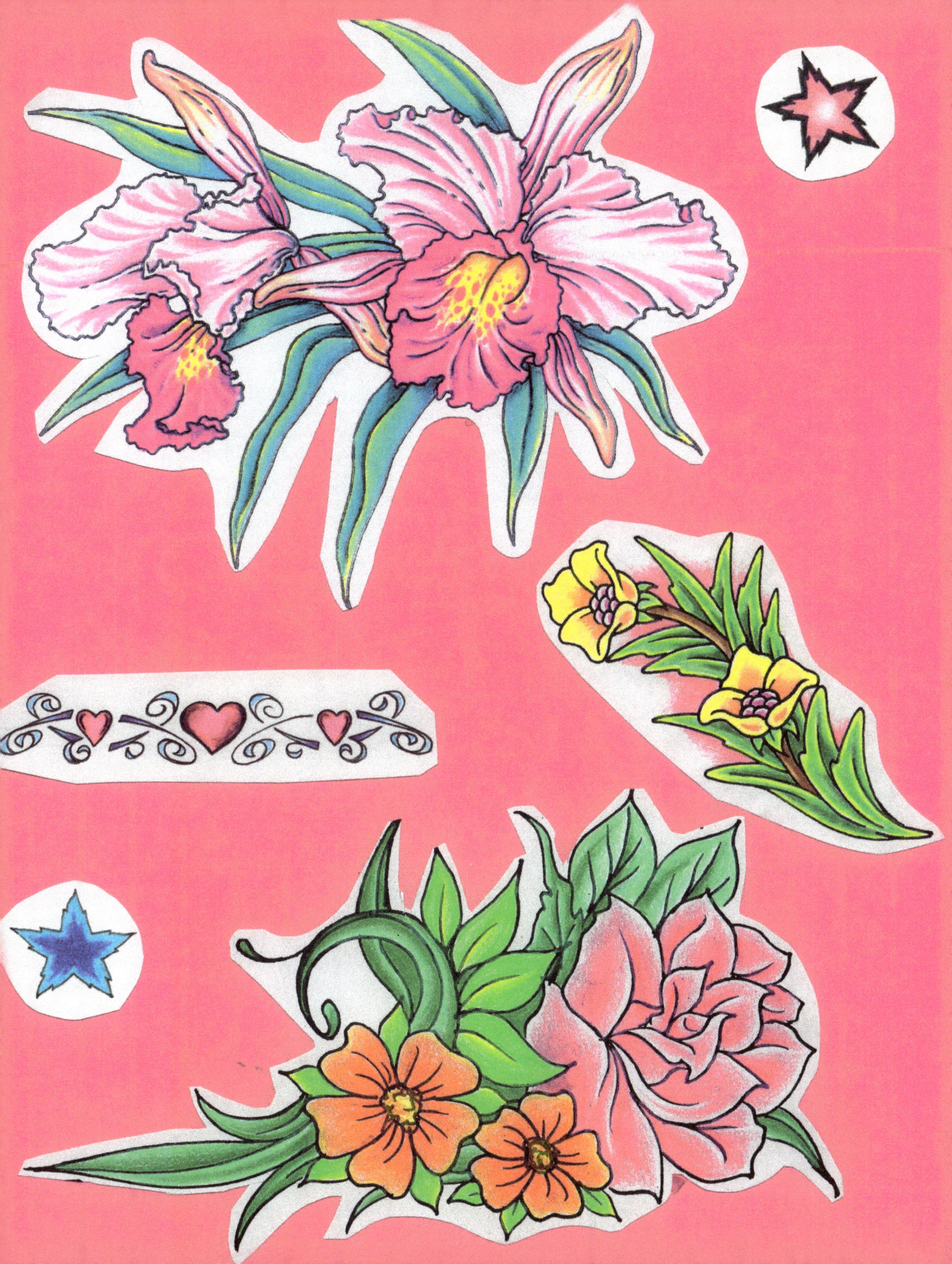

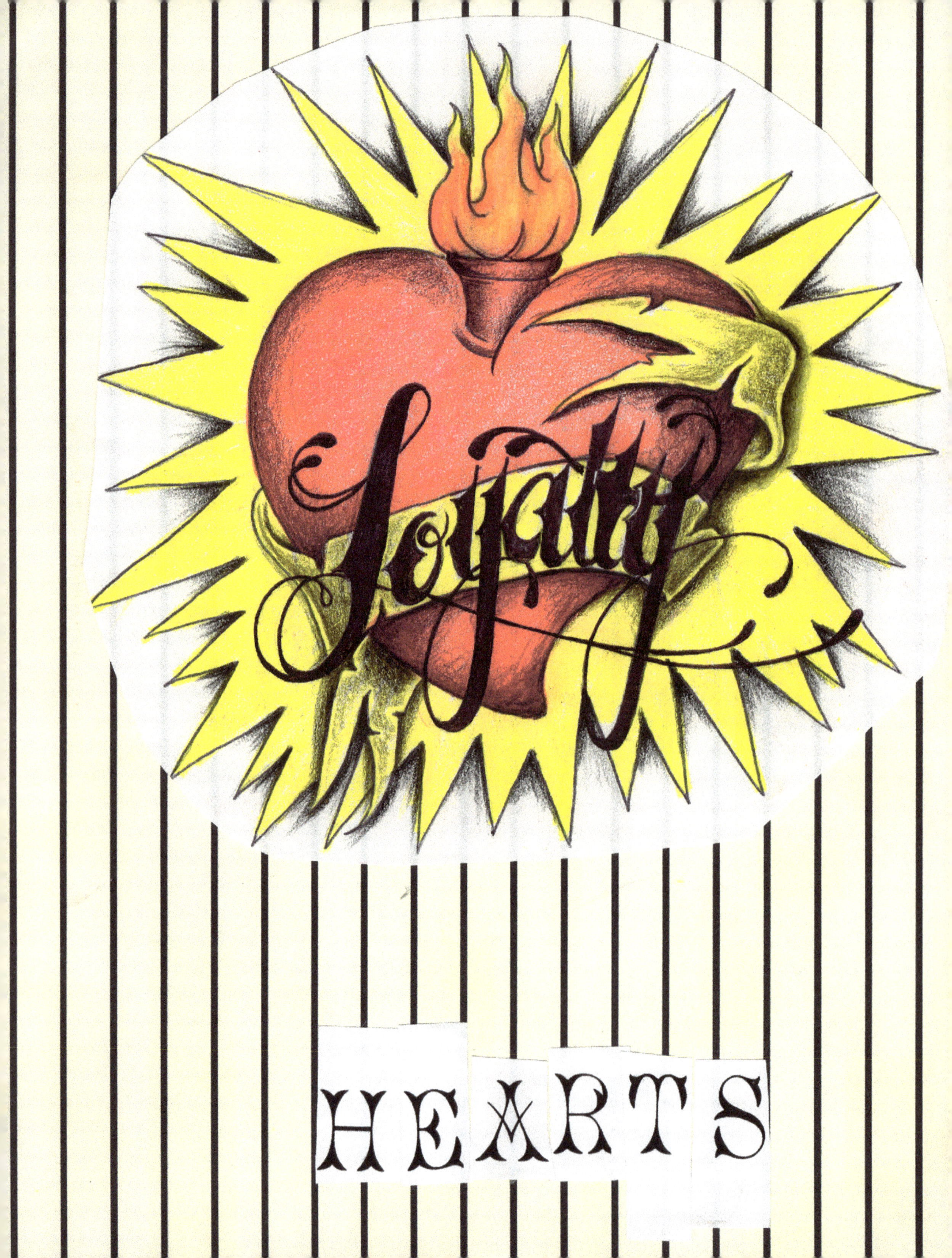
Loyalty
HEARTS

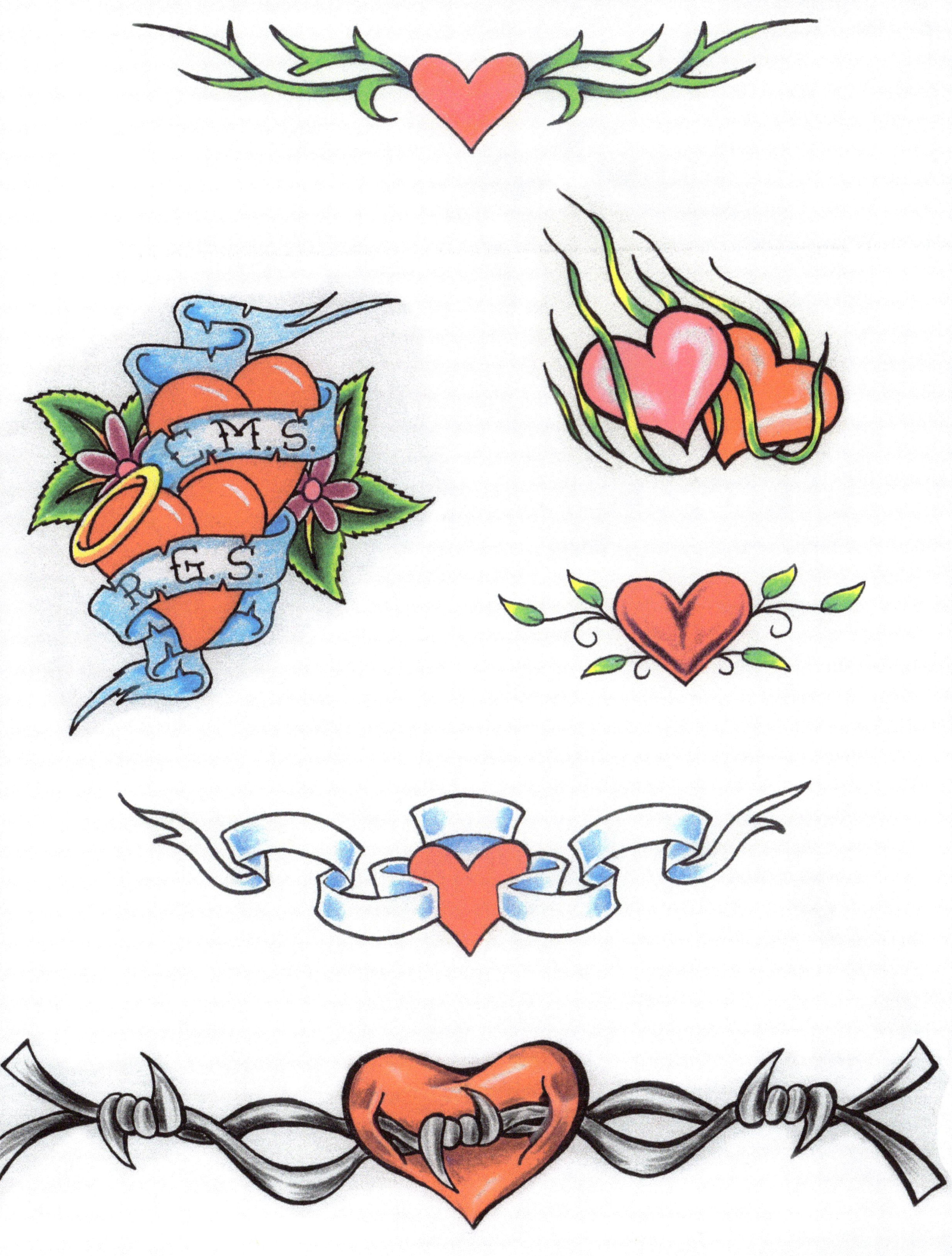

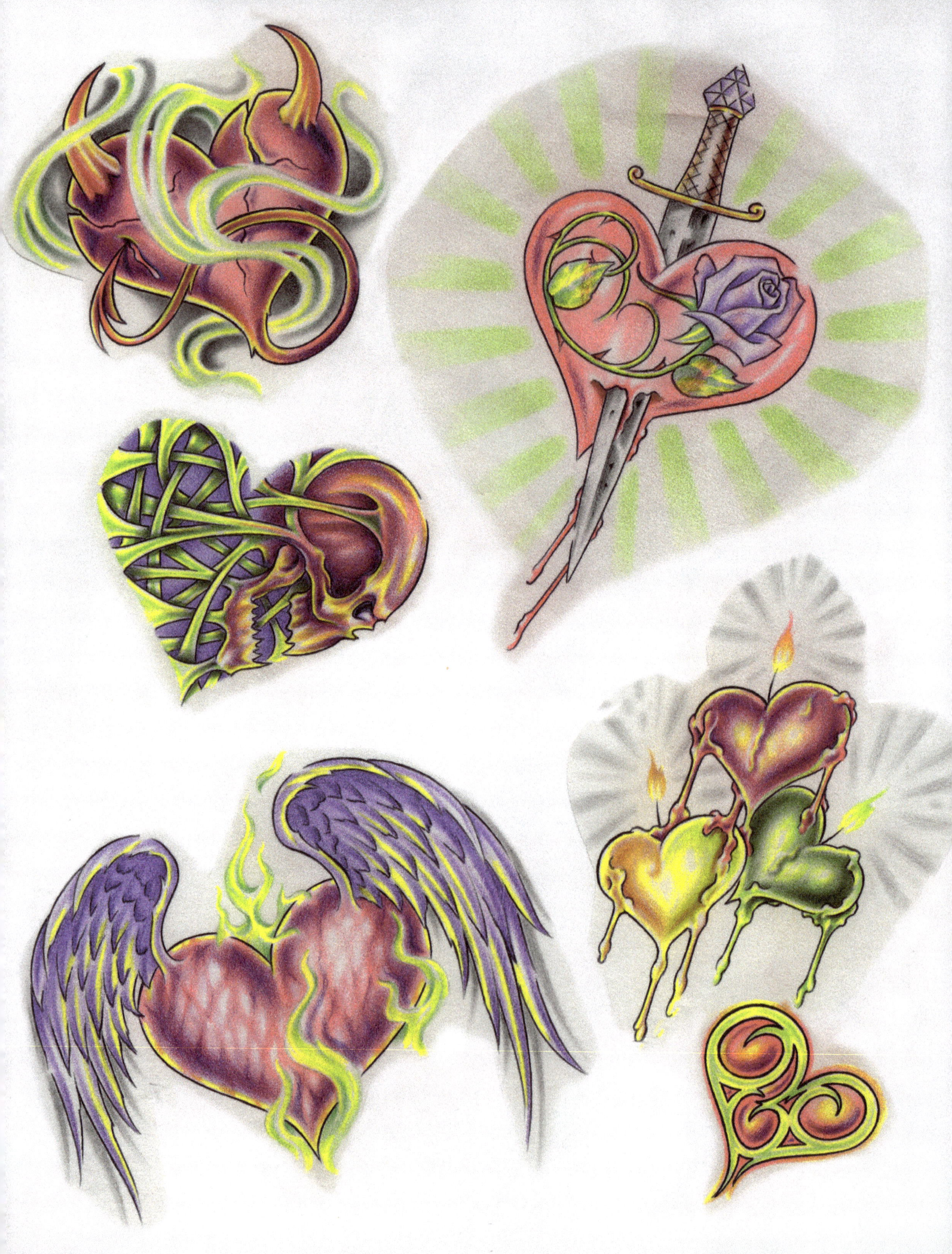

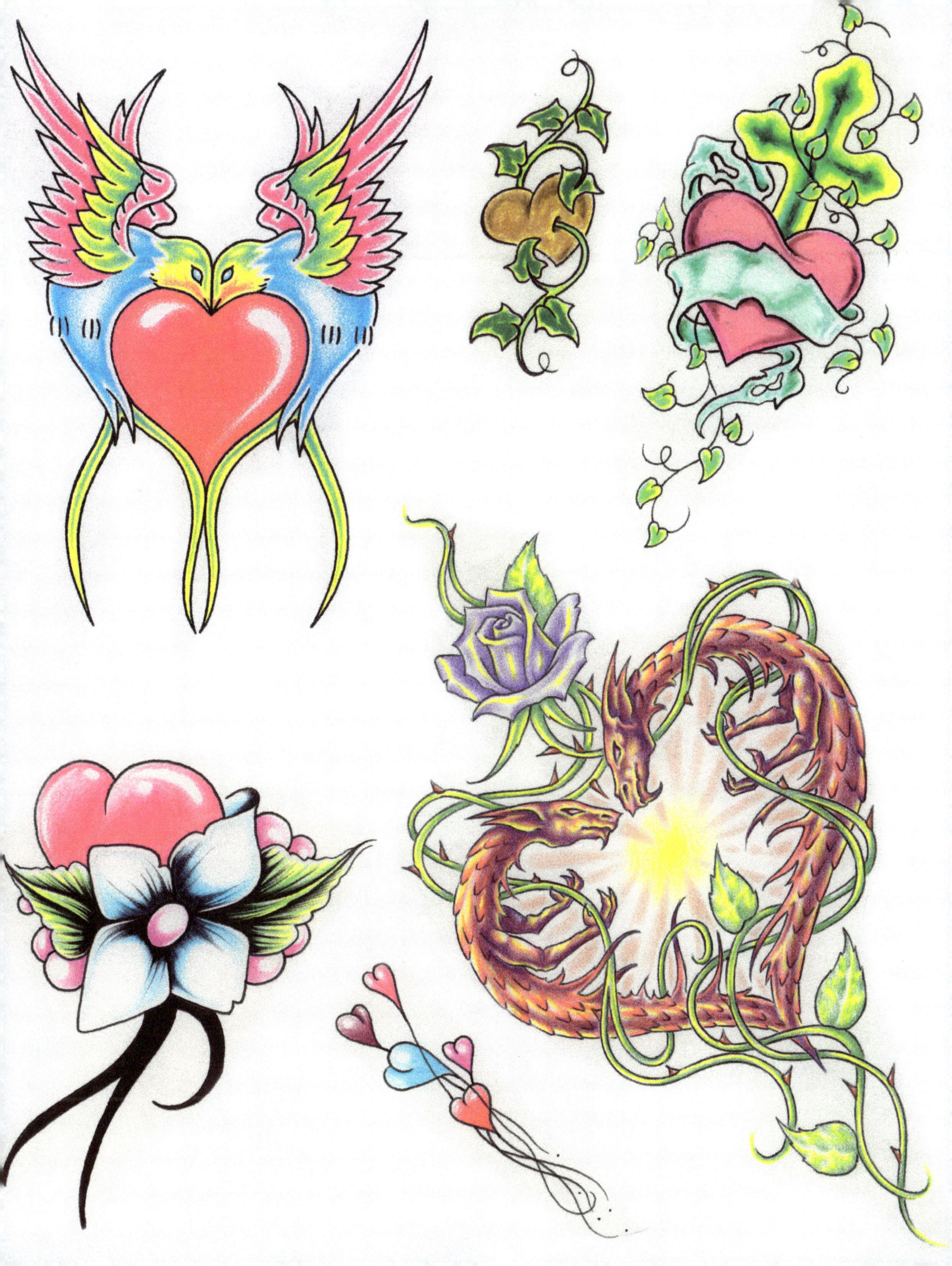

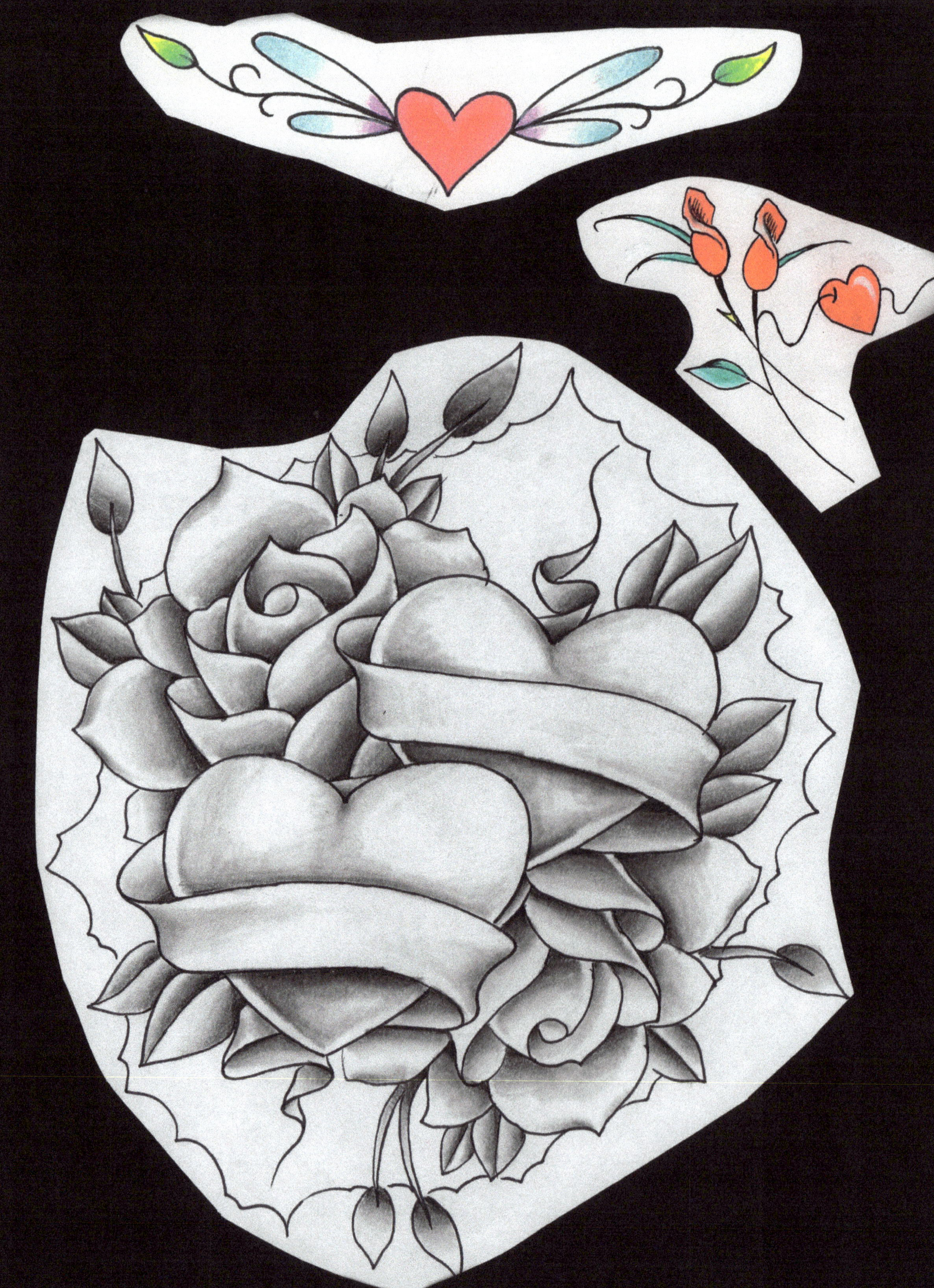

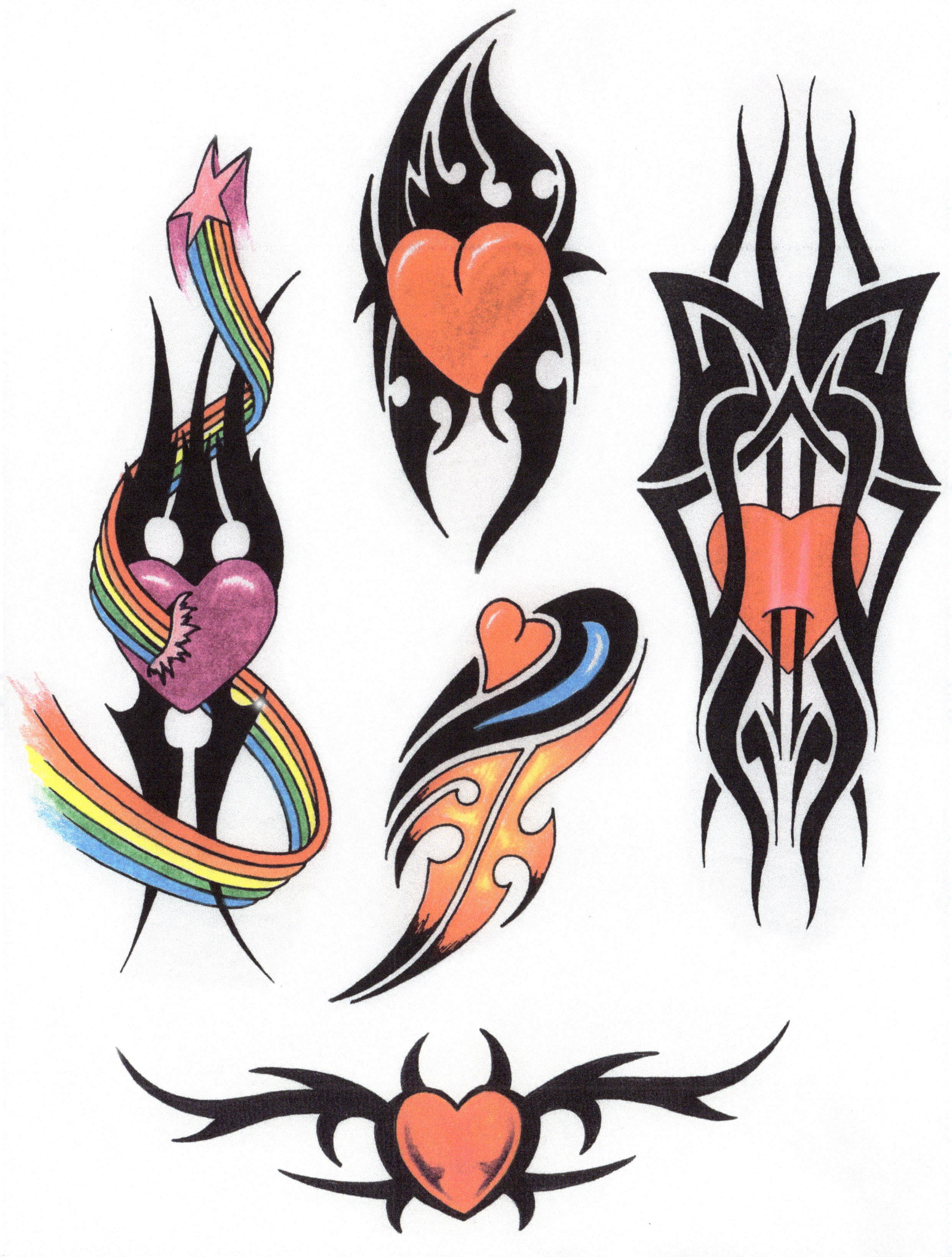

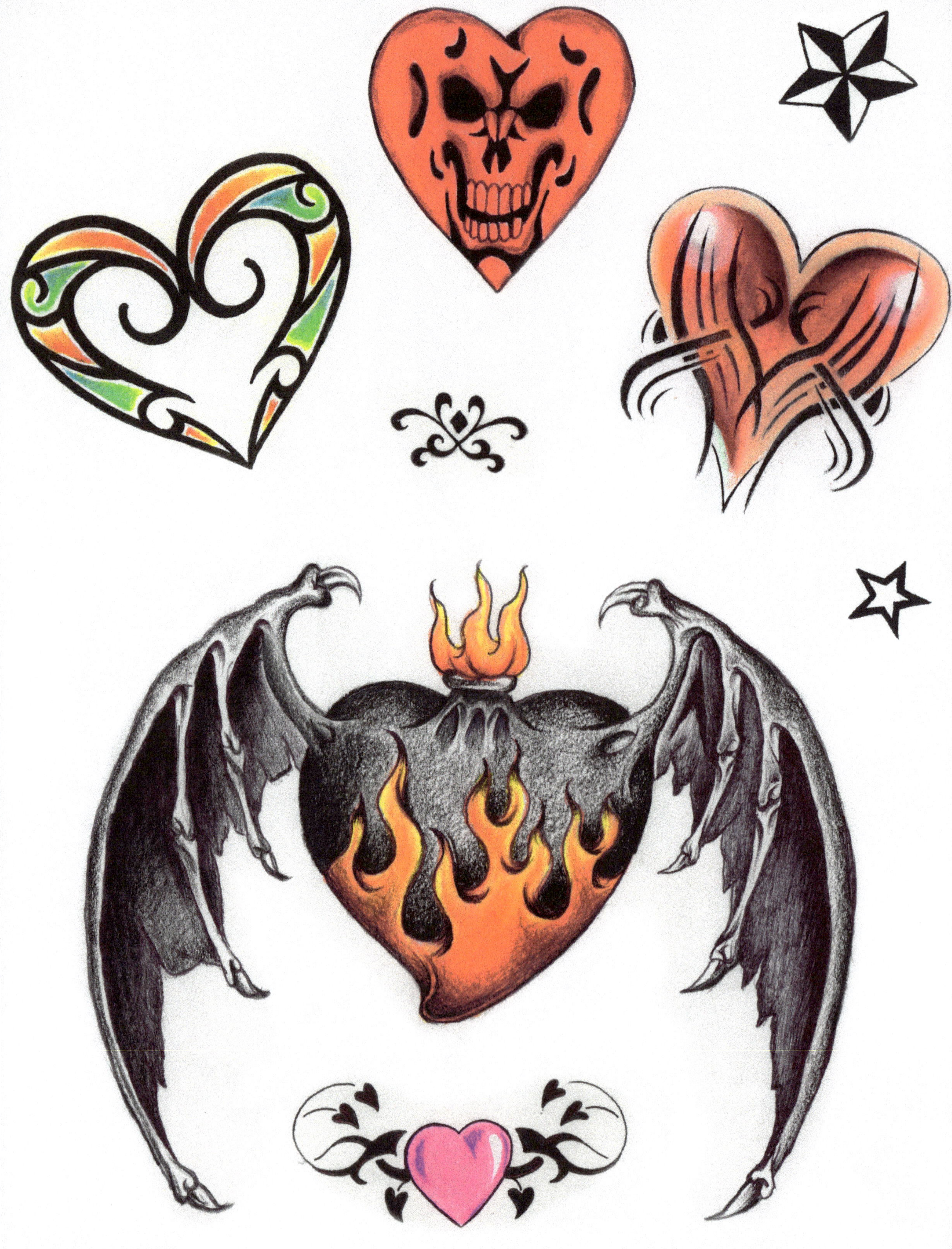

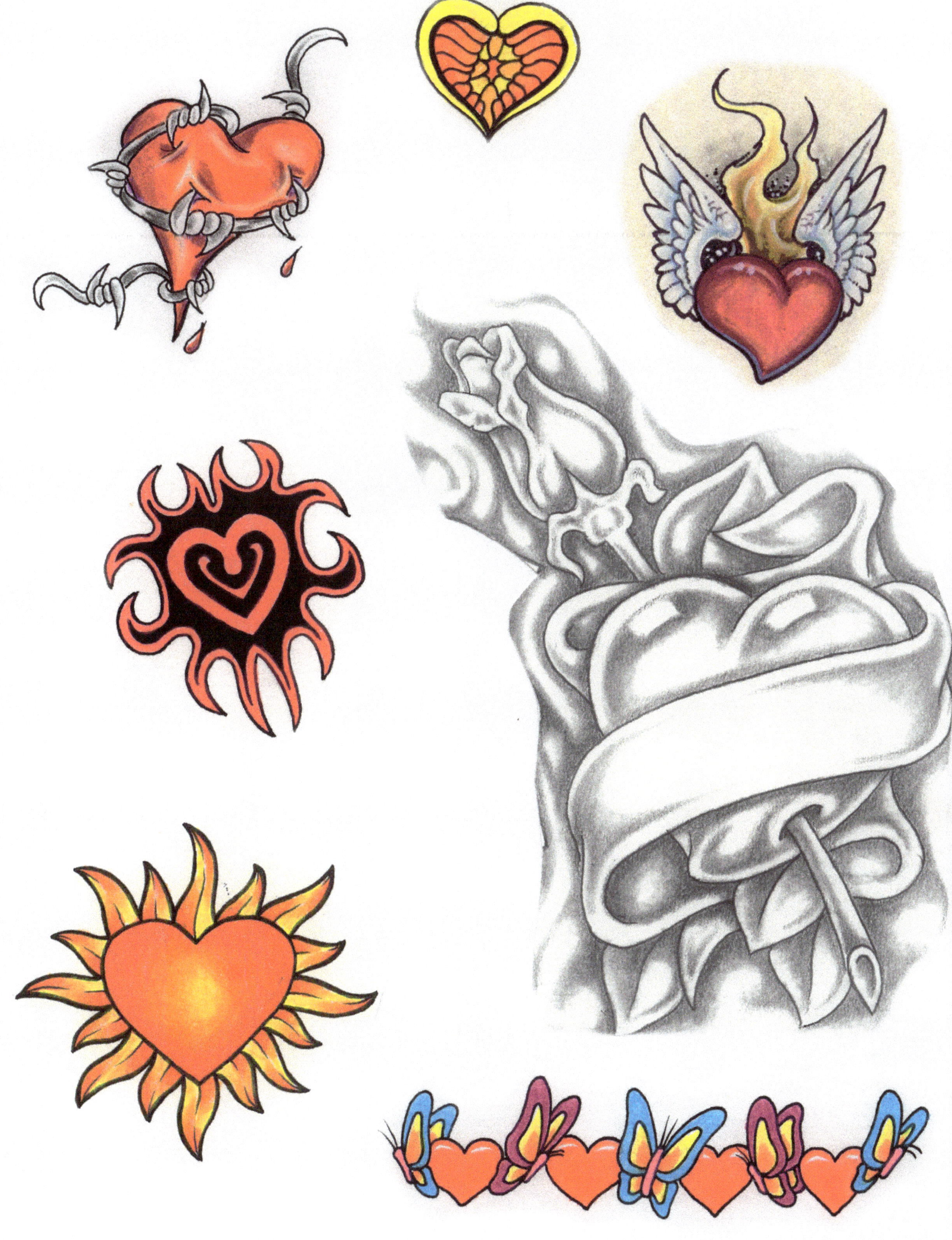

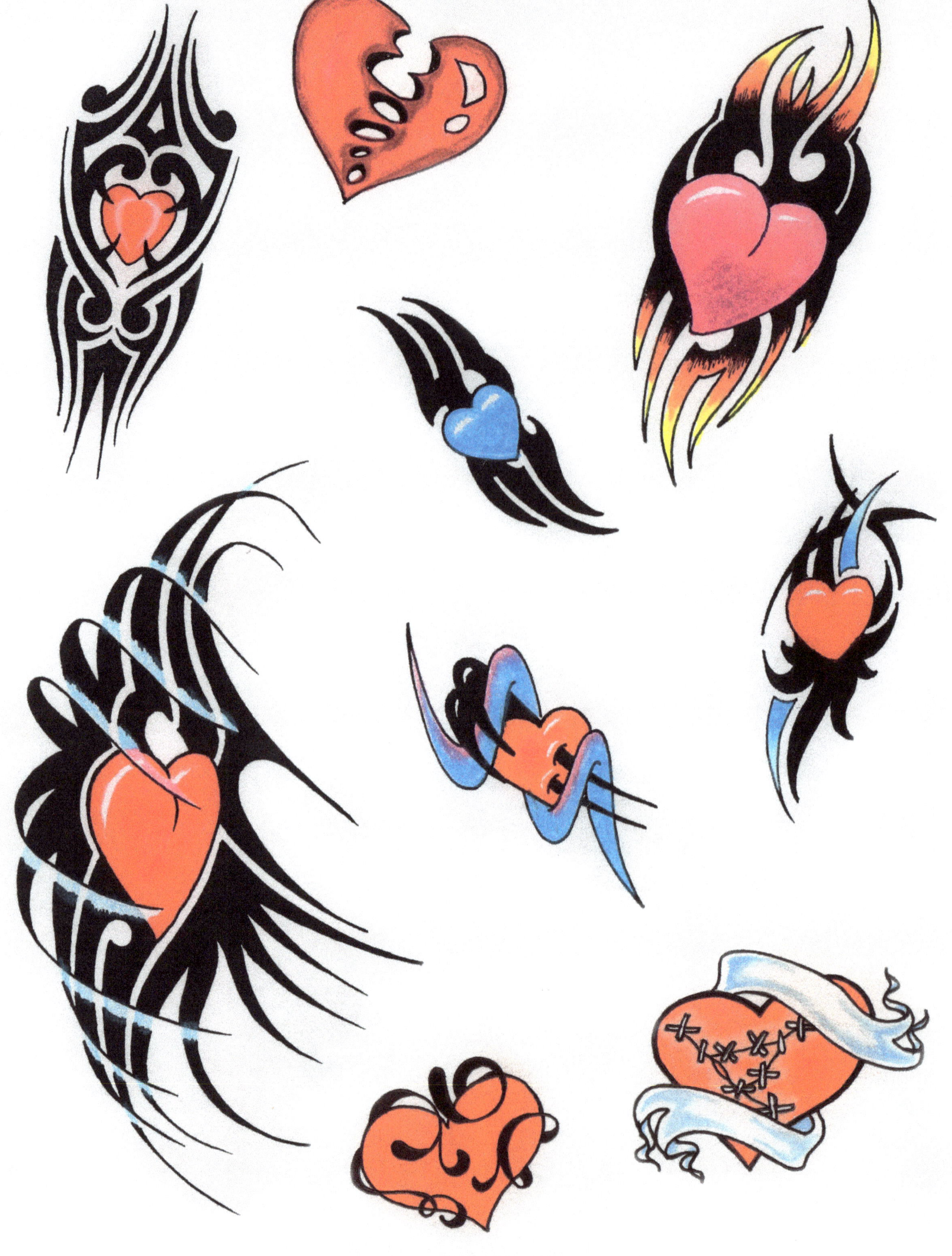

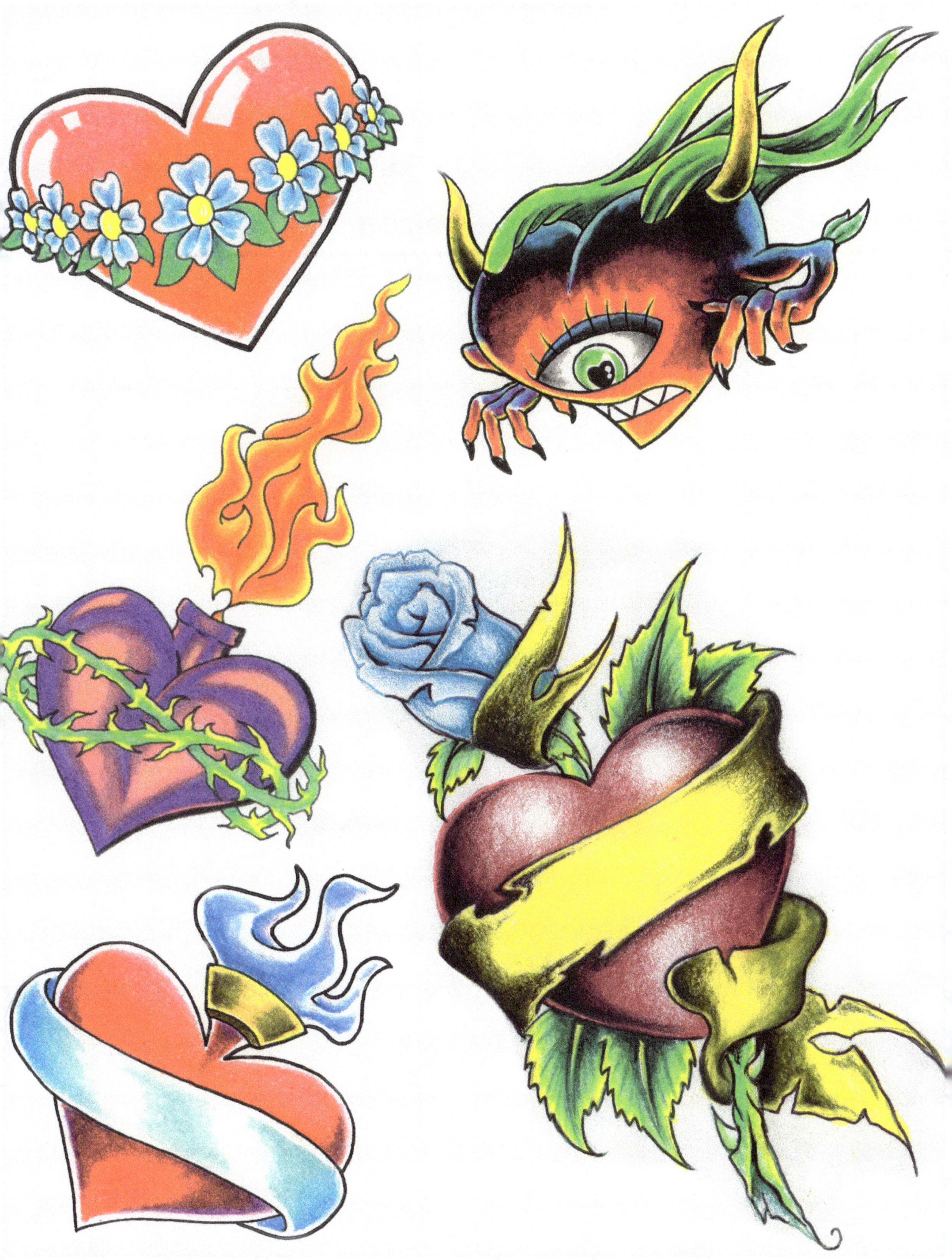

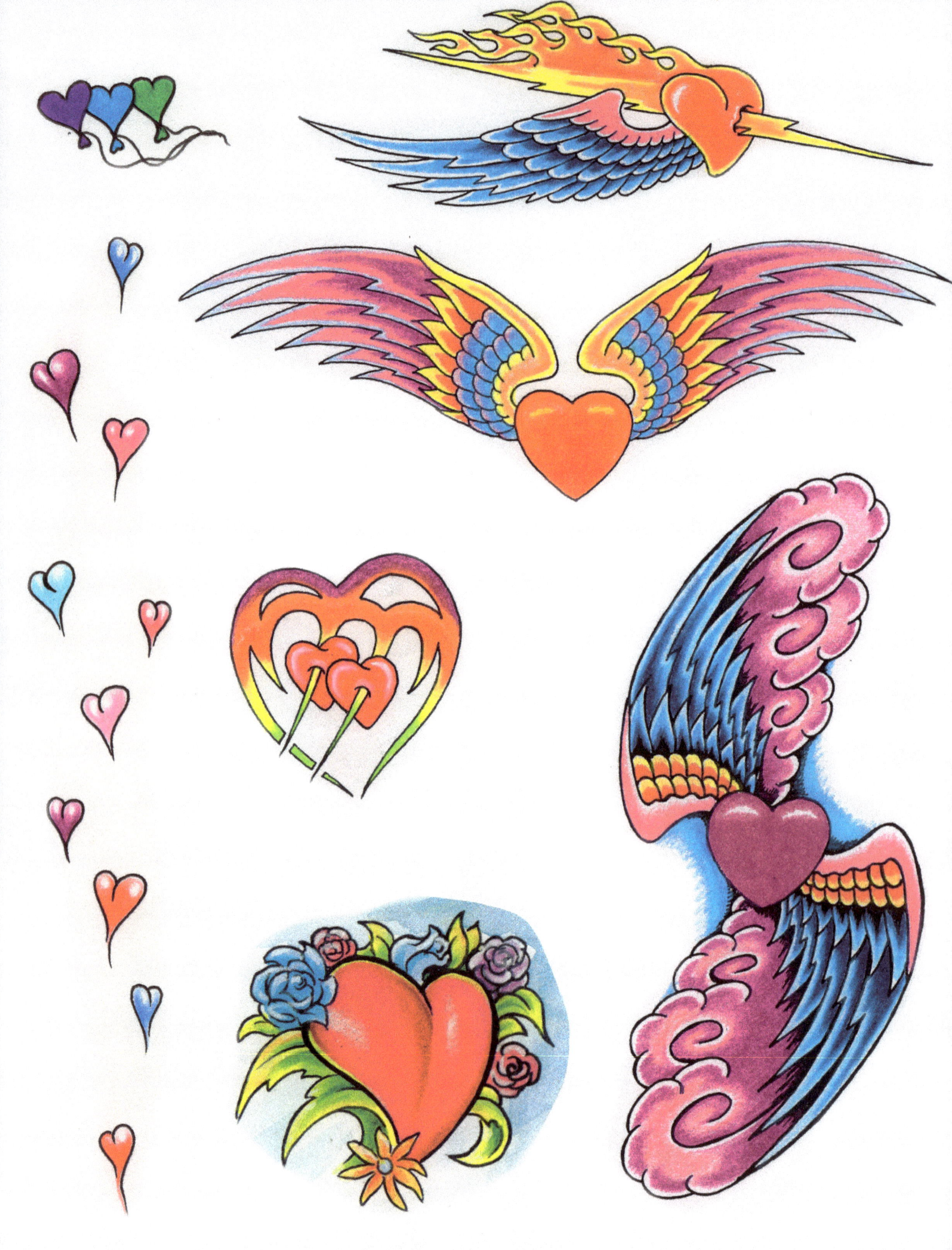

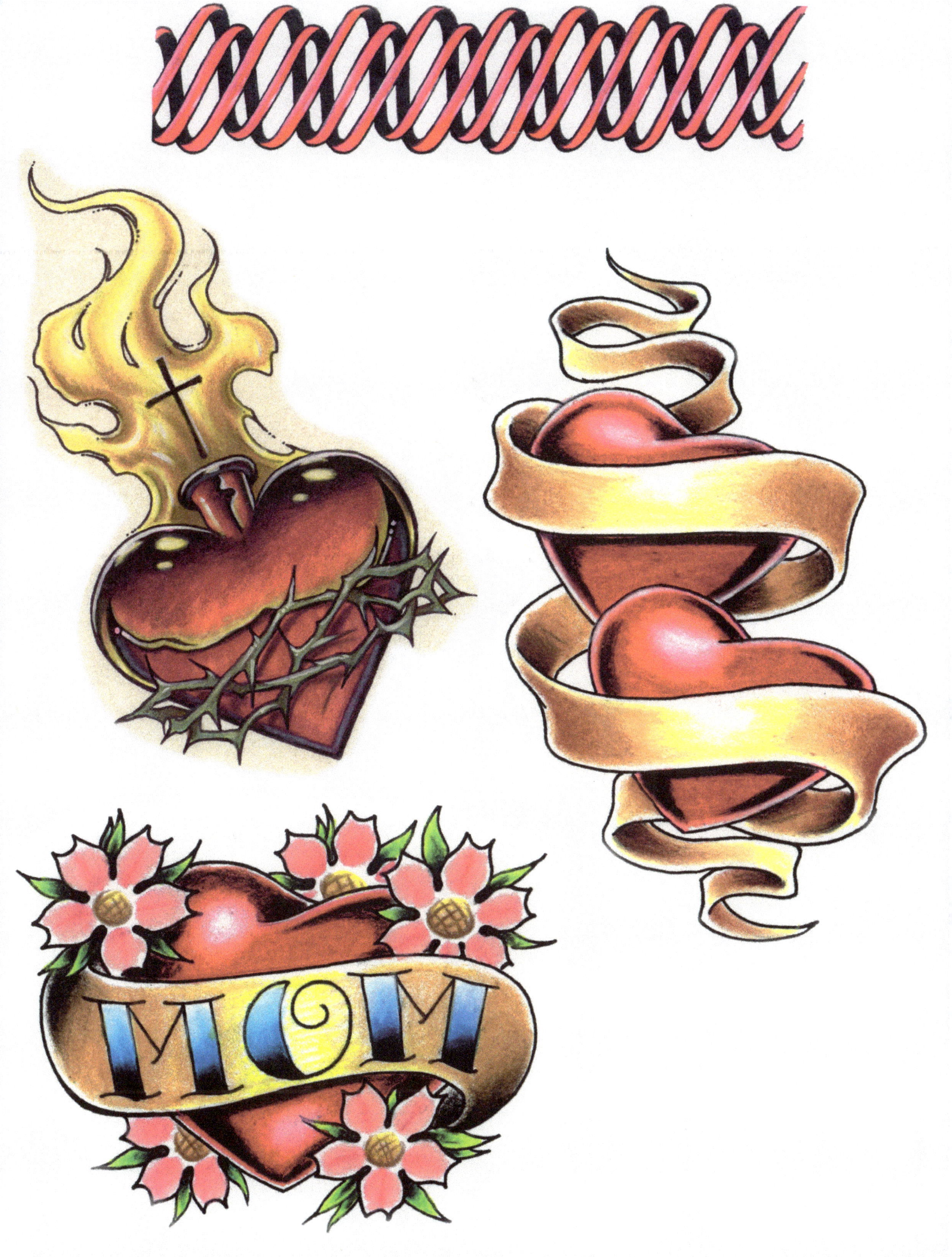

MOM

CROSSES

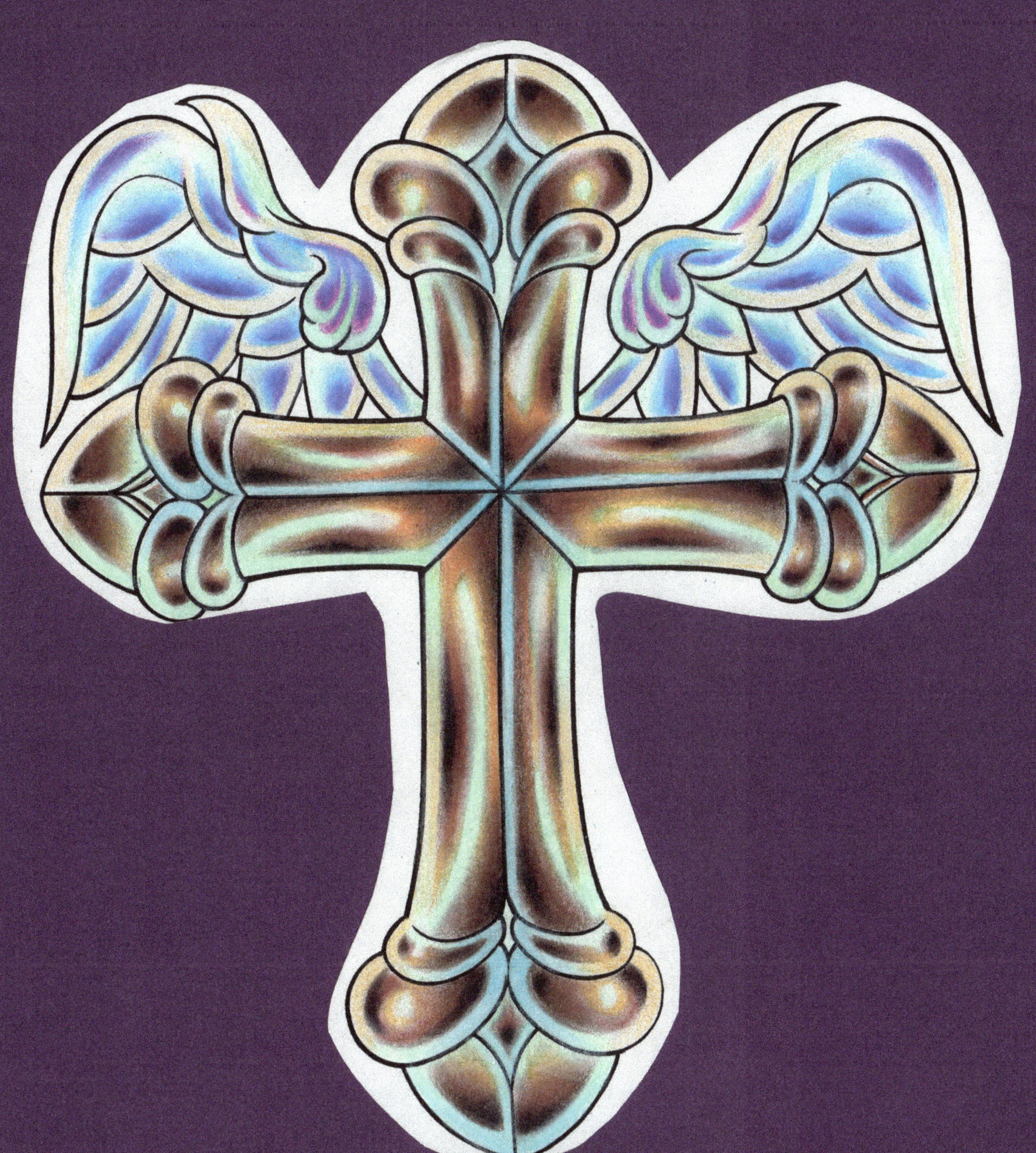

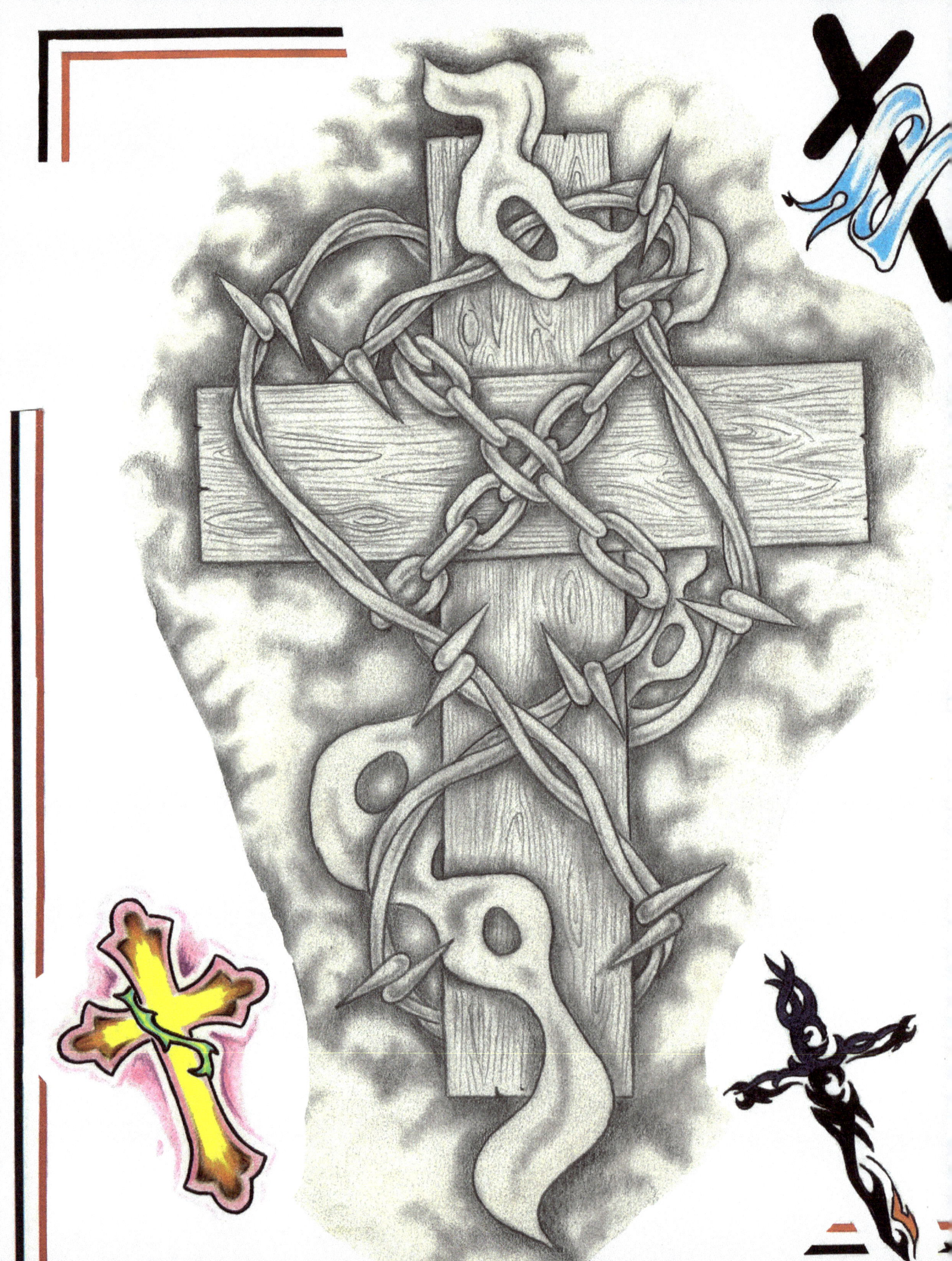

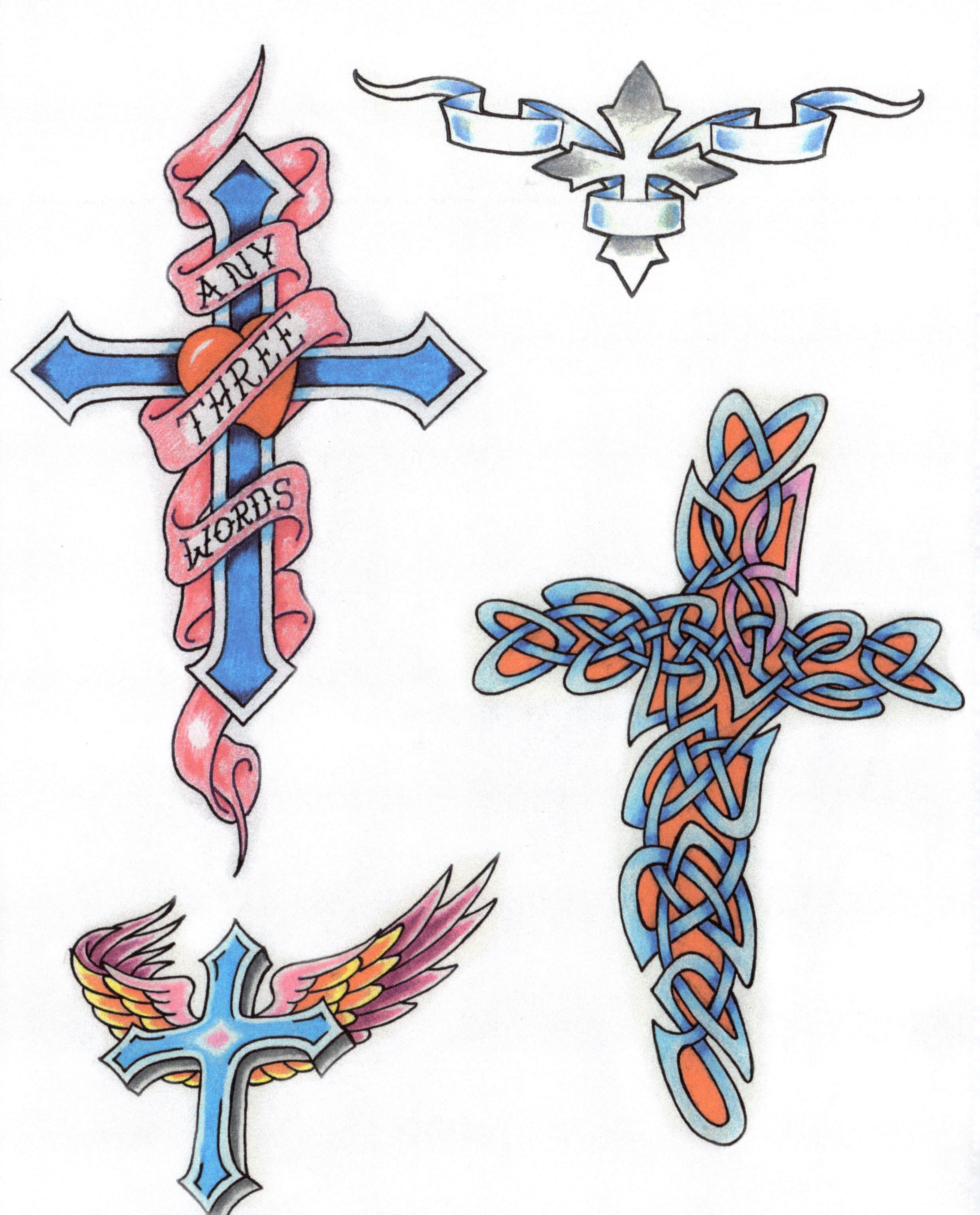

ANY
THREE
WORDS

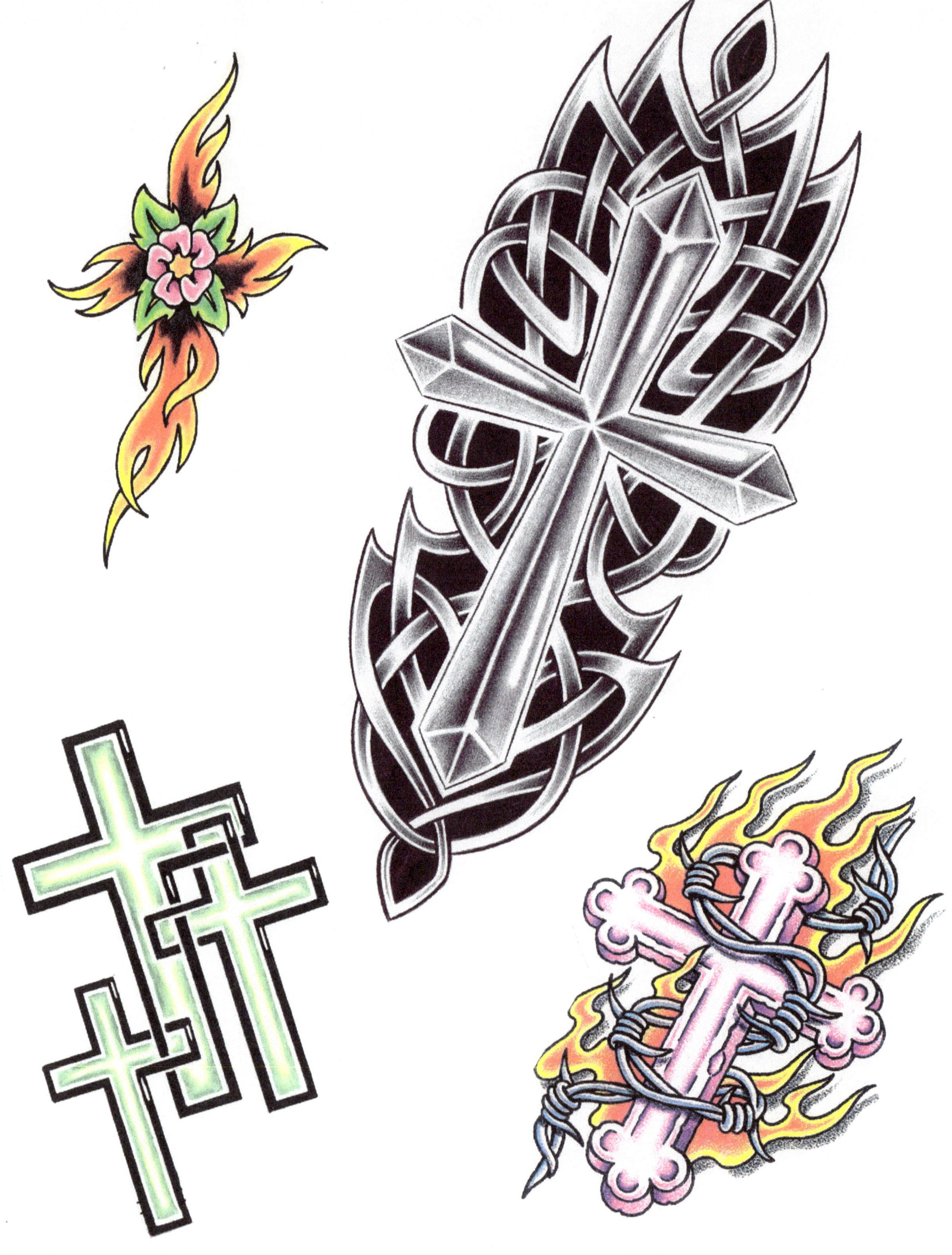

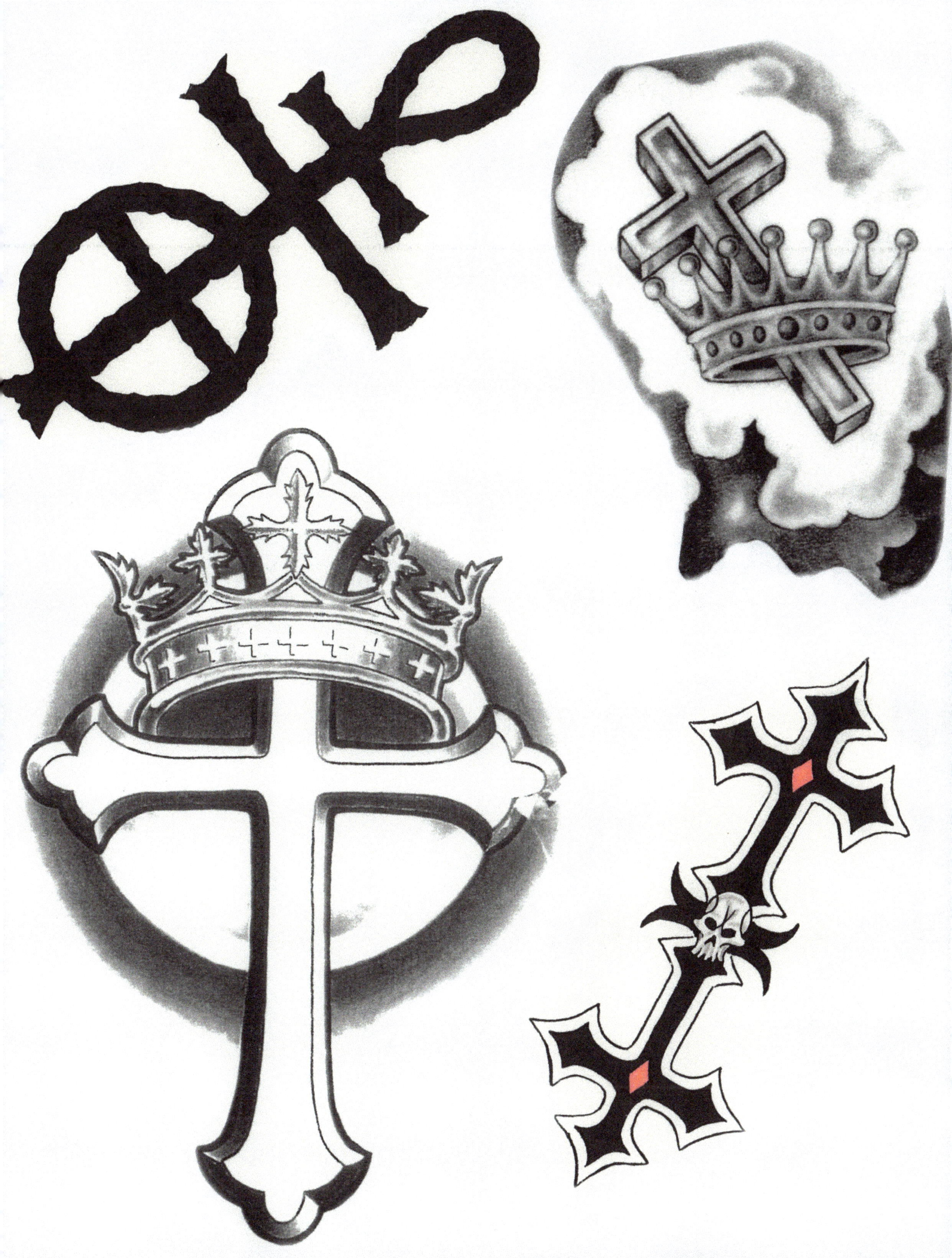

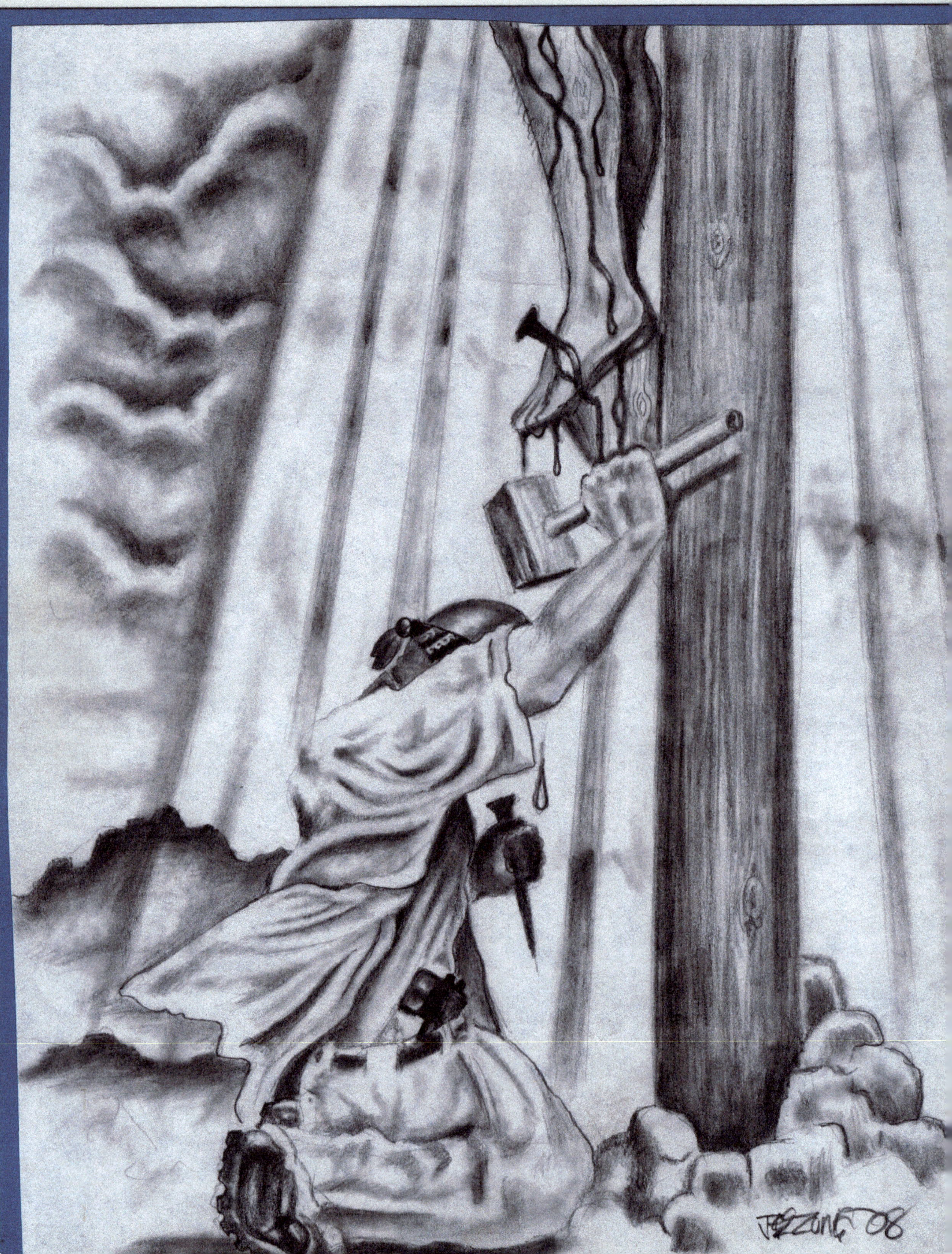

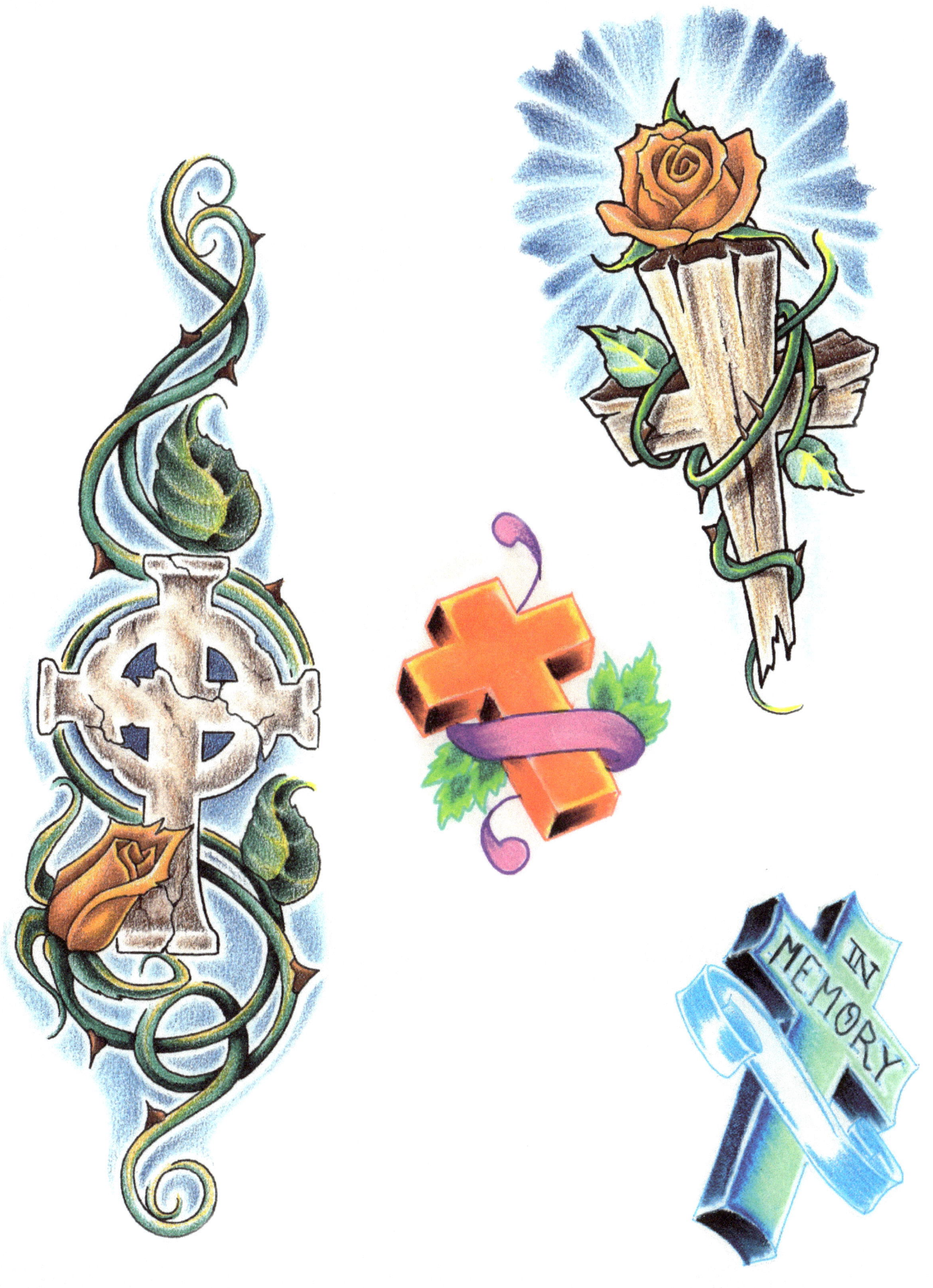

IN
MEMORY

DAWN
R.I.P.
MIKE

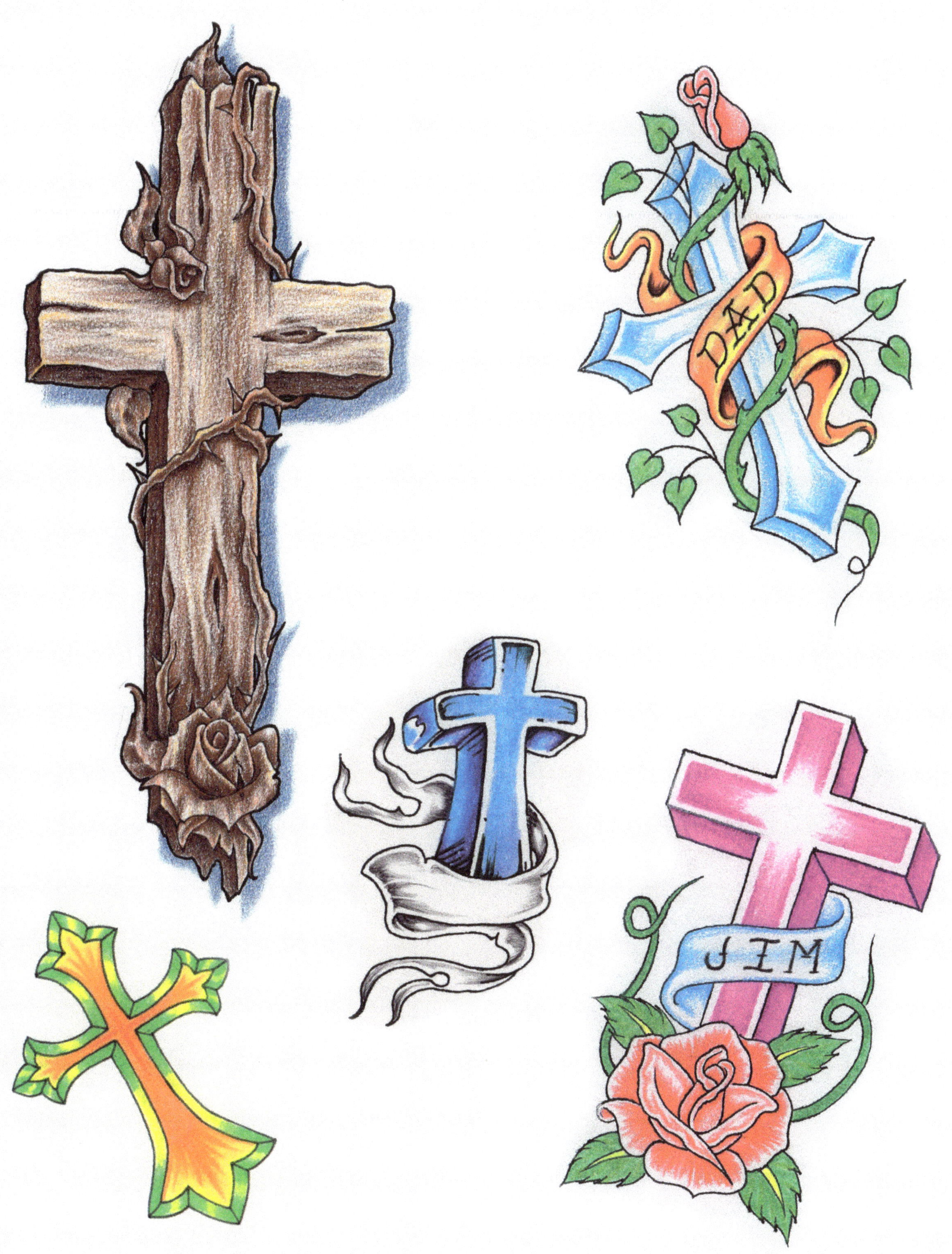
DAD
JIM

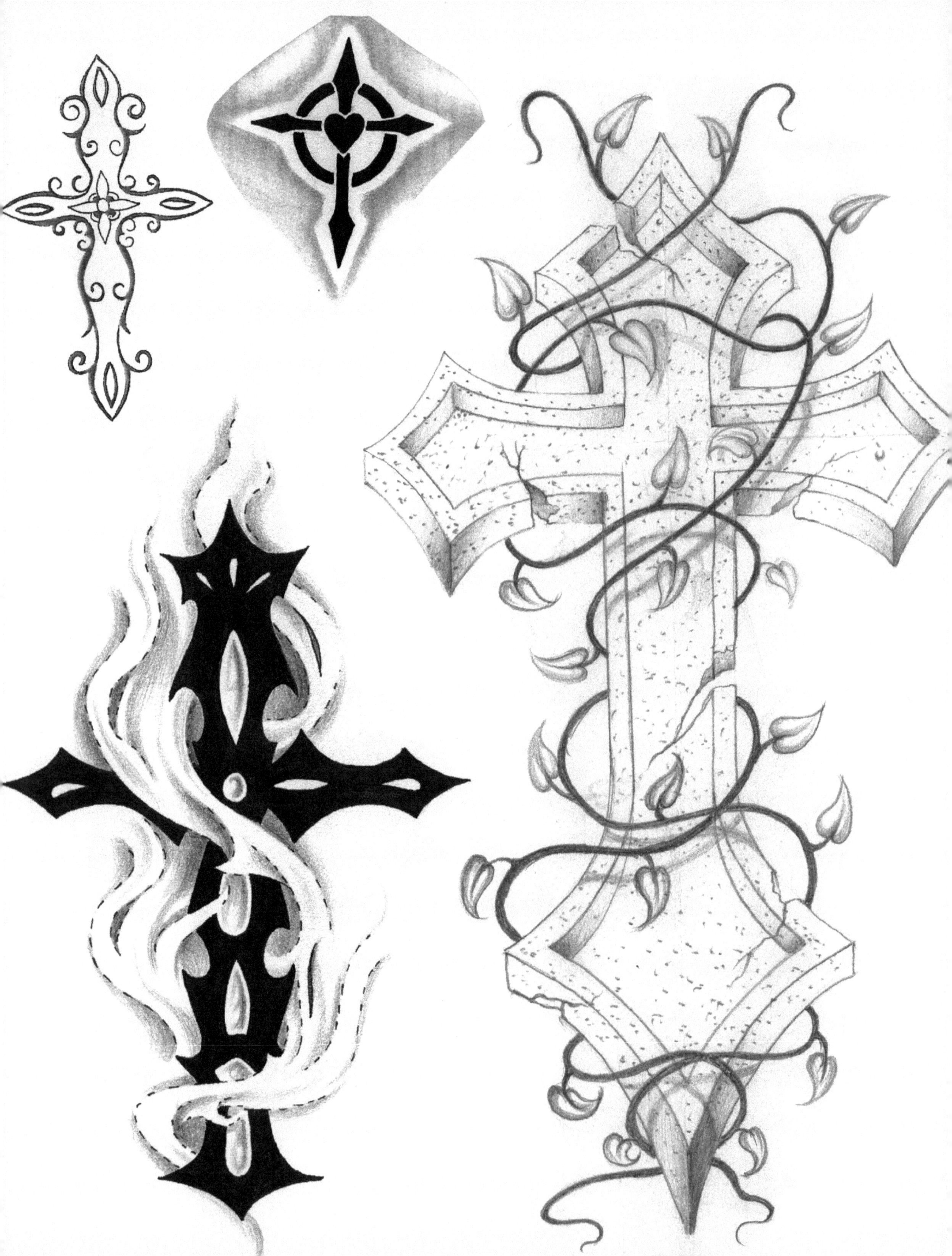

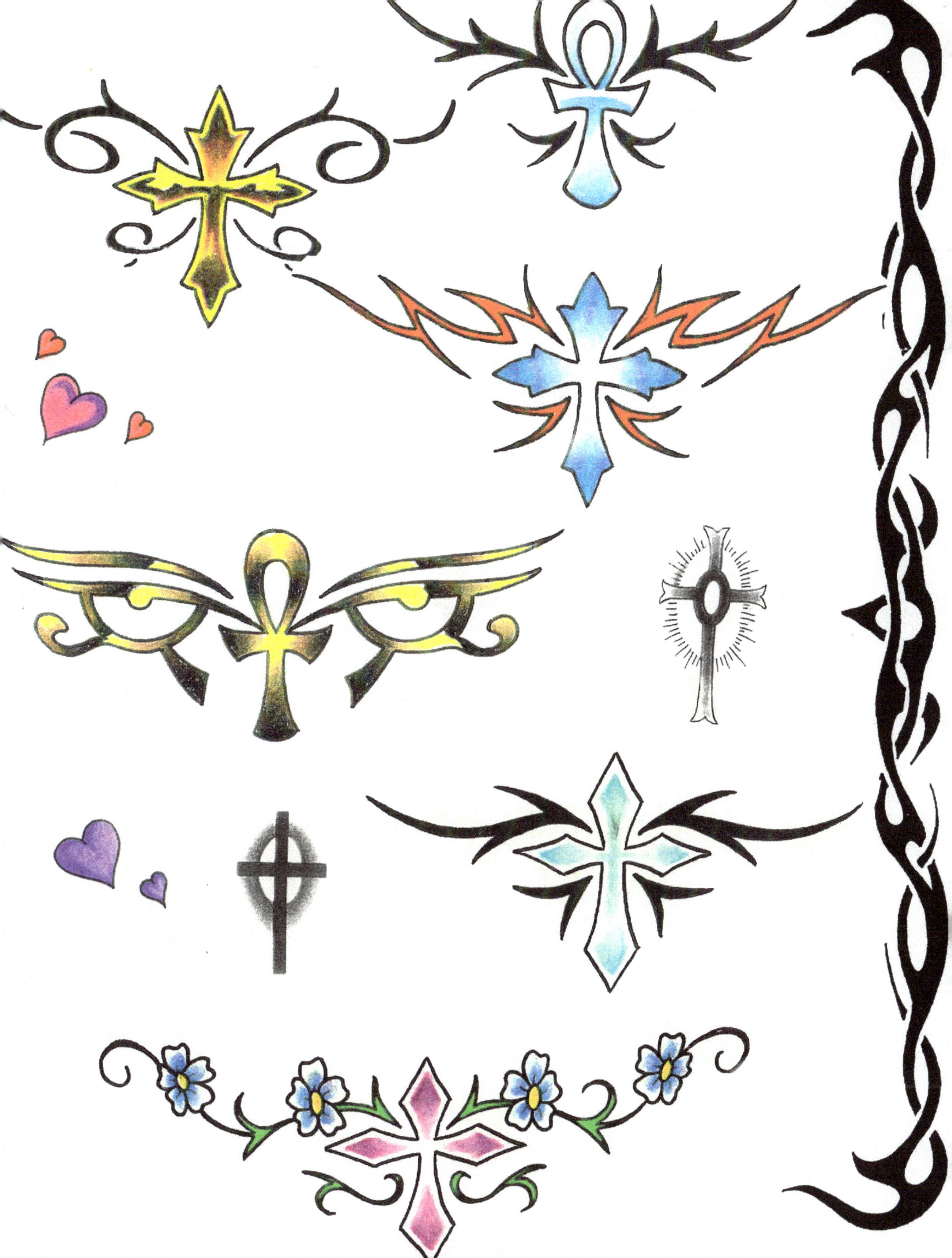

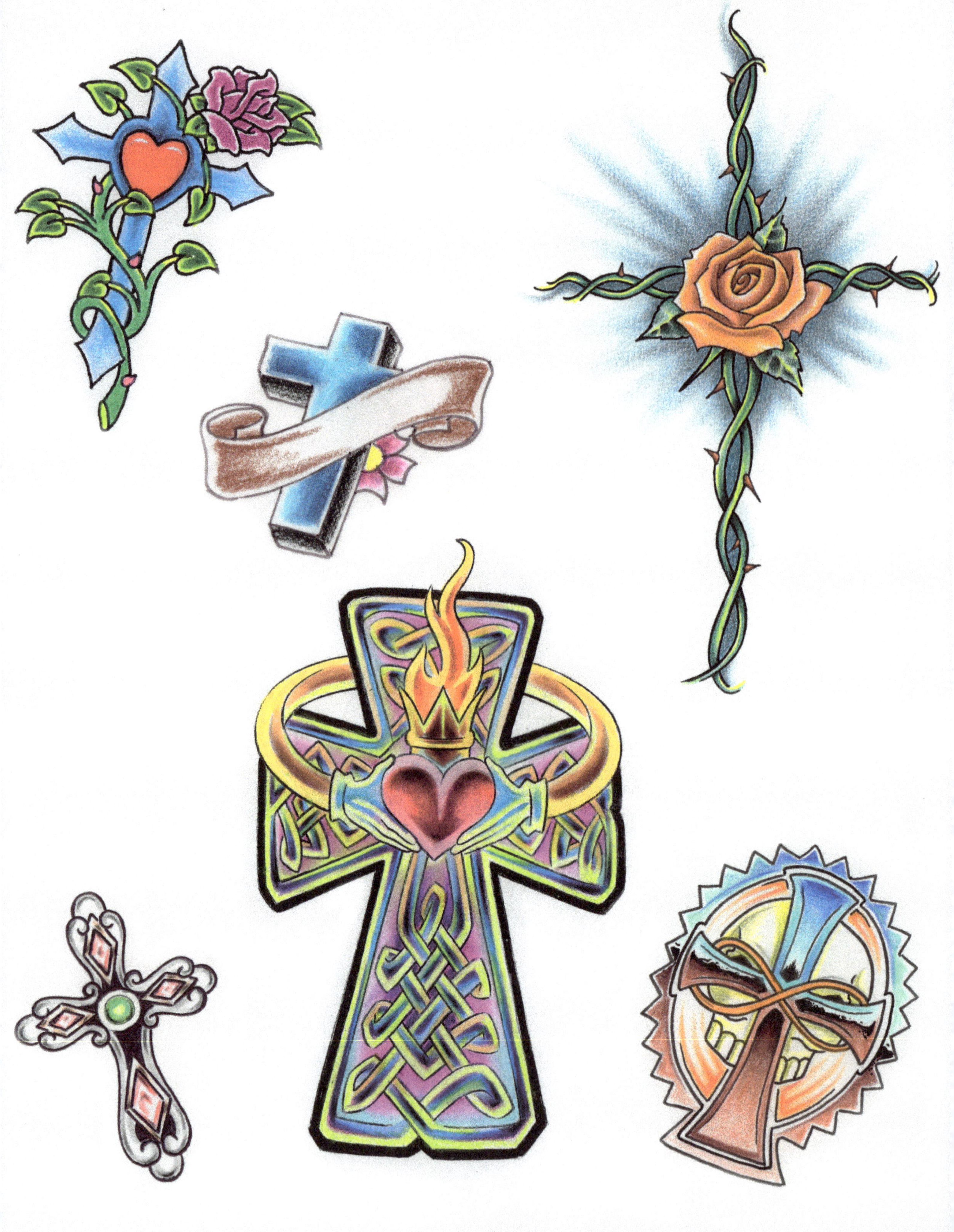

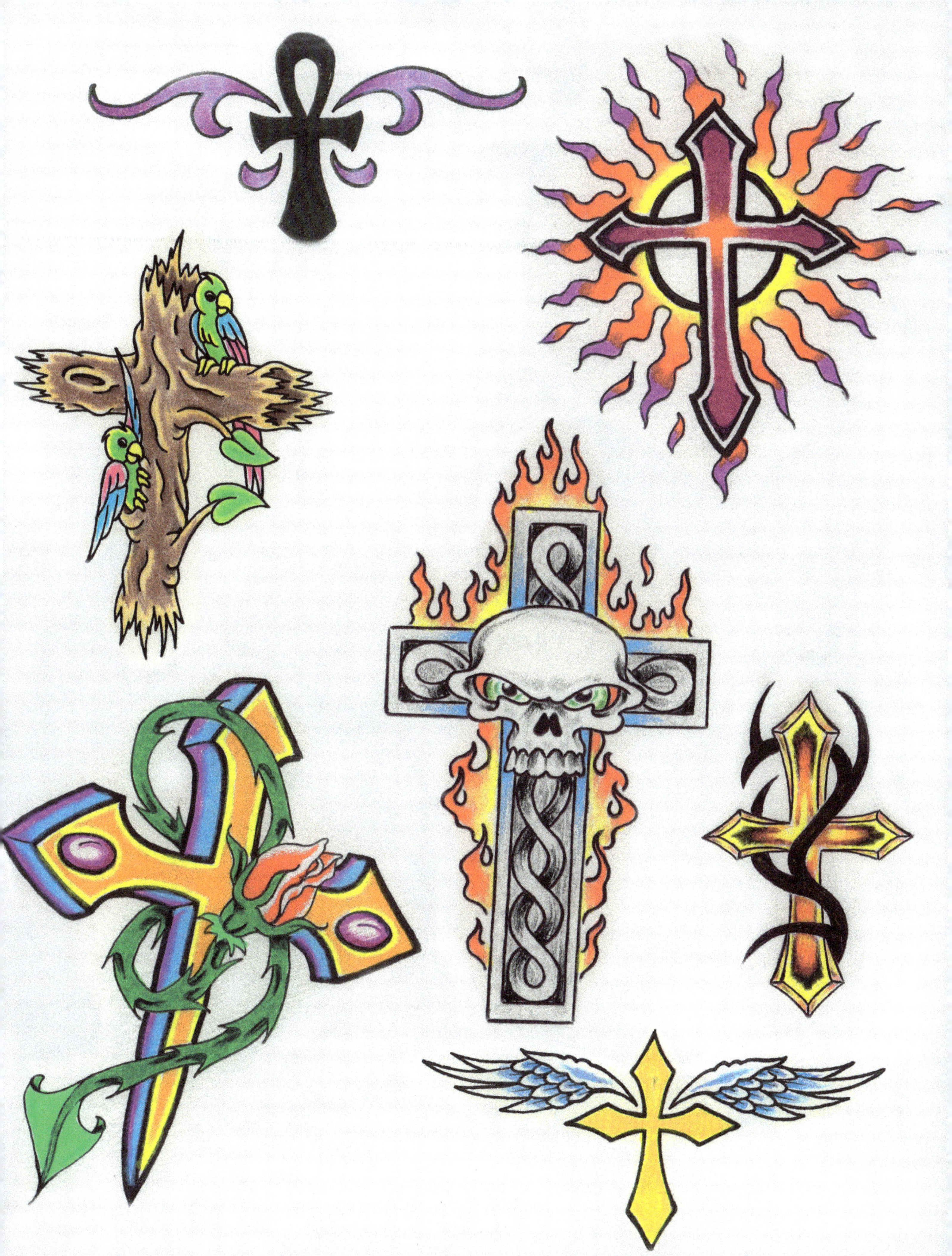

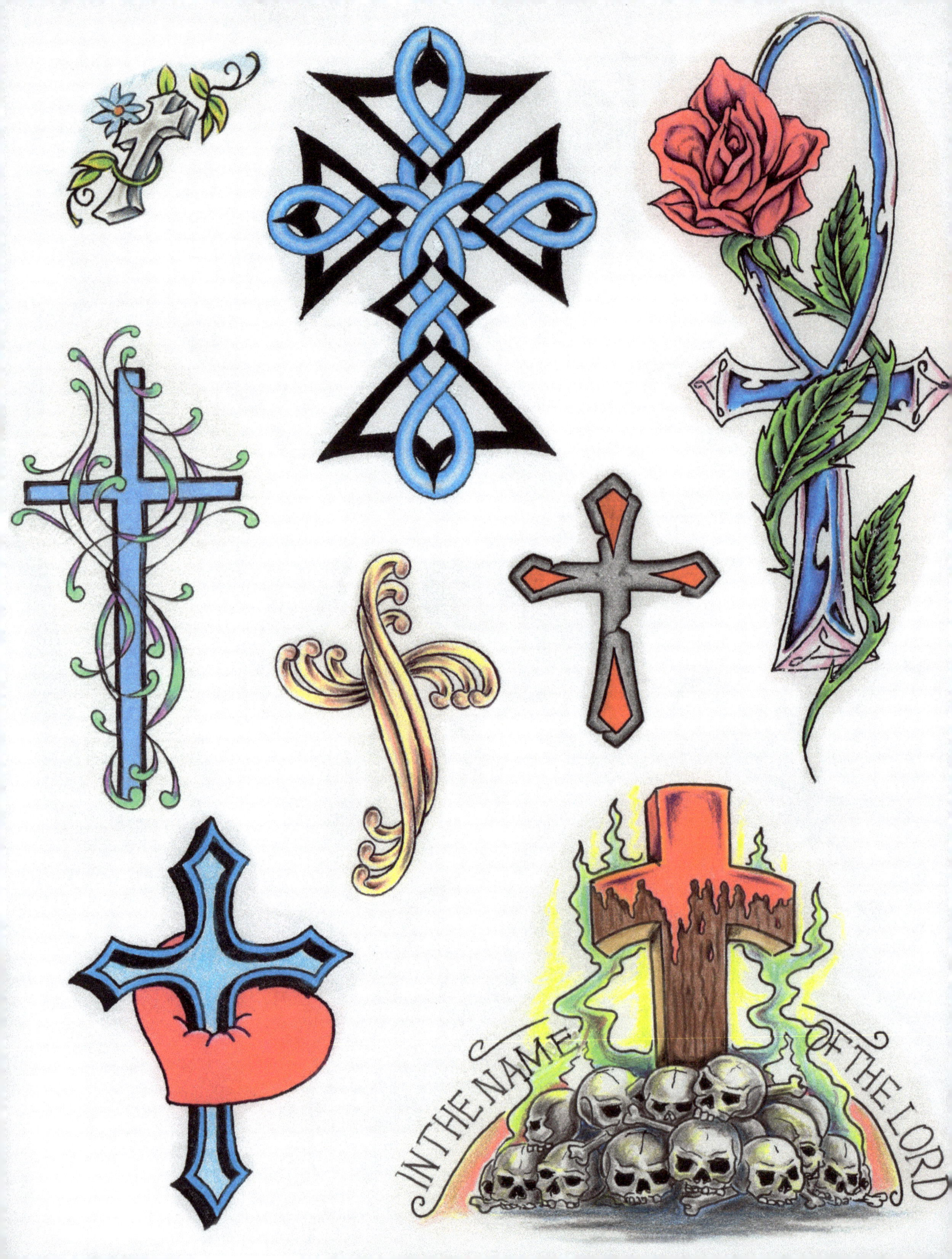
IN THE NAME
OF THE LORD

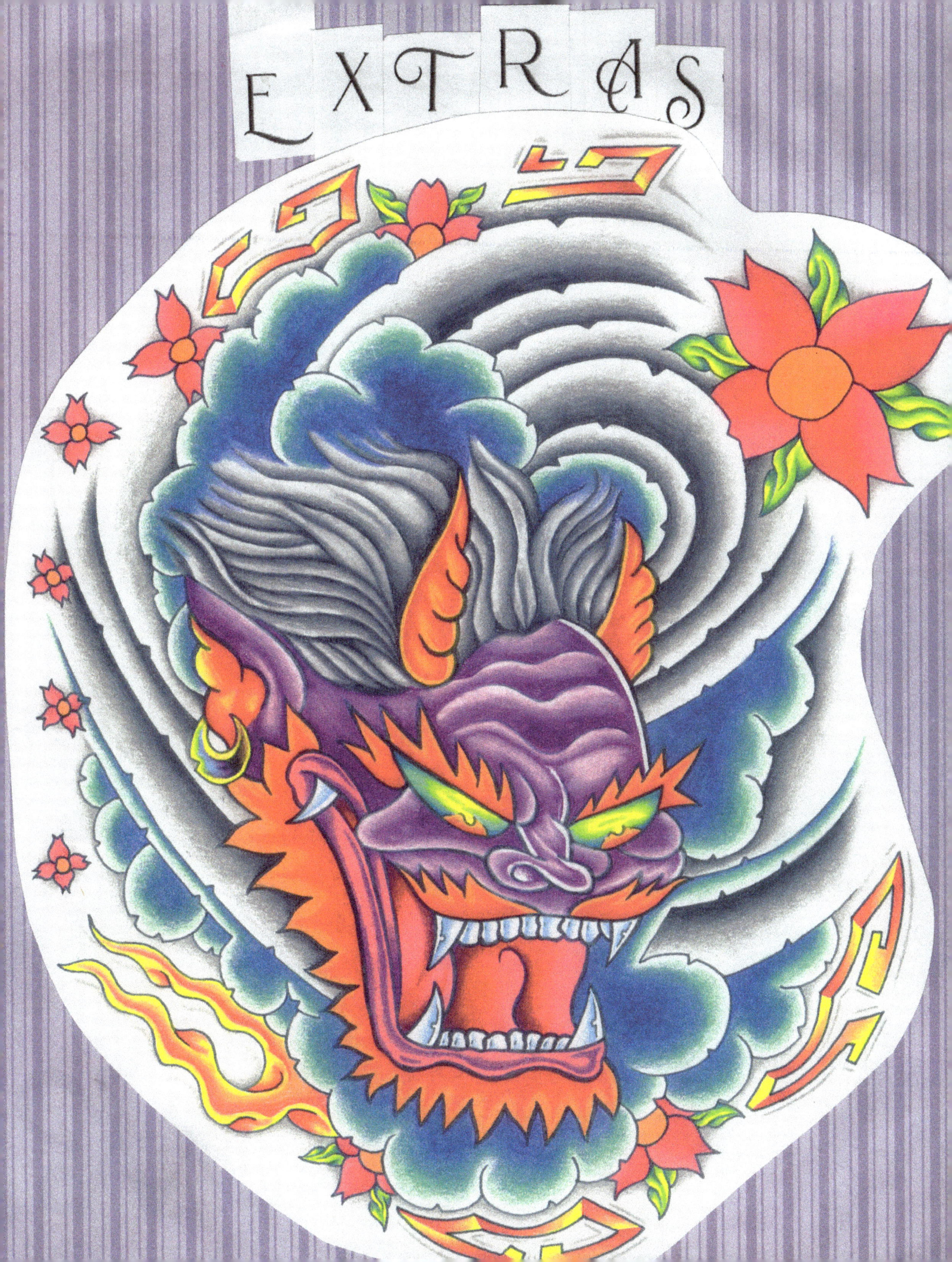

EXTRAS

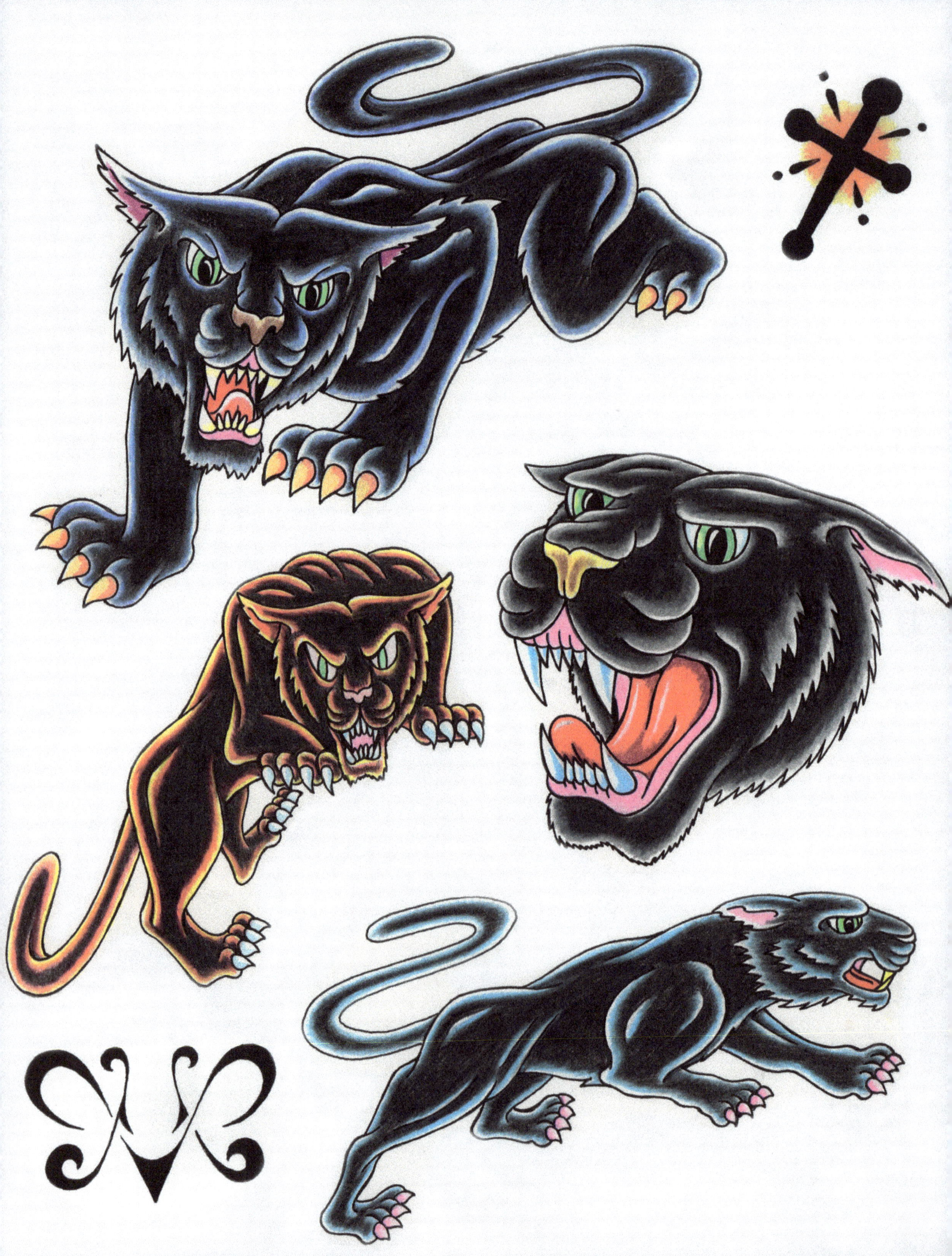

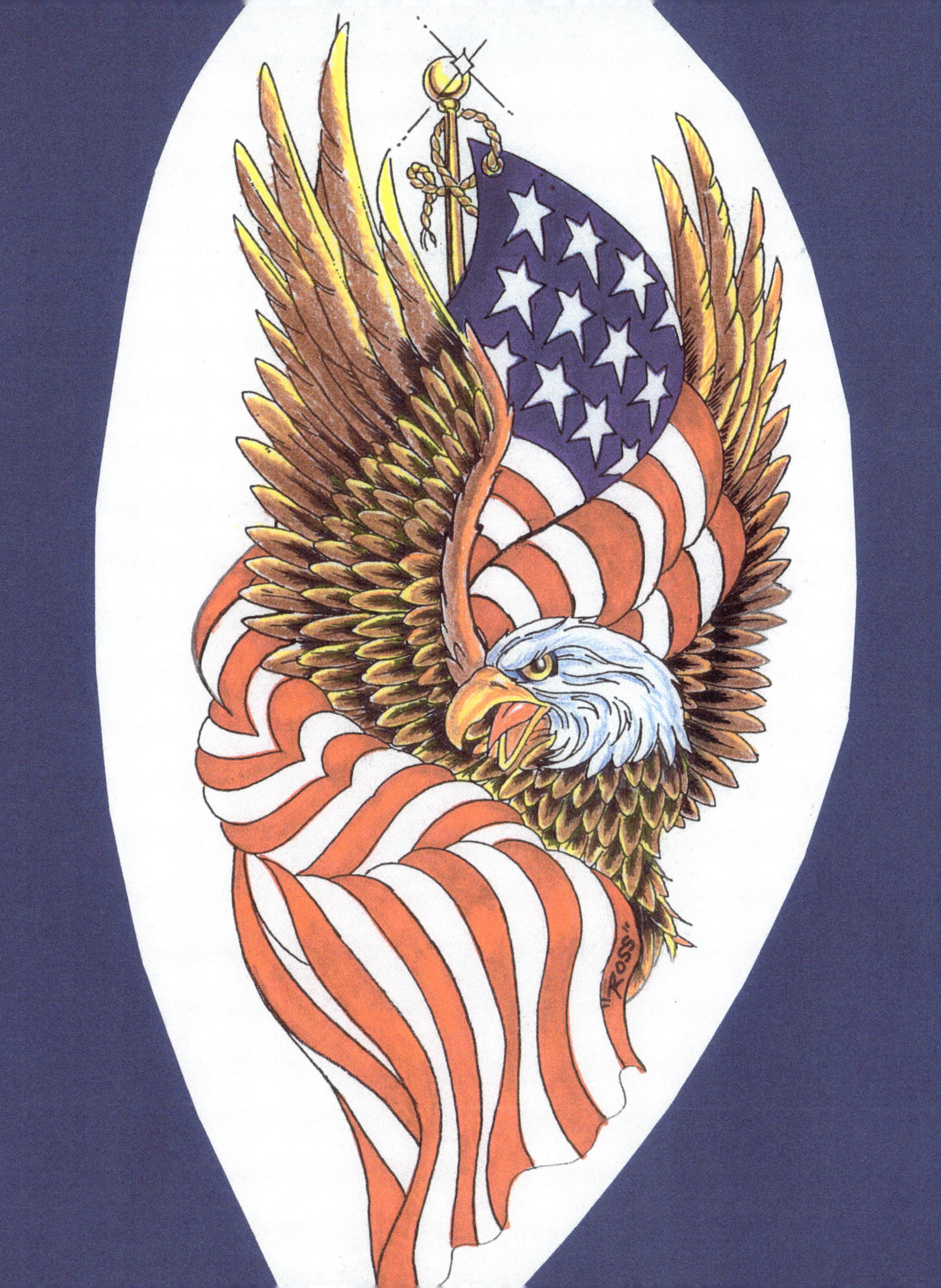

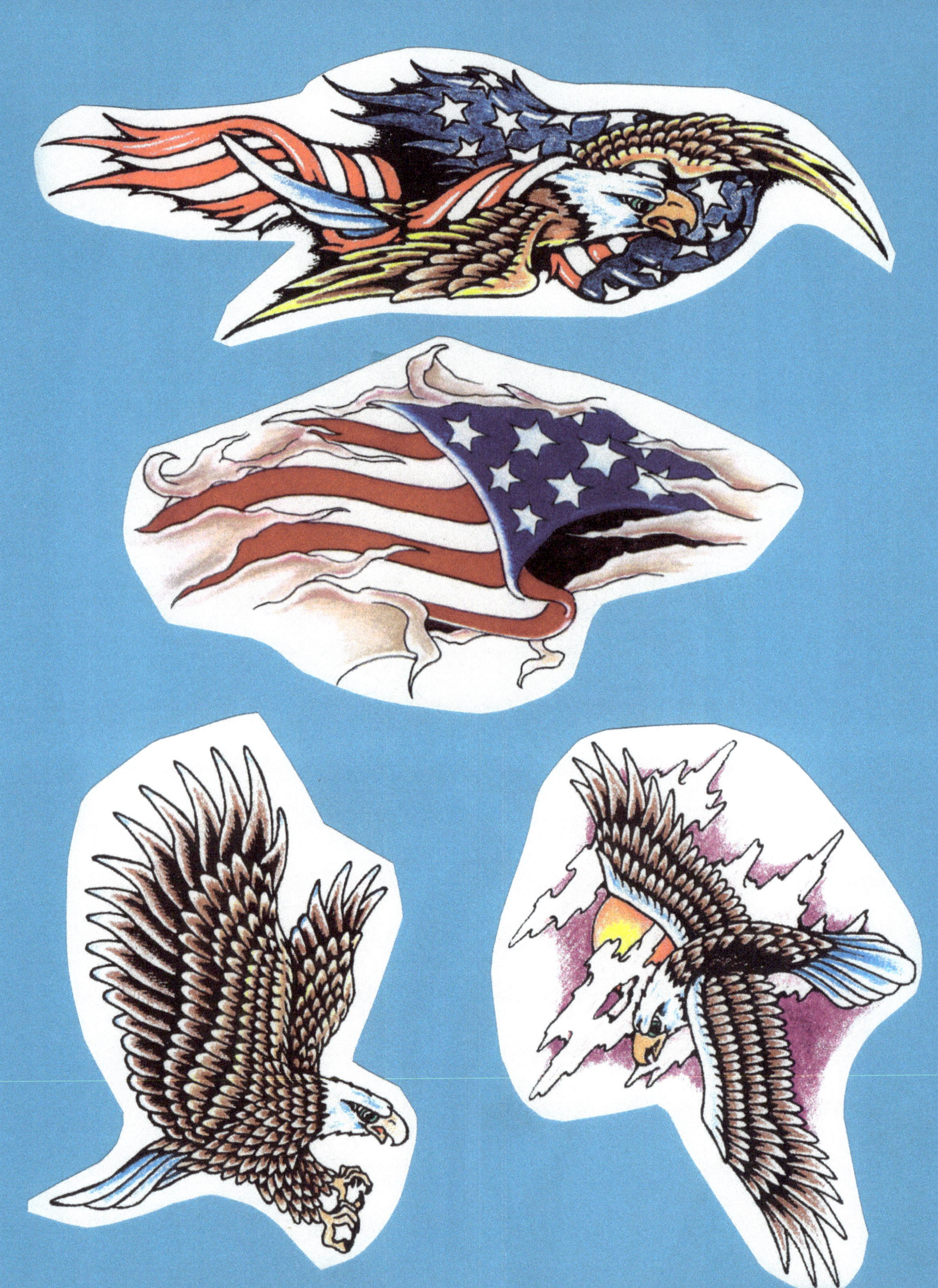

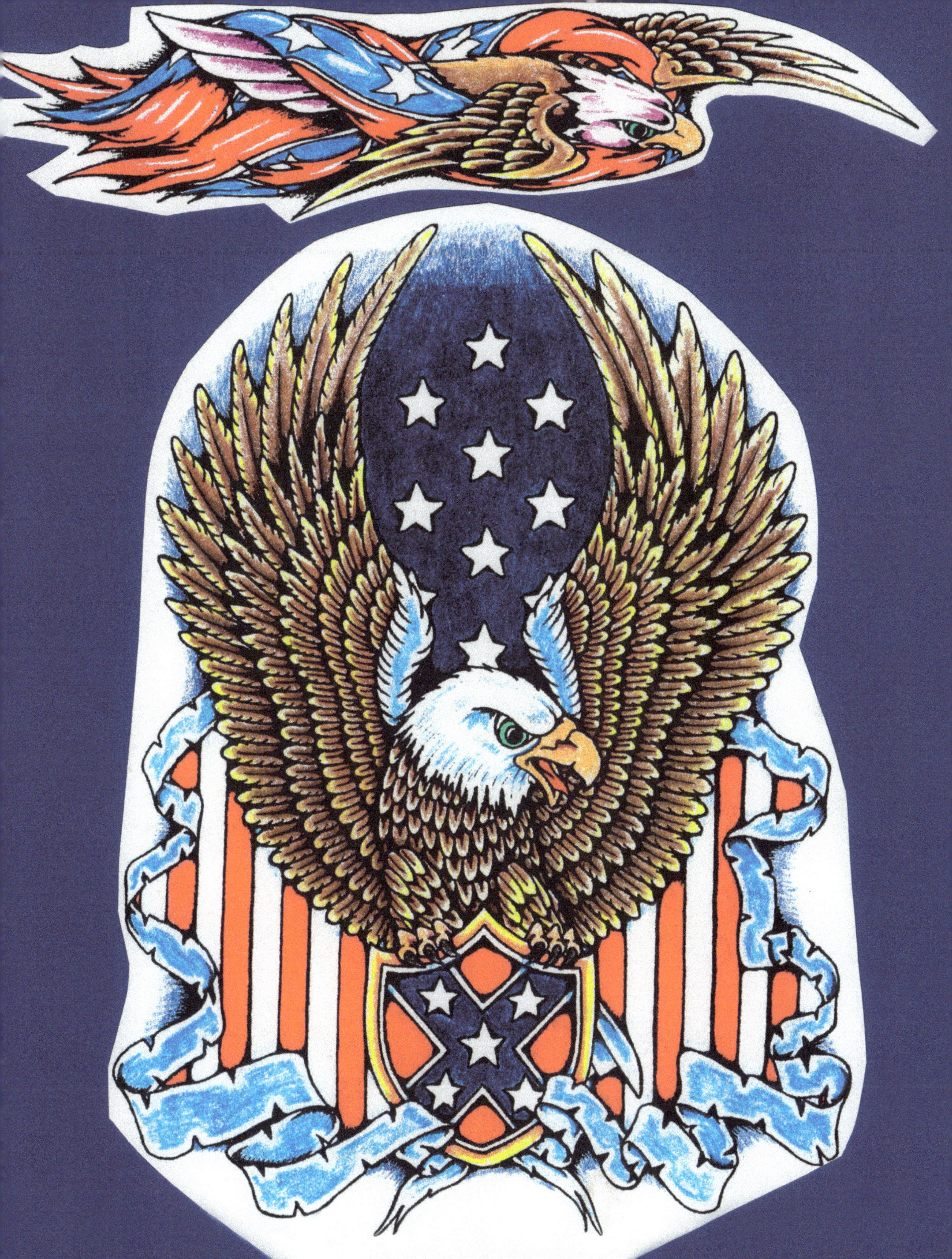

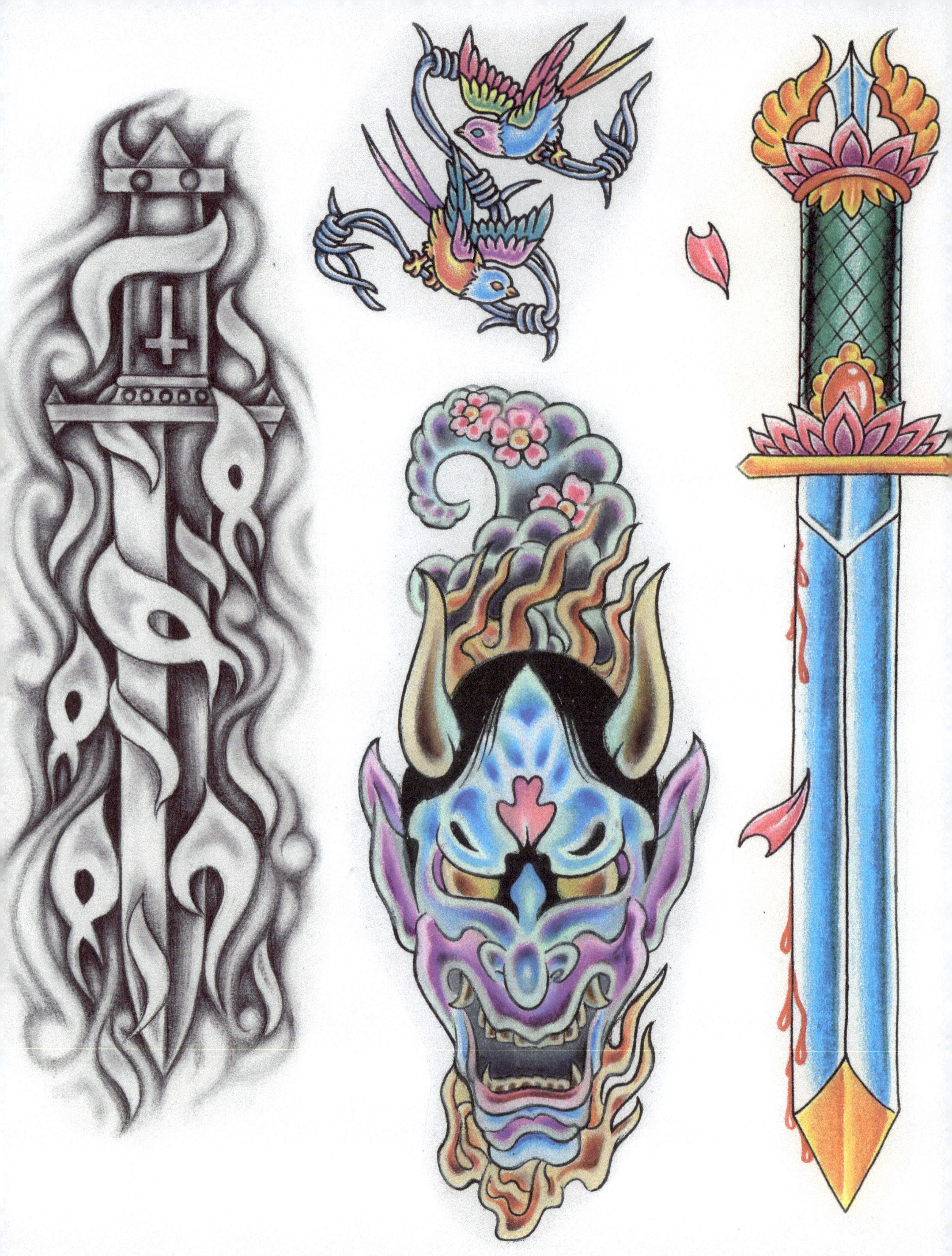

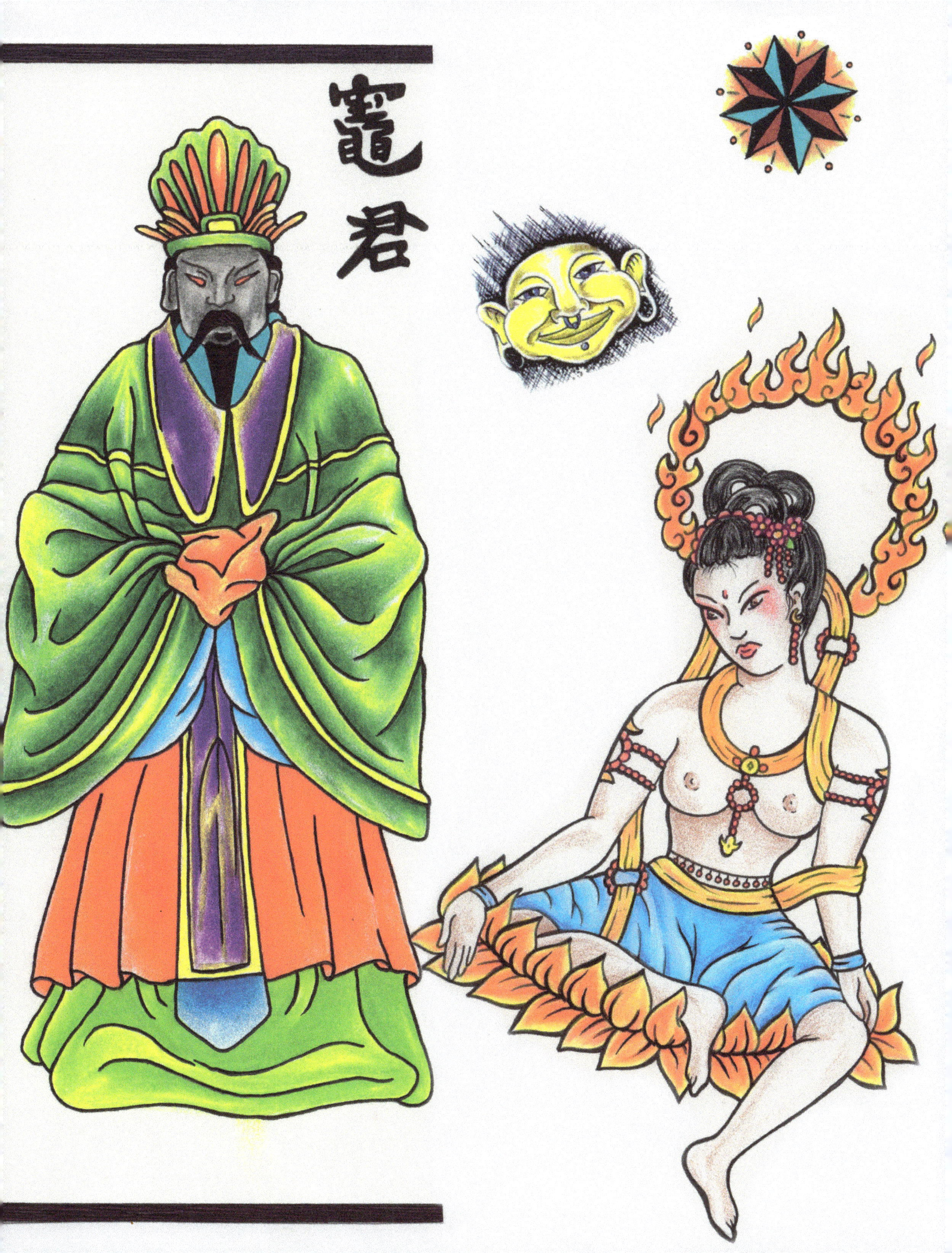

竈君

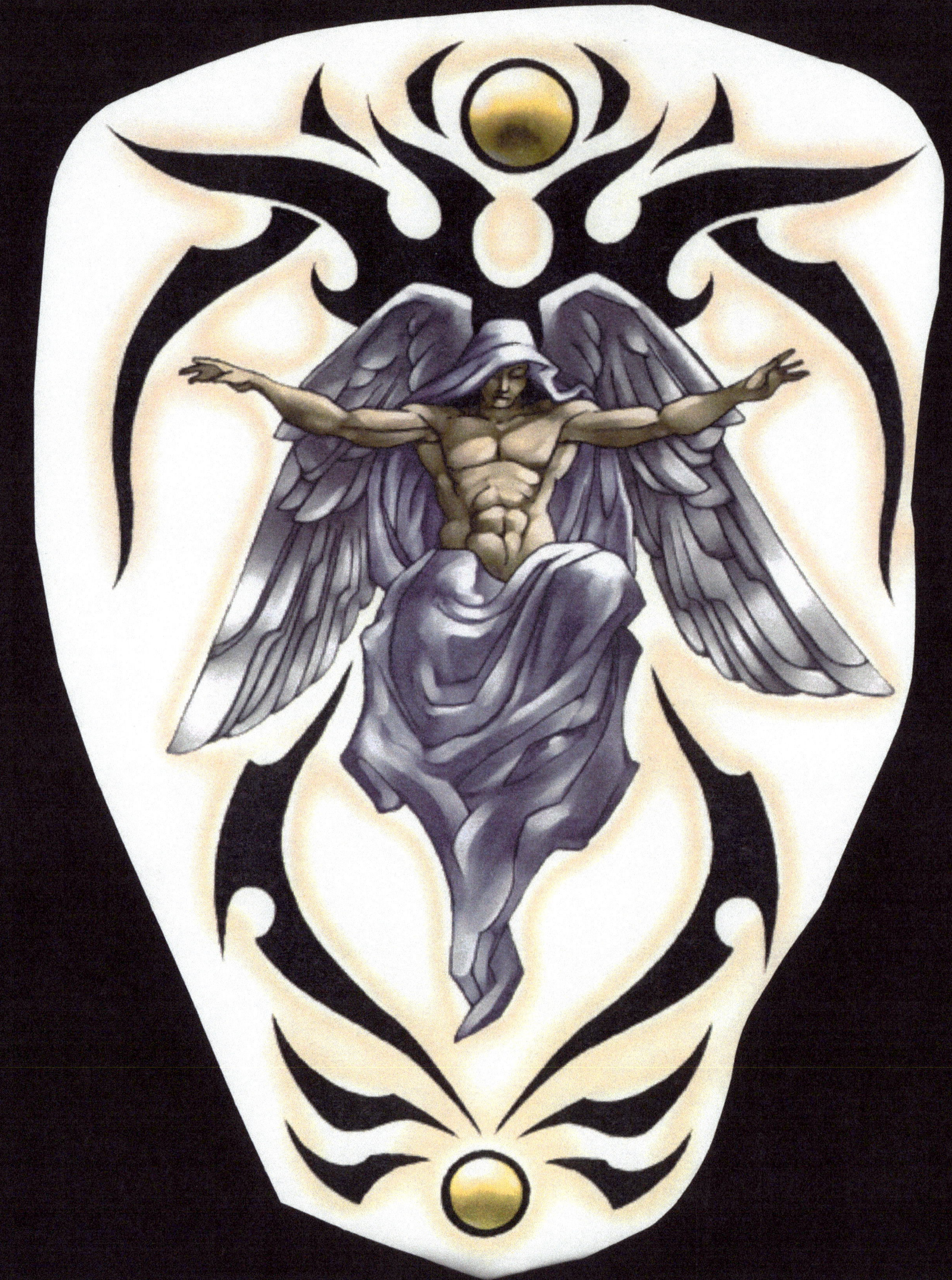

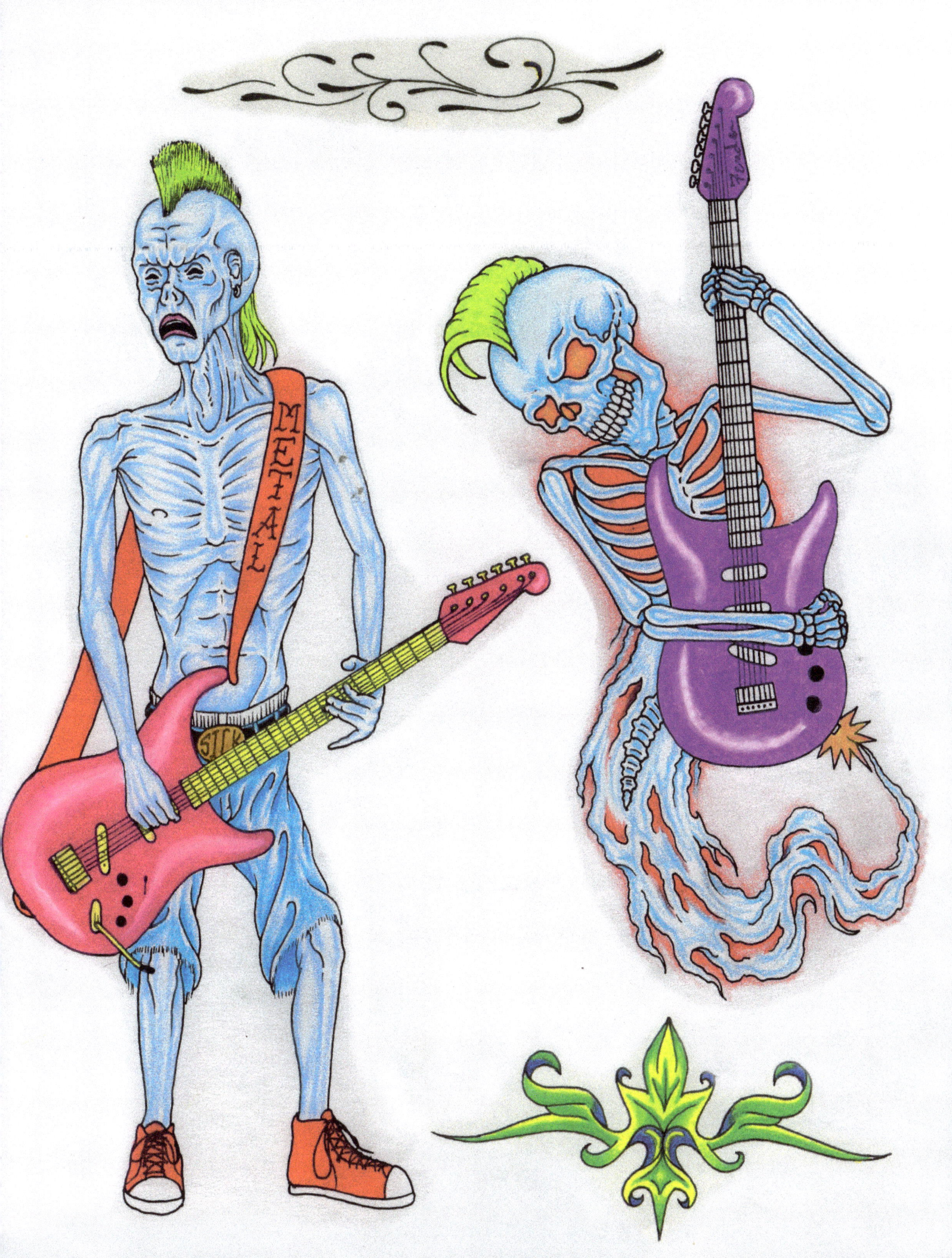

METAL
STICK
Fender

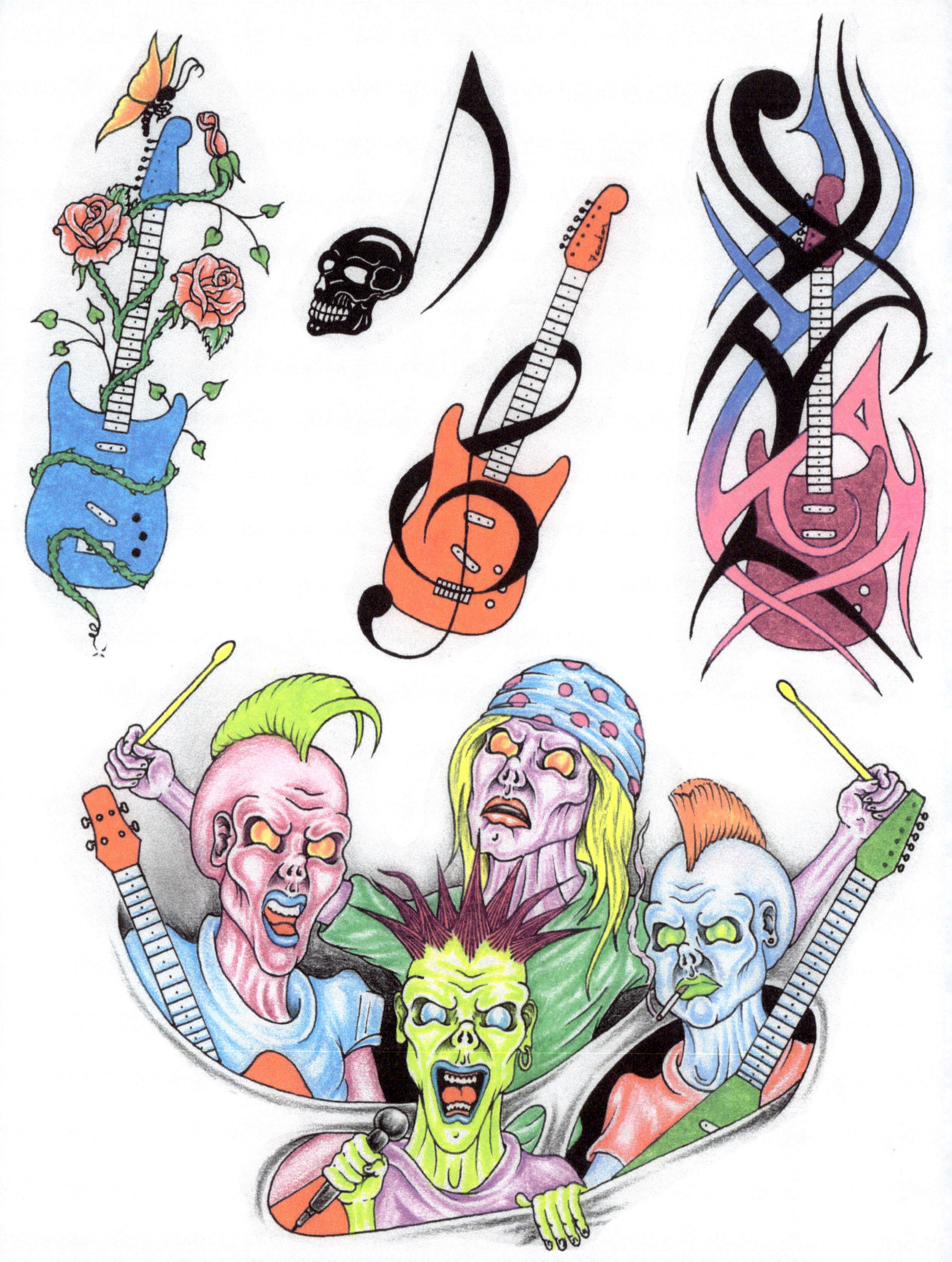

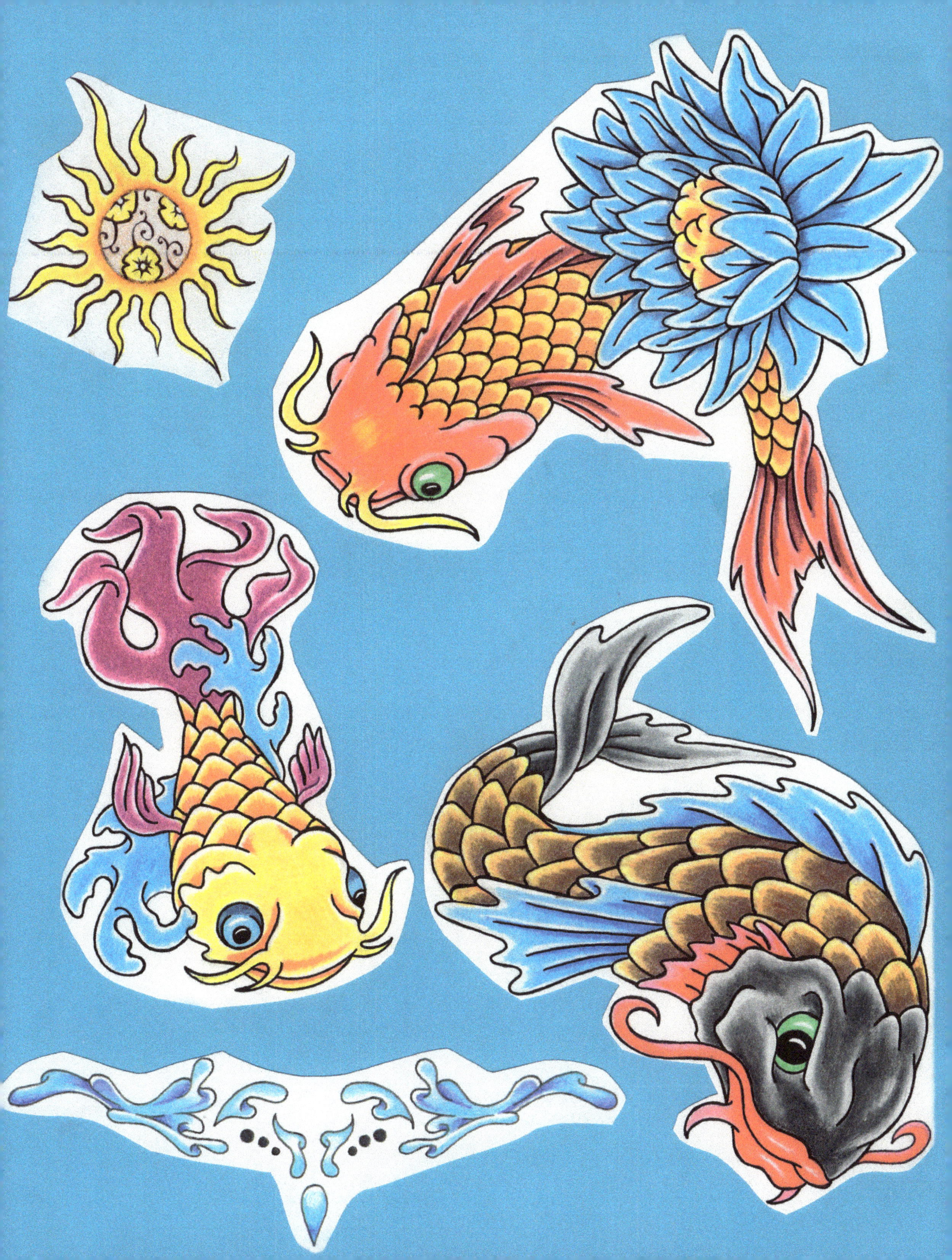

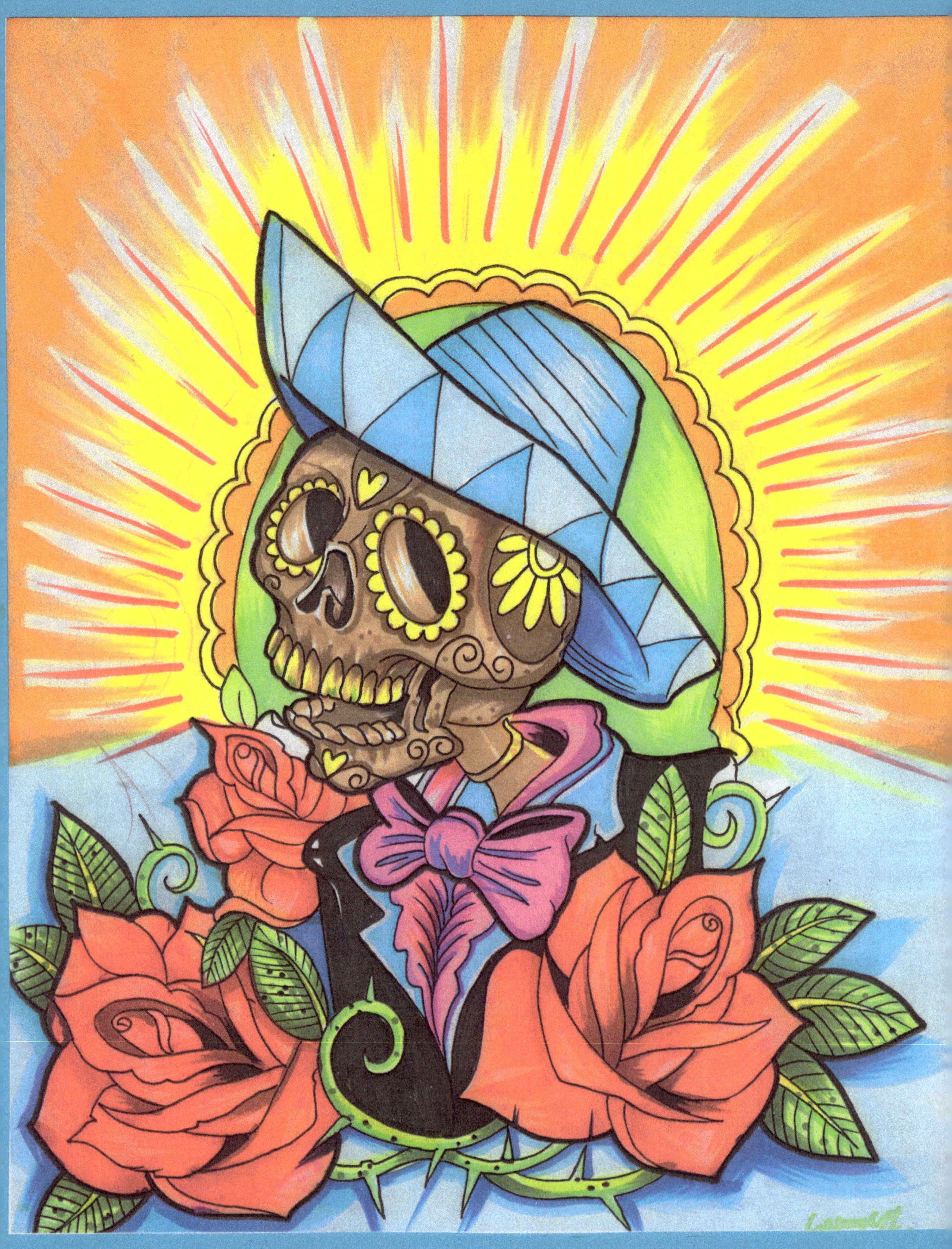

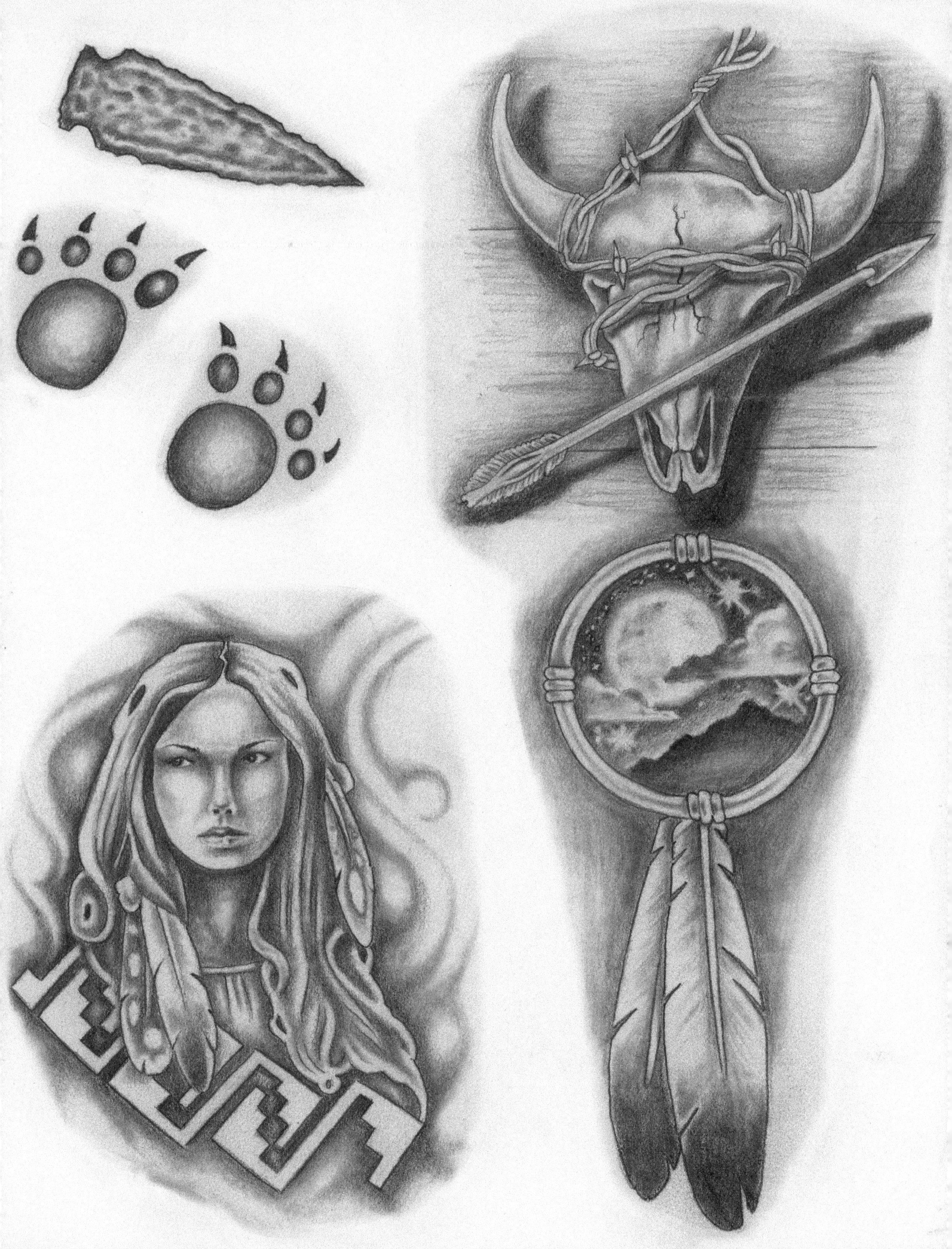

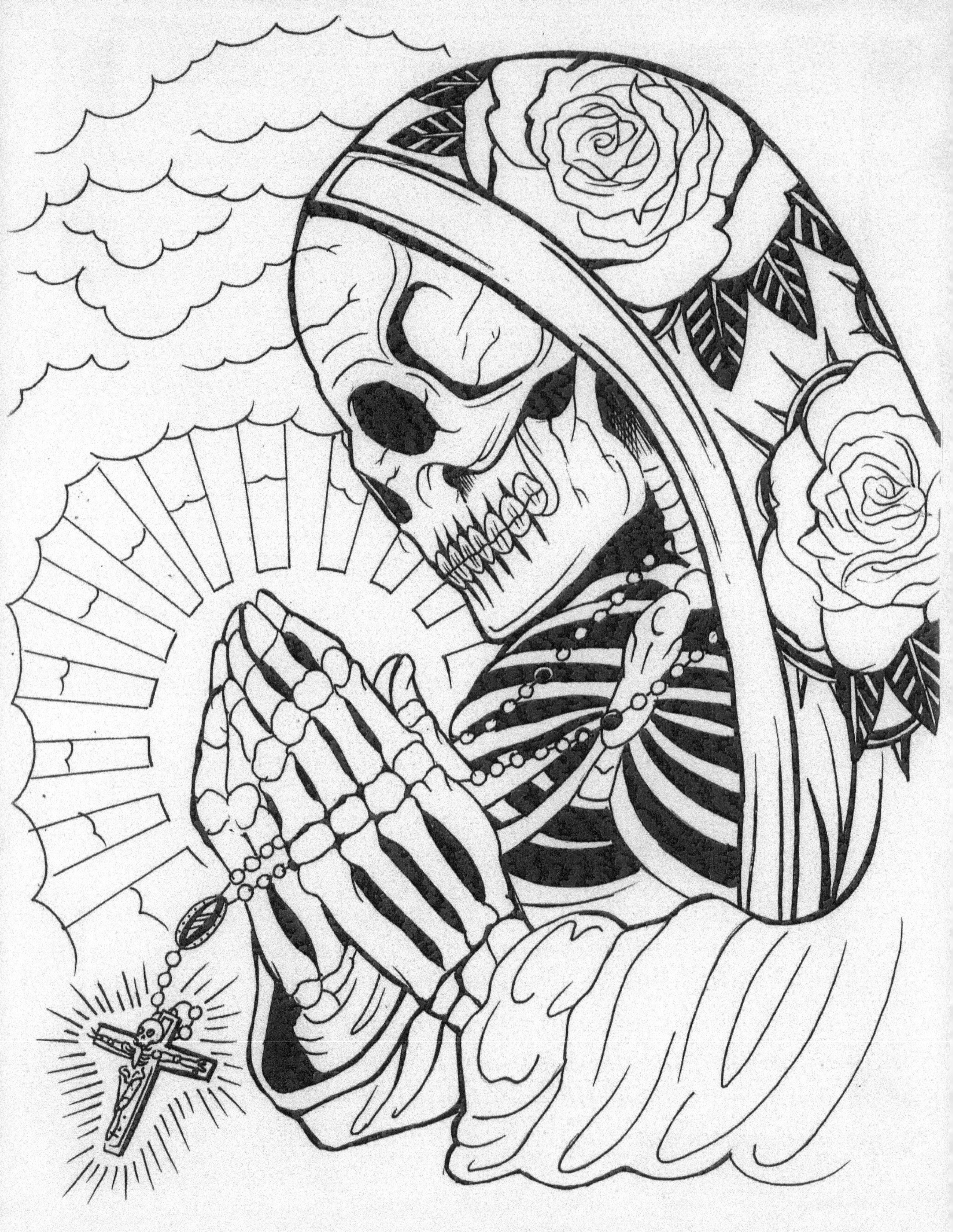

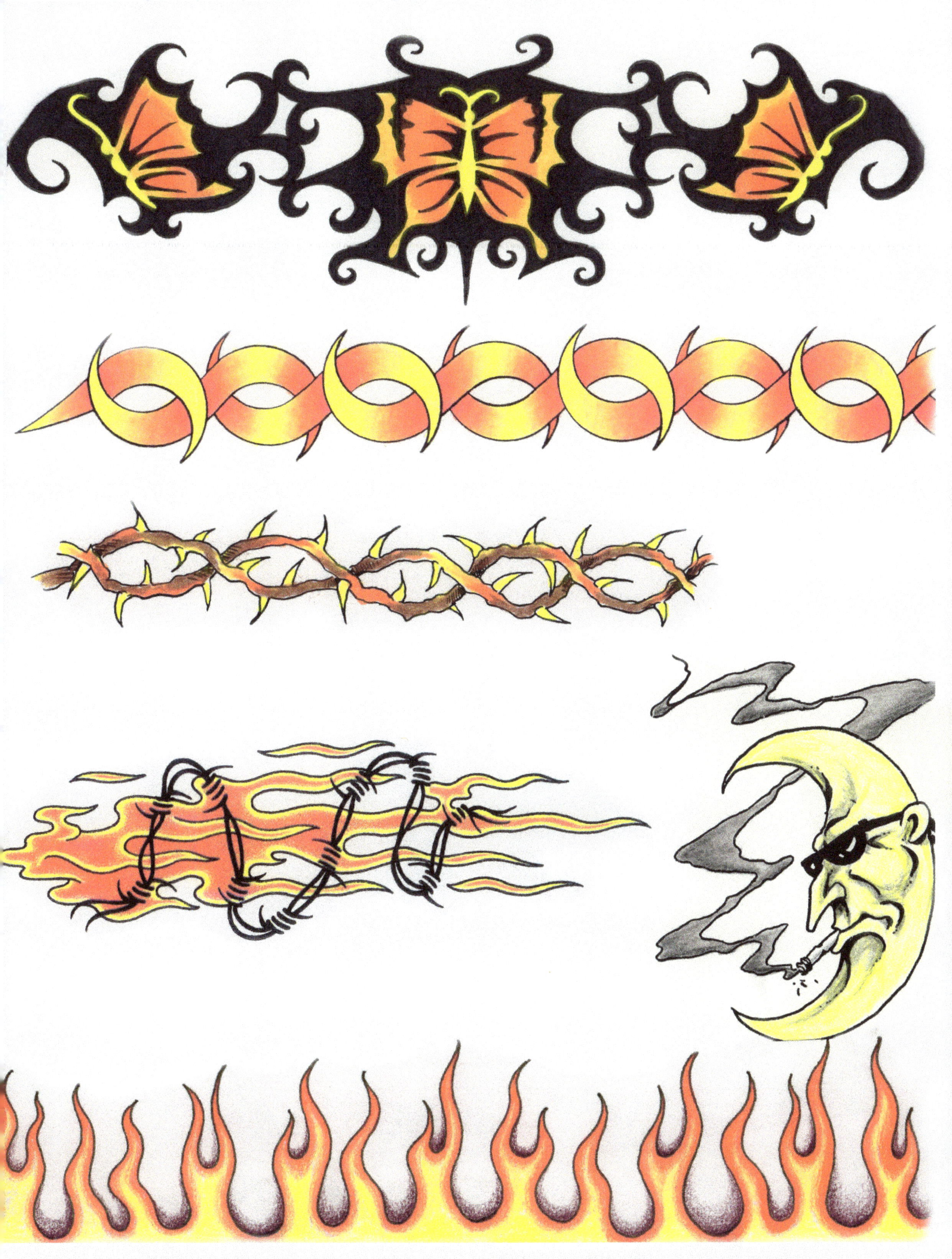

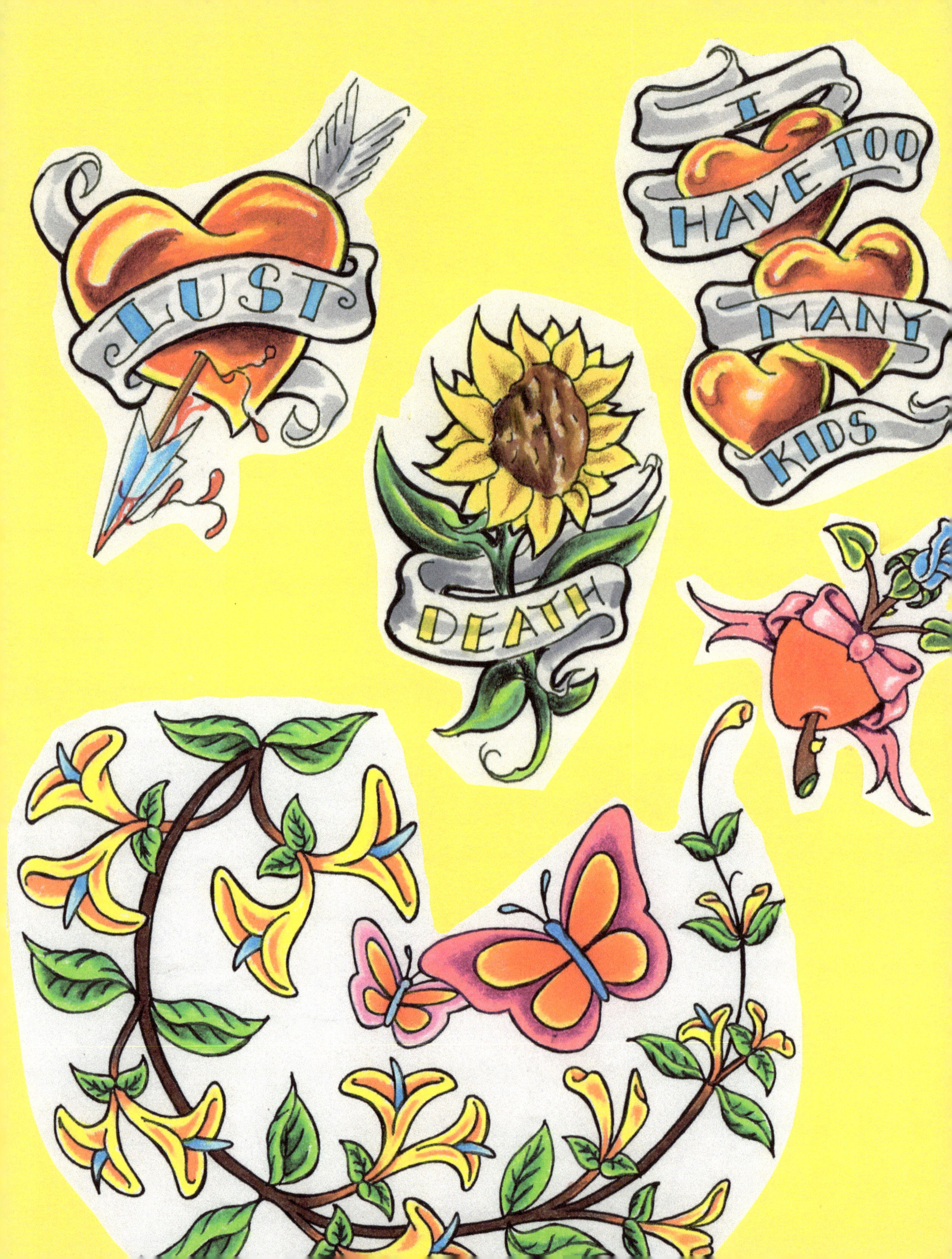

LUST
DEATH
I HAVE TOO MANY KIDS

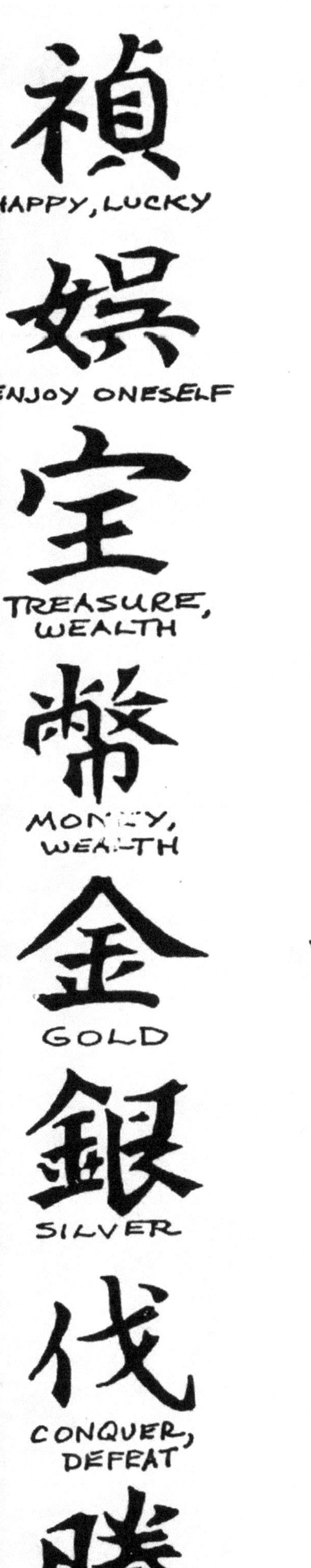

HAPPY, LUCKY

ENJOY ONESELF

TREASURE, WEALTH

MON[E]Y, WEALTH

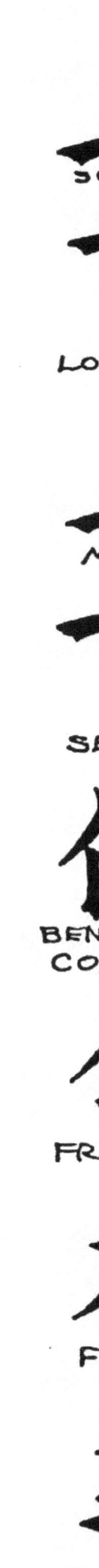

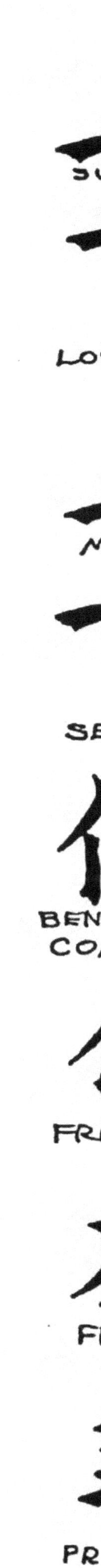

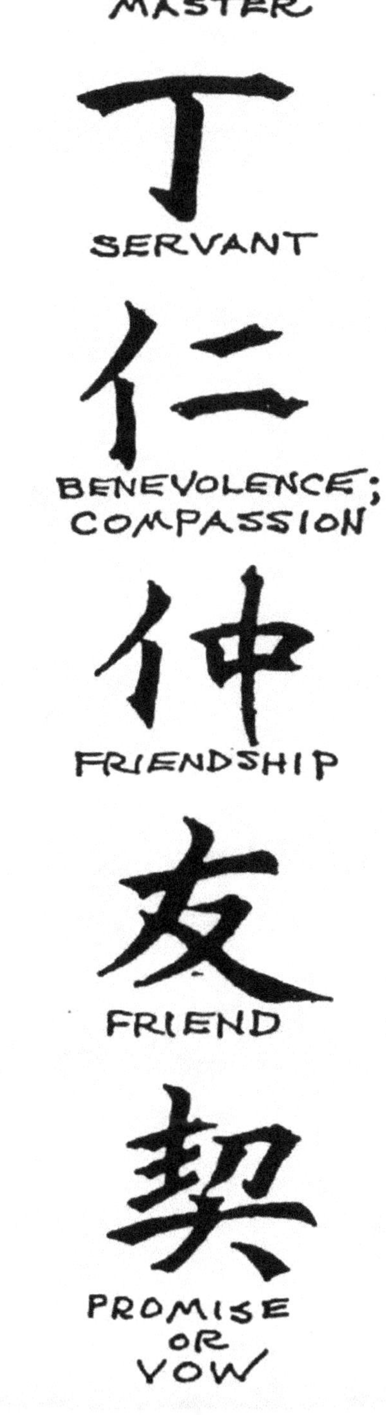

GOLD

SILVER

CONQUER, DEFEAT

TO WIN

SUPERIOR

LOW CLASS

MASTER

SERVANT

BENEVOLENCE; COMPASSION

FRIENDSHIP

FRIEND

PROMISE OR VOW

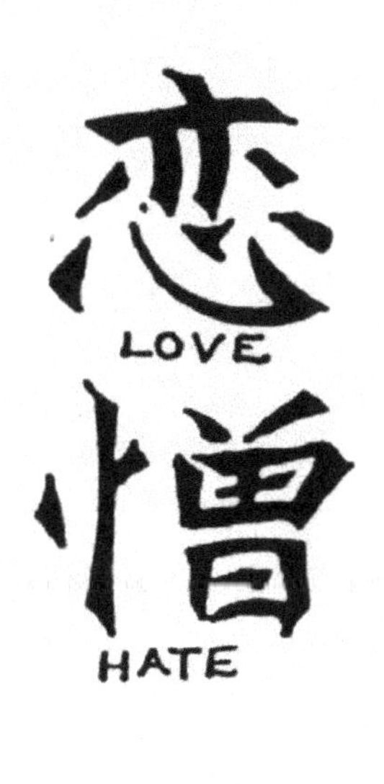

LOVE

HATE

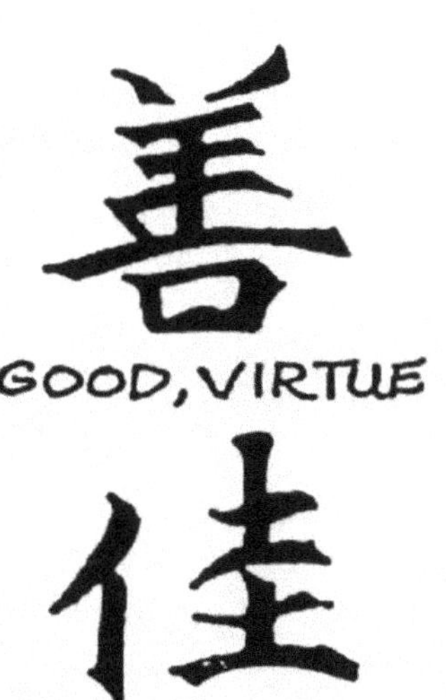

GOOD, VIRTUE

BEAUTIFUL, EXCELLENT

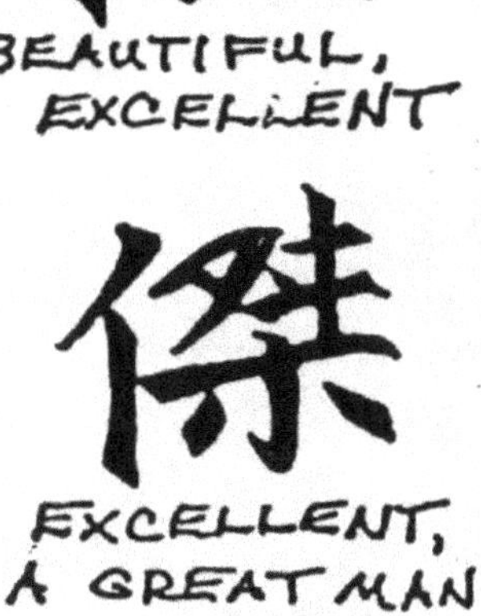

EXCELLENT, A GREAT MAN

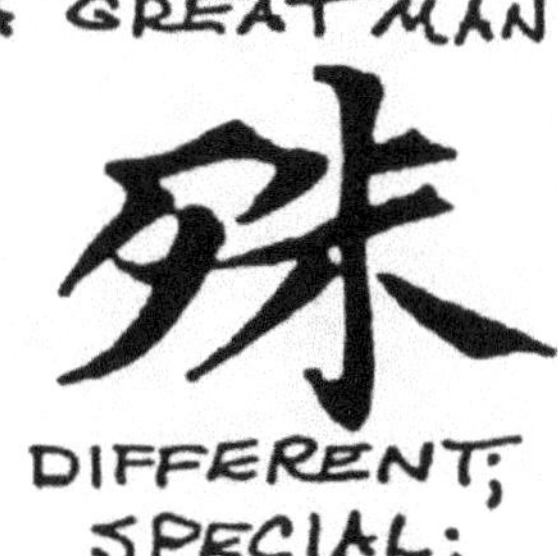

DIFFERENT; SPECIAL; TO EXCEL

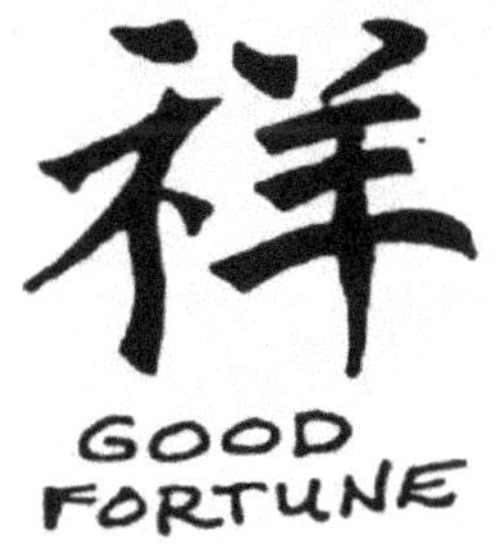

GOOD FORTUNE

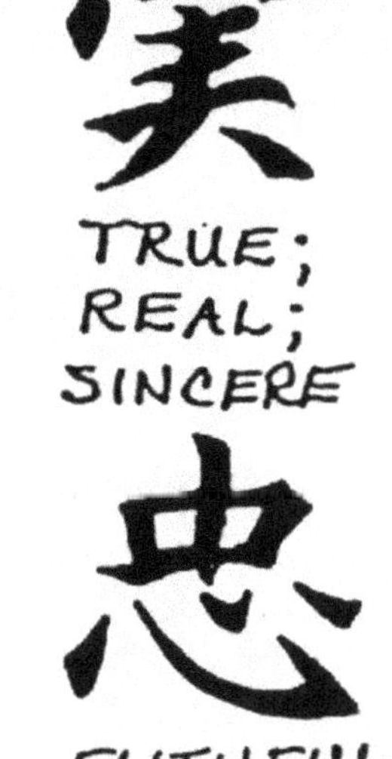

TRUE; REAL; SINCERE

FAITHFUL; LOYAL

HARD & STRONG

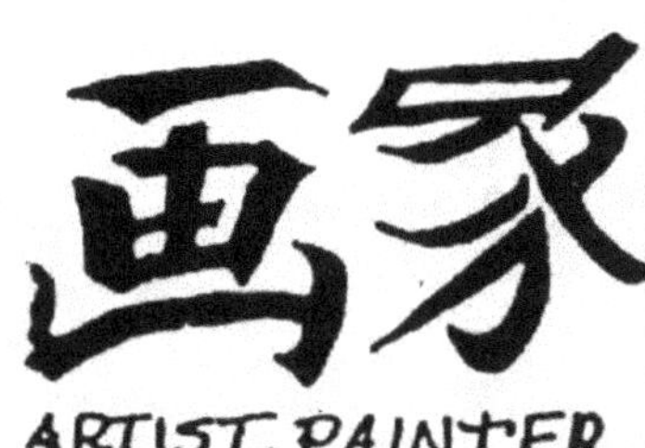

ARTIST, PAINTER

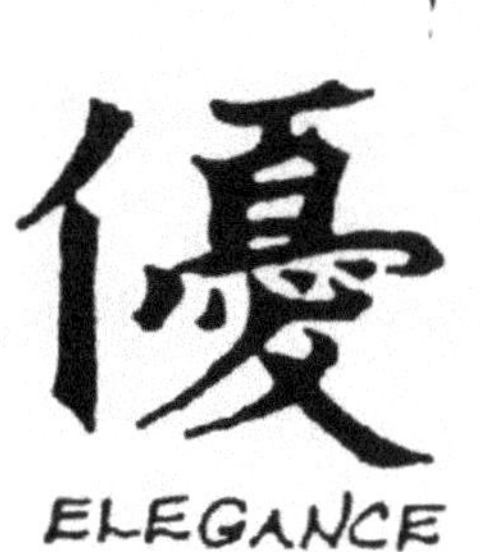

ELEGANCE

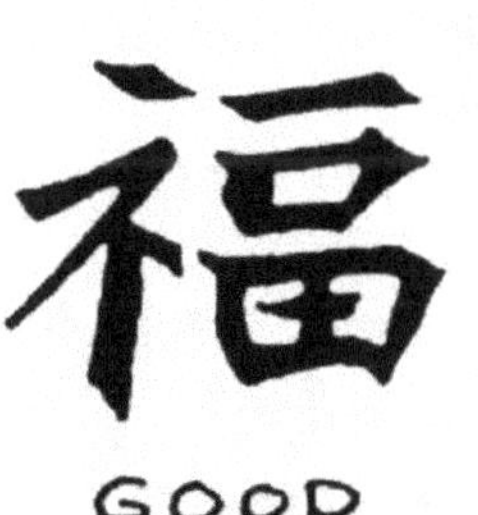

GOOD LUCK

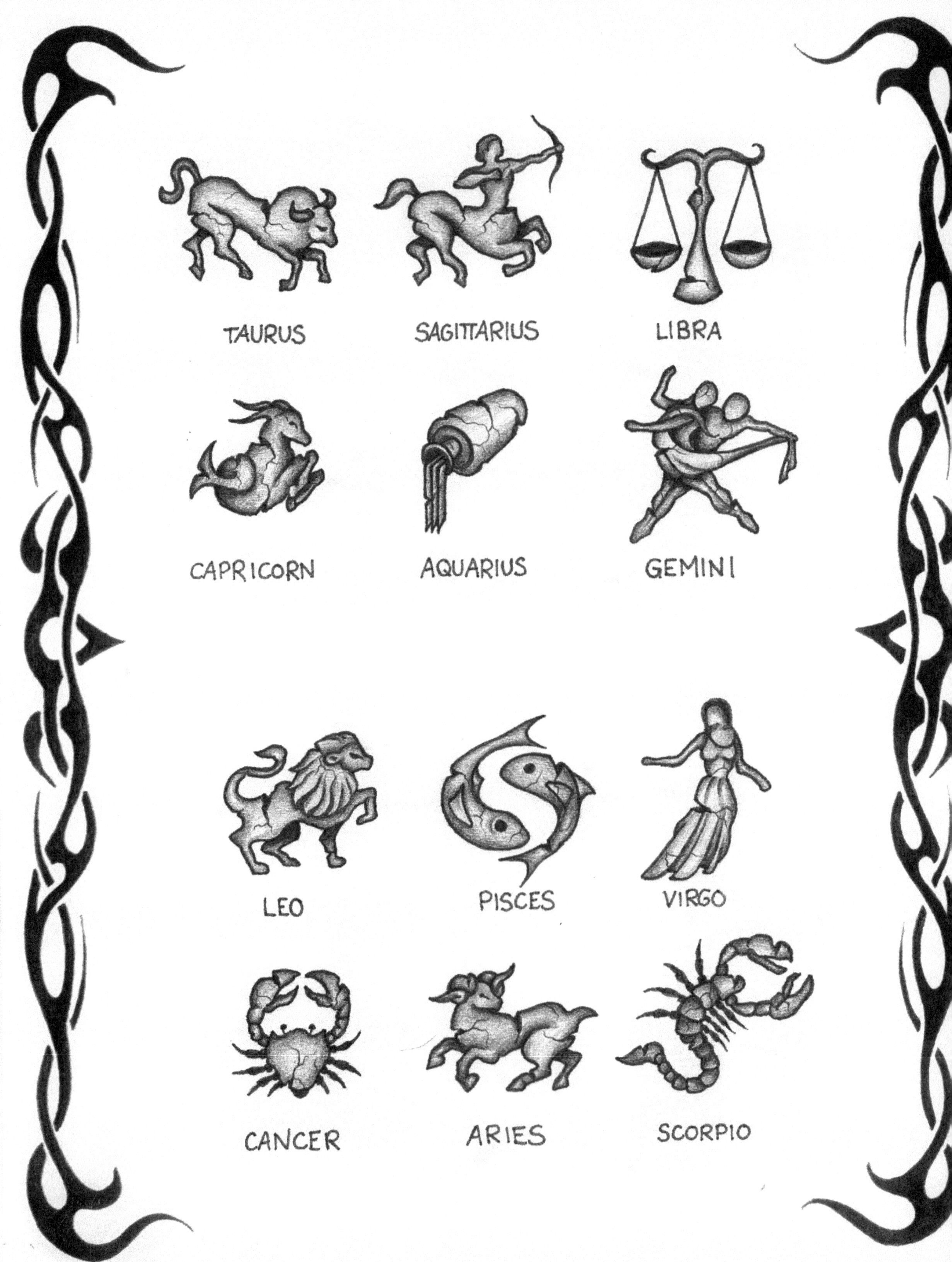

TAURUS
SAGITTARIUS
LIBRA
CAPRICORN
AQUARIUS
GEMINI
LEO
PISCES
VIRGO
CANCER
ARIES
SCORPIO

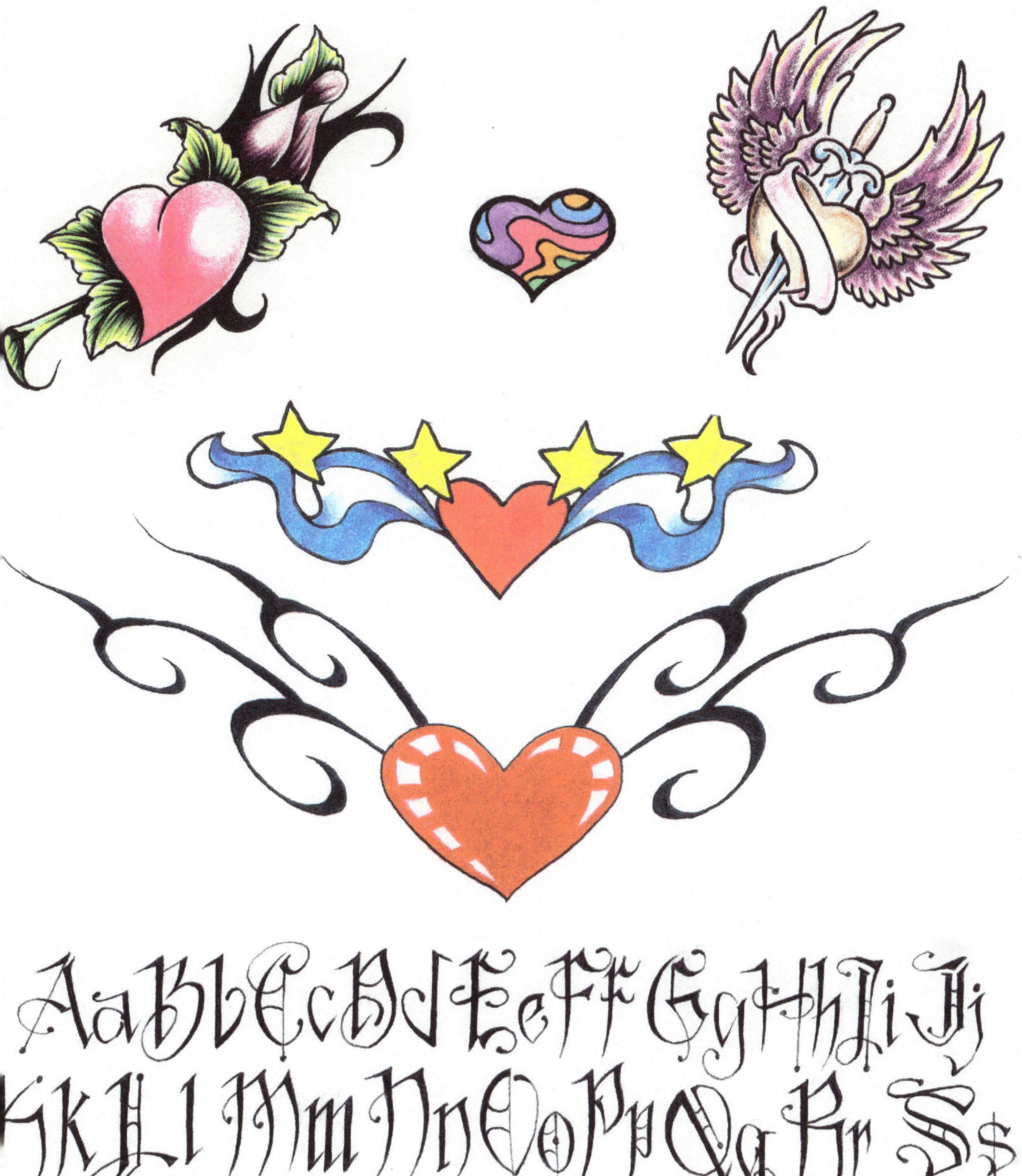

Aa Bb Cc Dd Ee Ff Gg Hh Ii Jj
Kk Ll Mm Nn Oo Pp Qq Rr Ss $
Tt Uu Vv Ww Xx Yy Zz

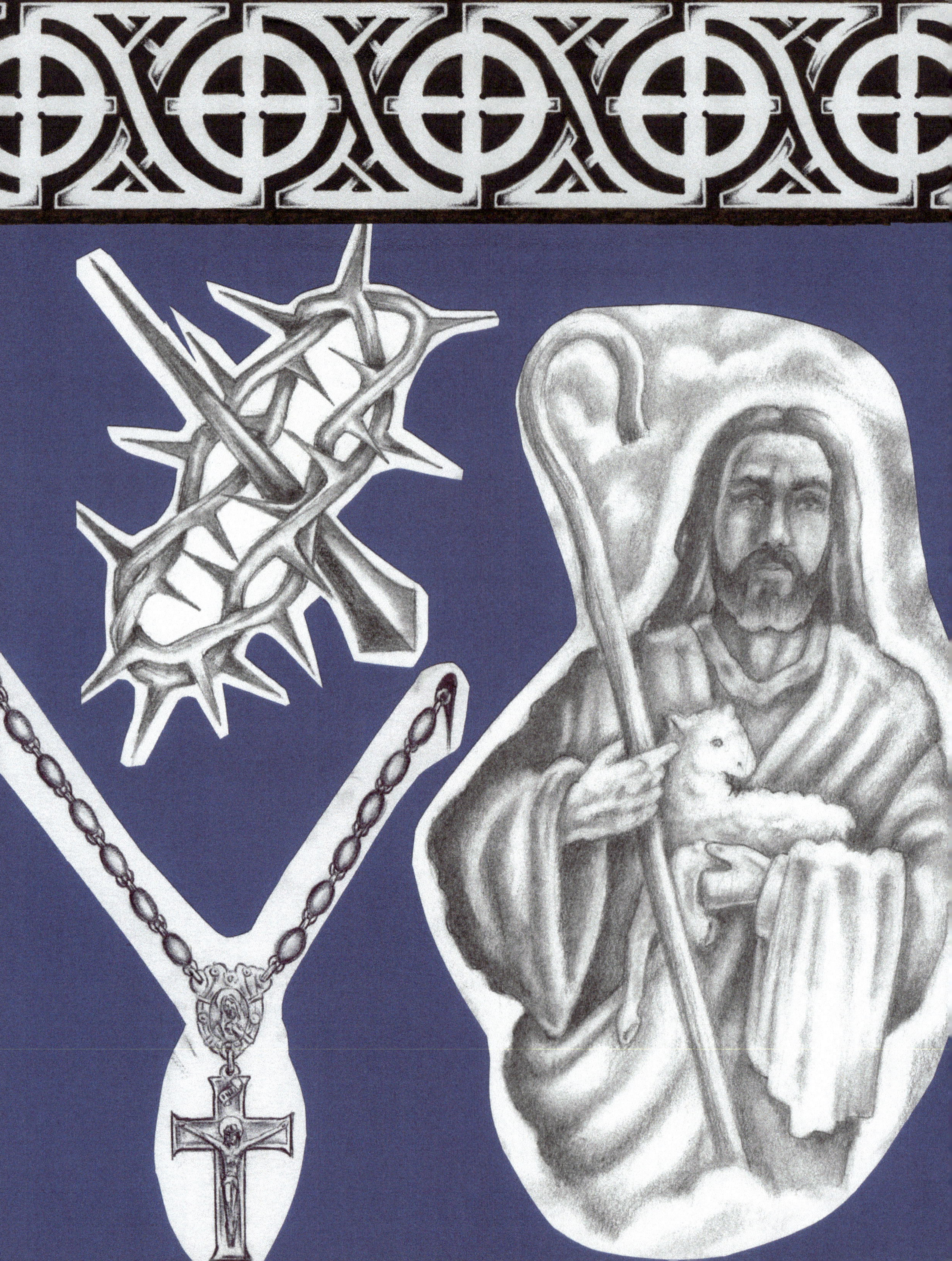

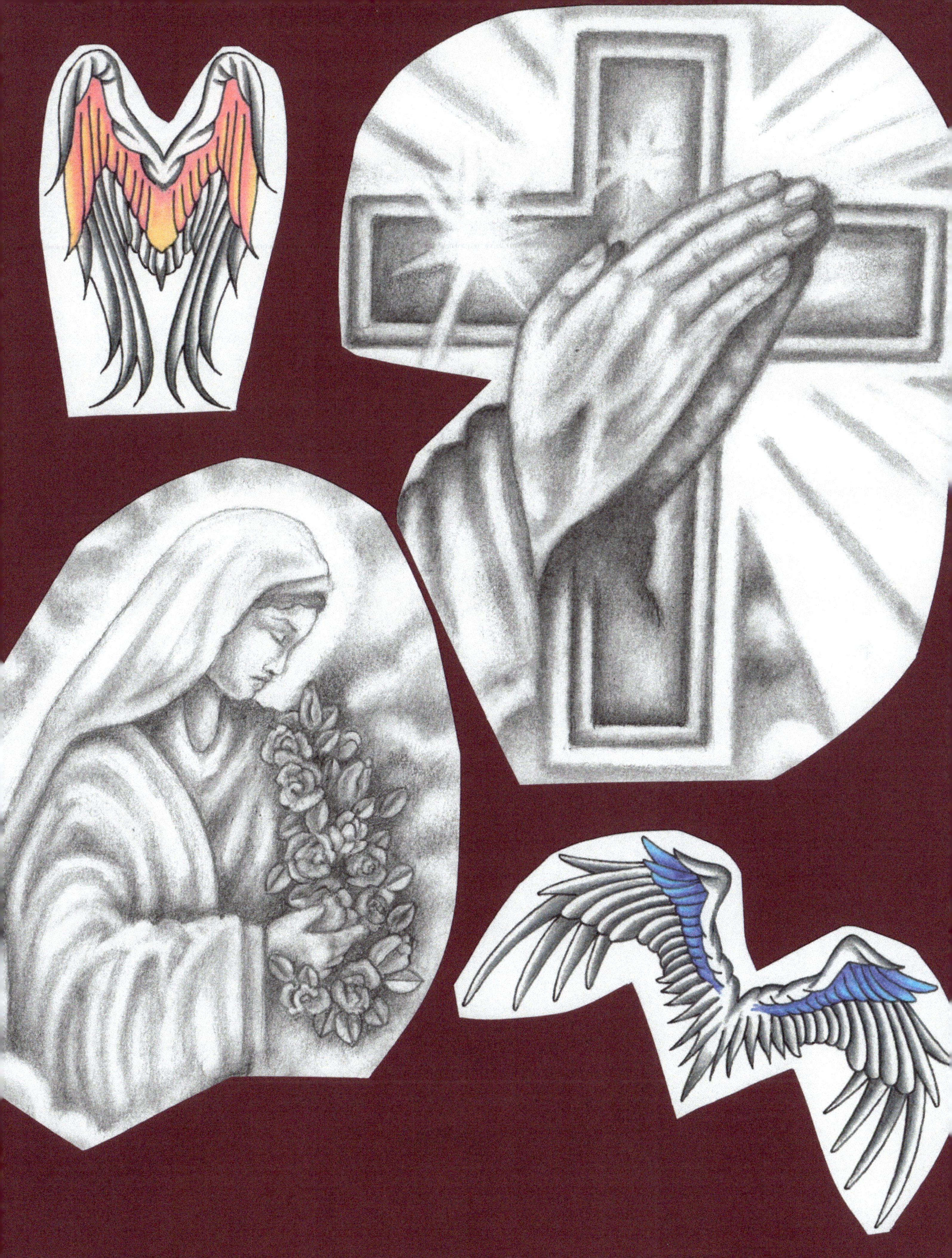

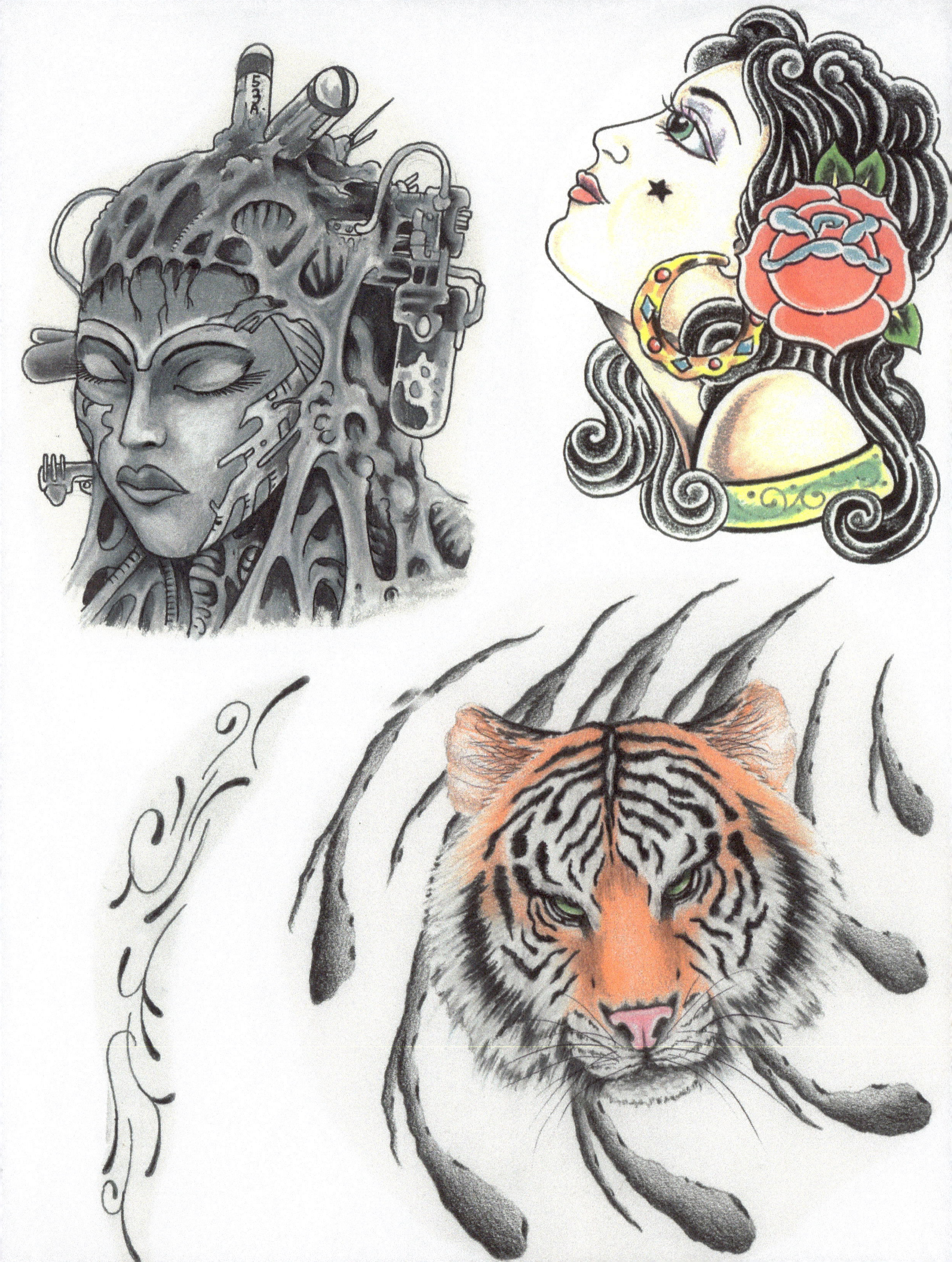

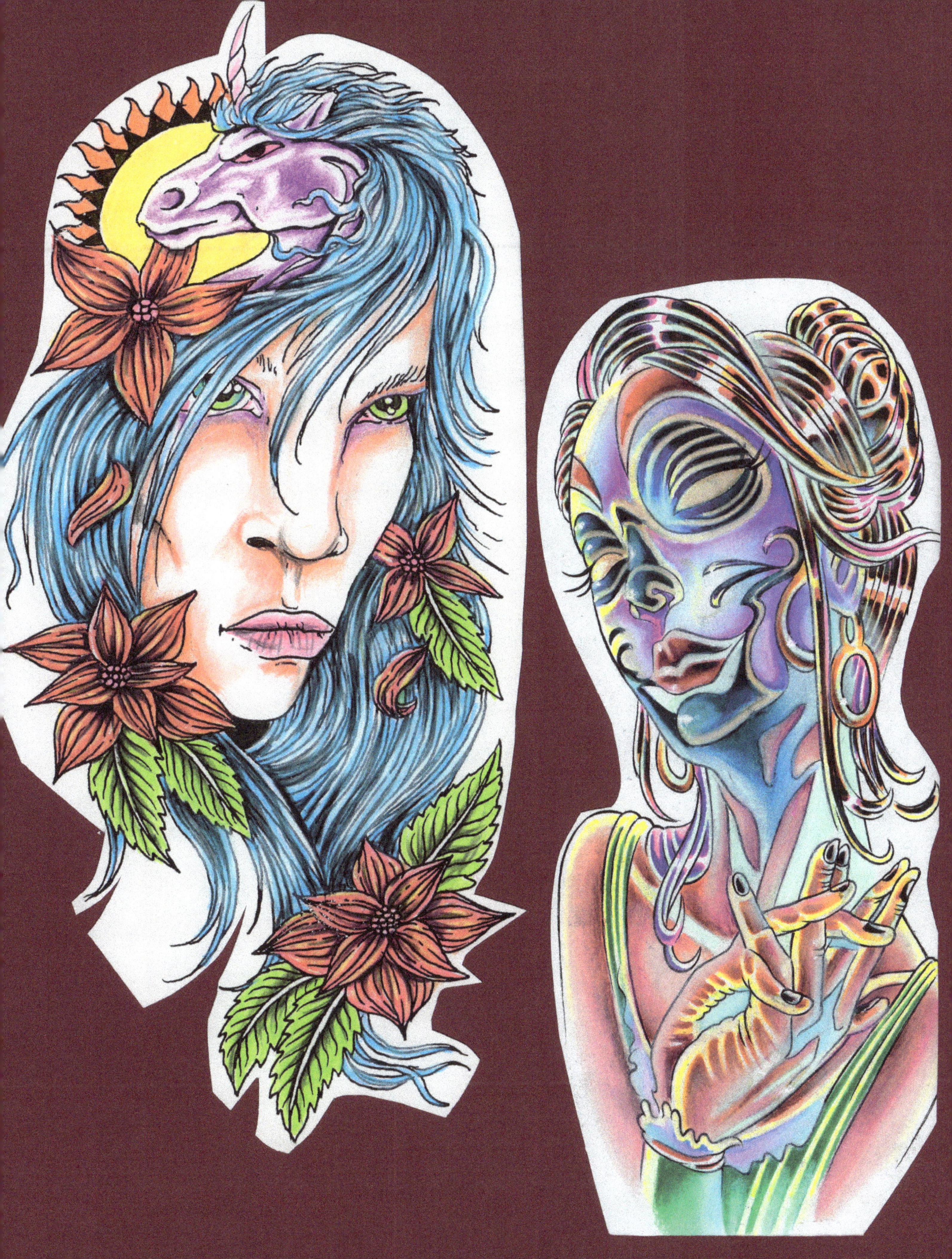

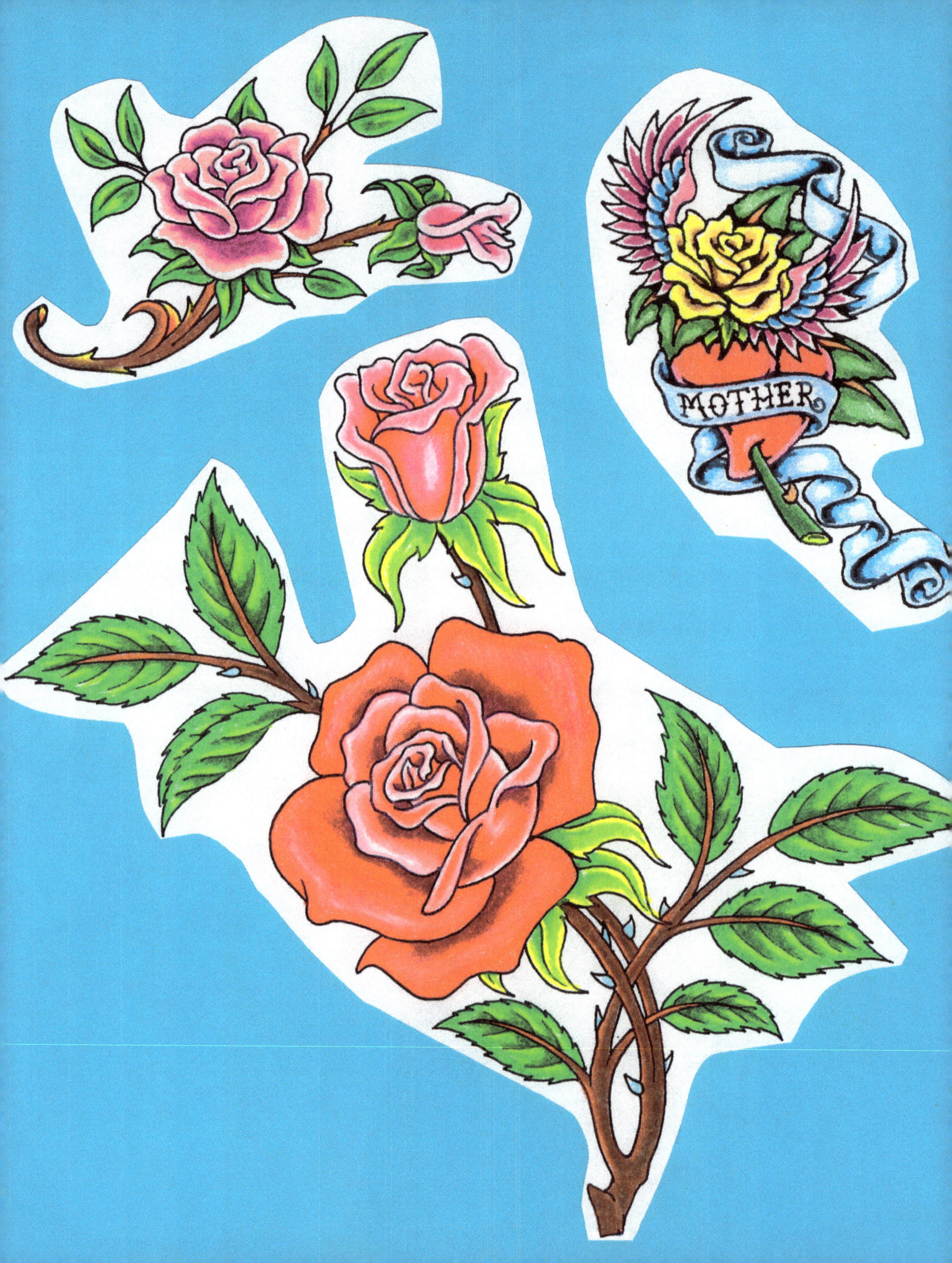
MOTHER

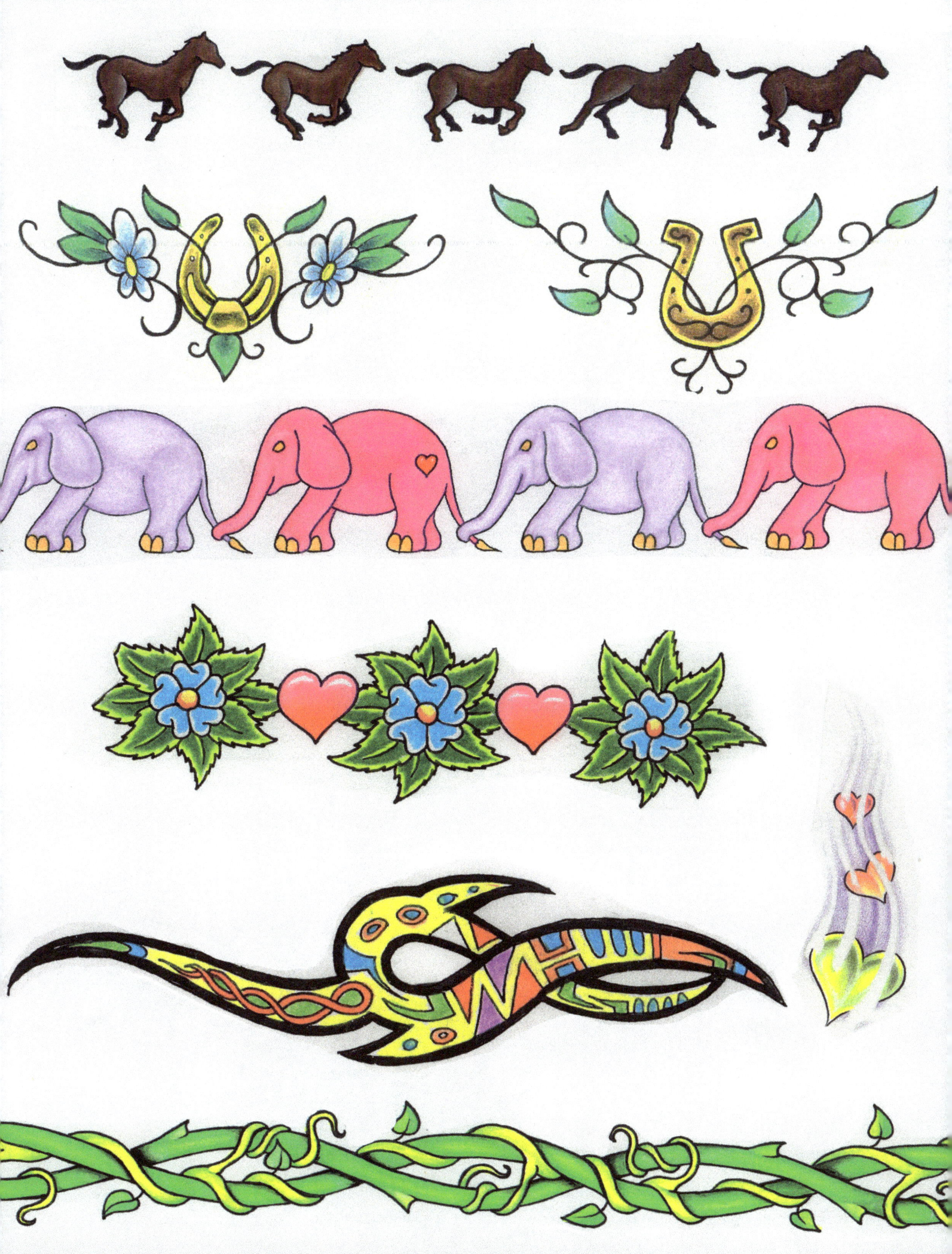

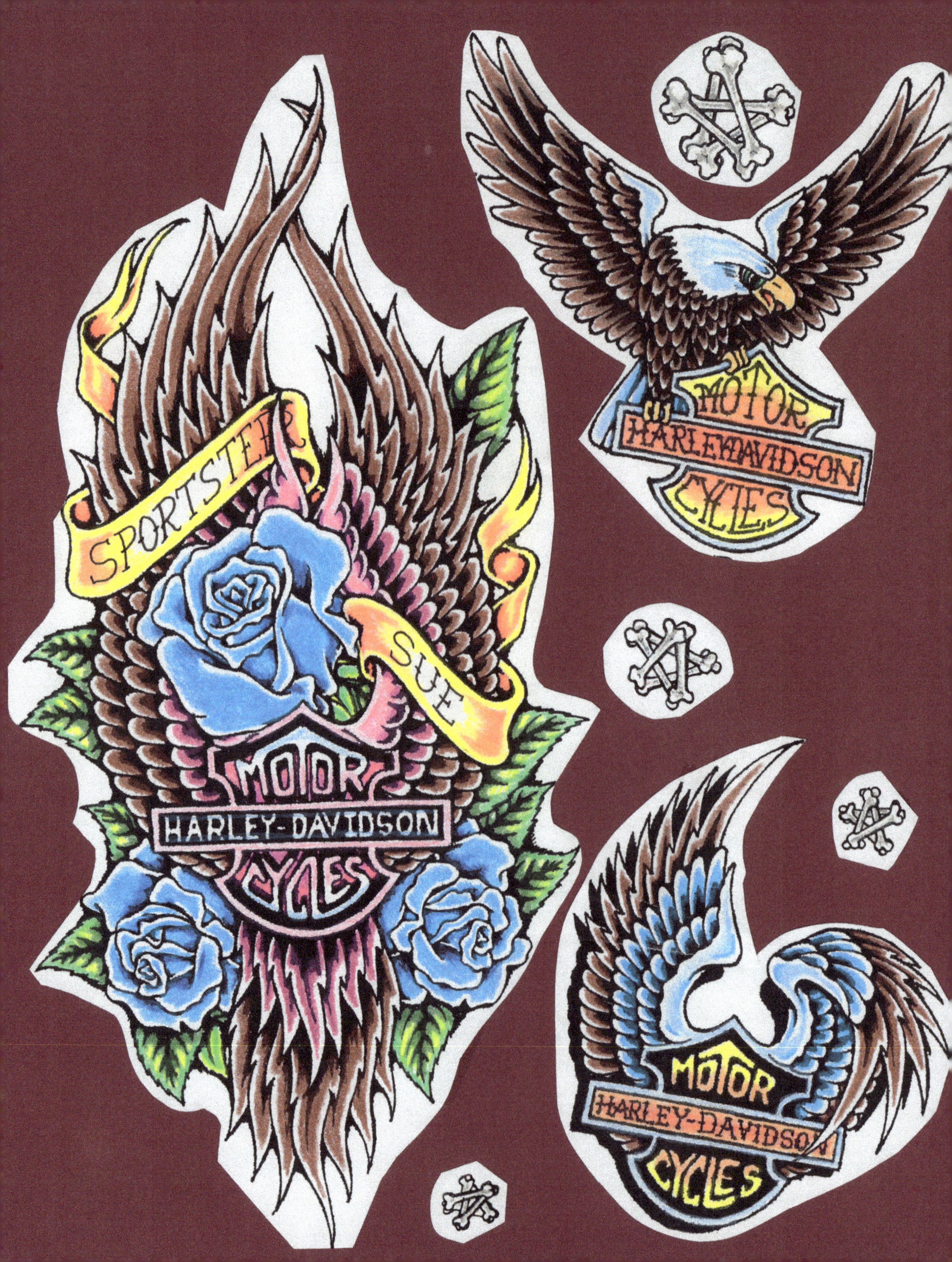
SPORTSTER
SUE
MOTOR
HARLEY-DAVIDSON
CYCLES
MOTOR
HARLEY-DAVIDSON
CYCLES
MOTOR
HARLEY-DAVIDSON
CYCLES

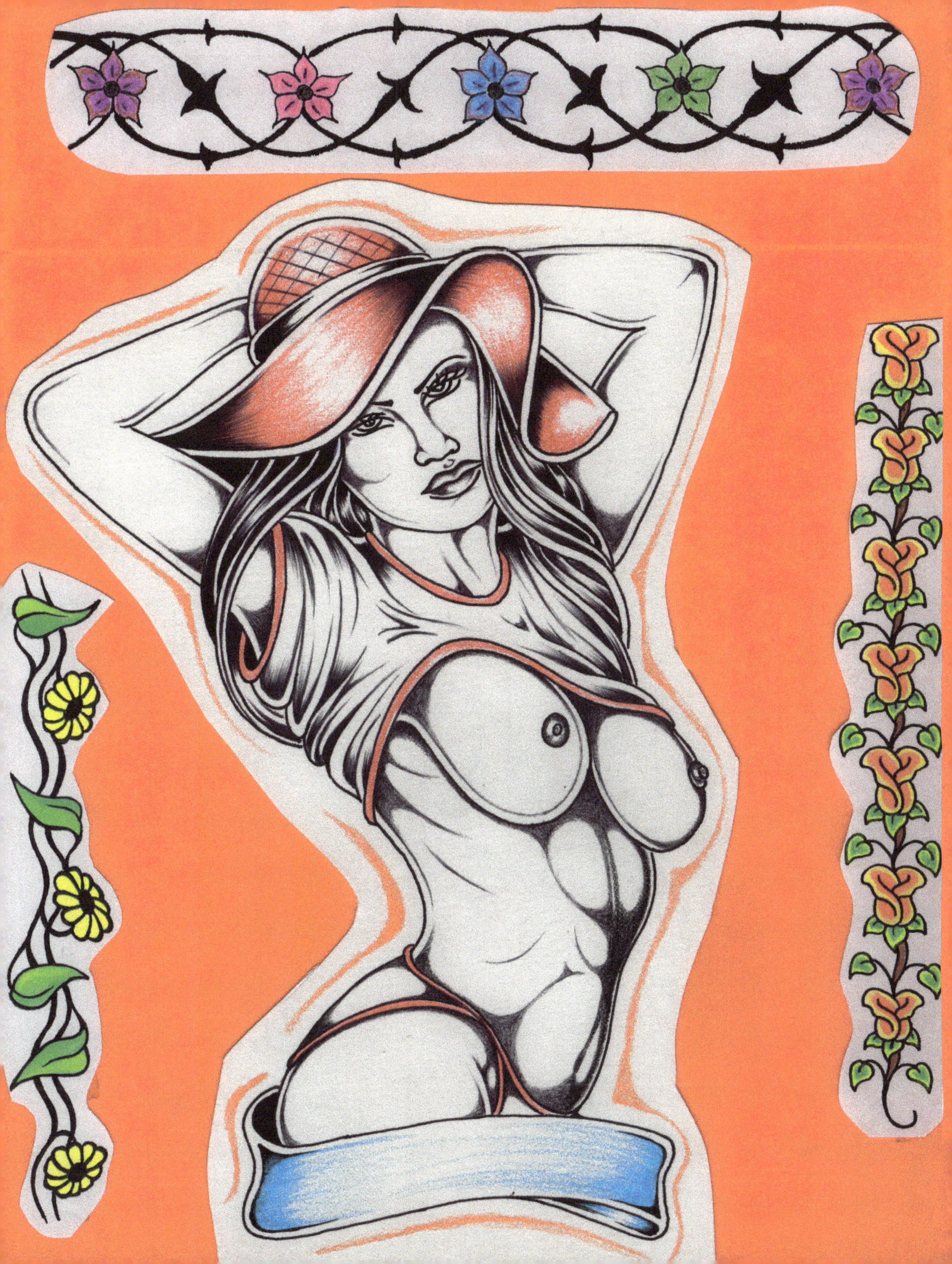

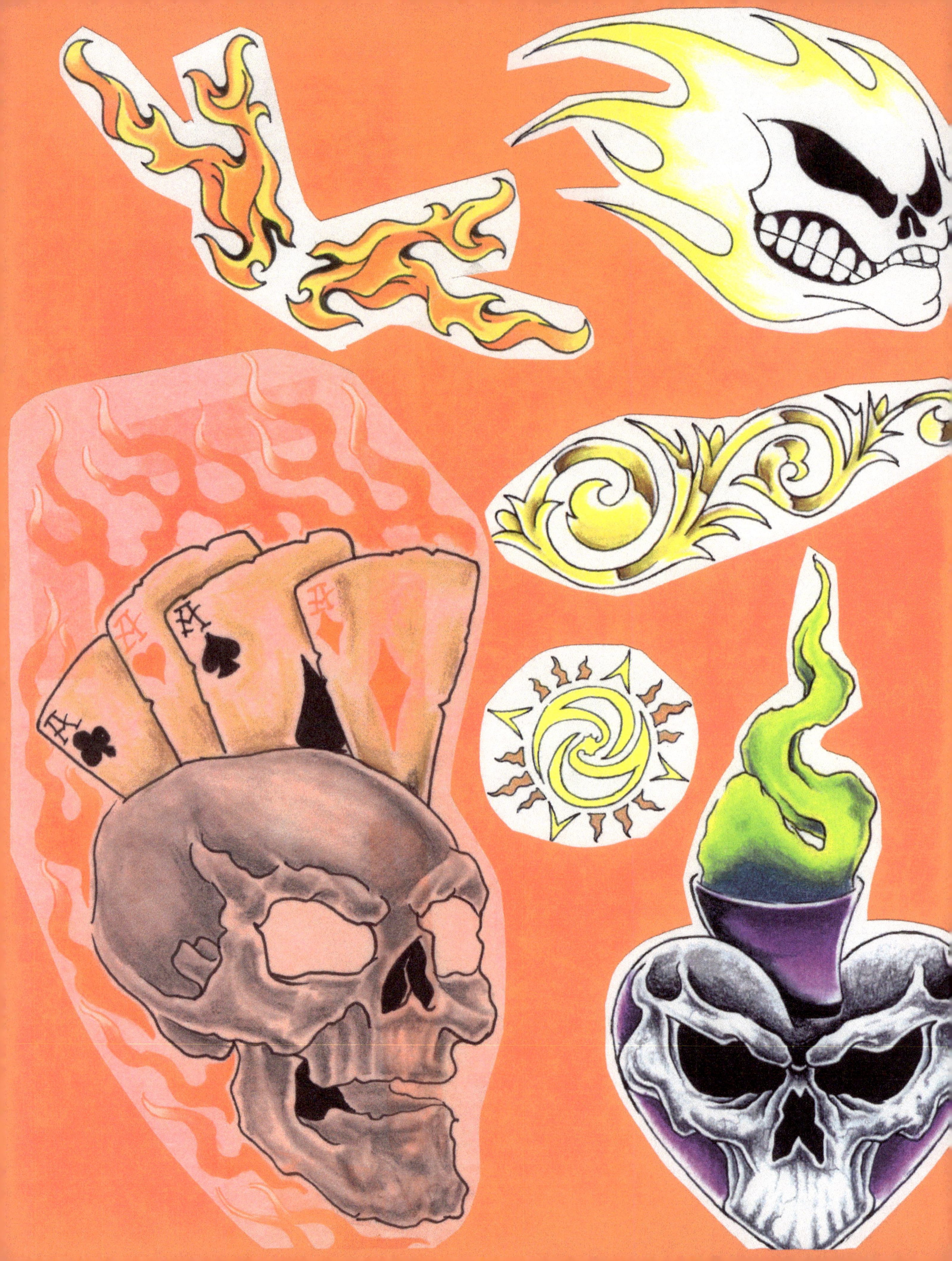

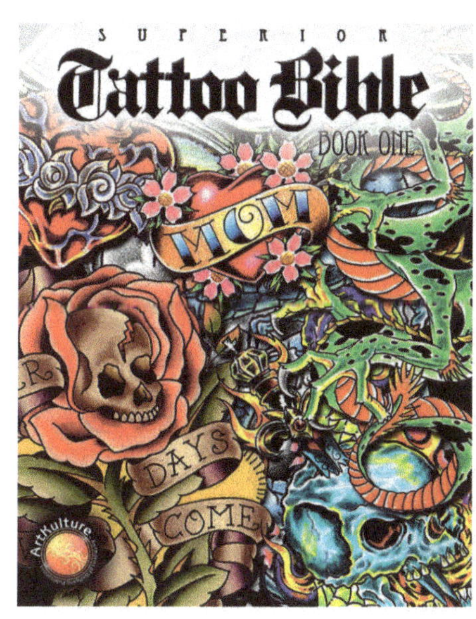
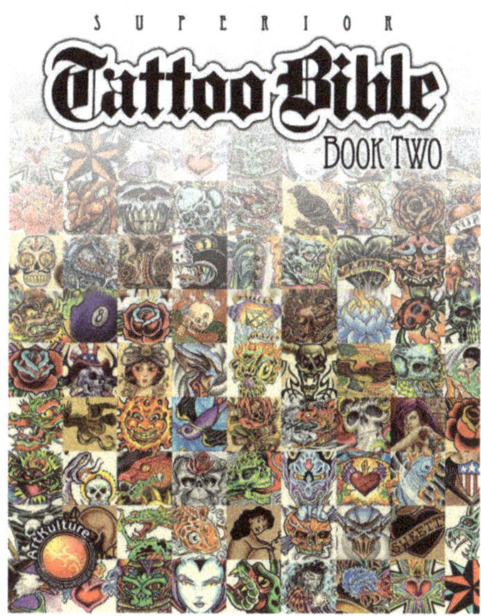
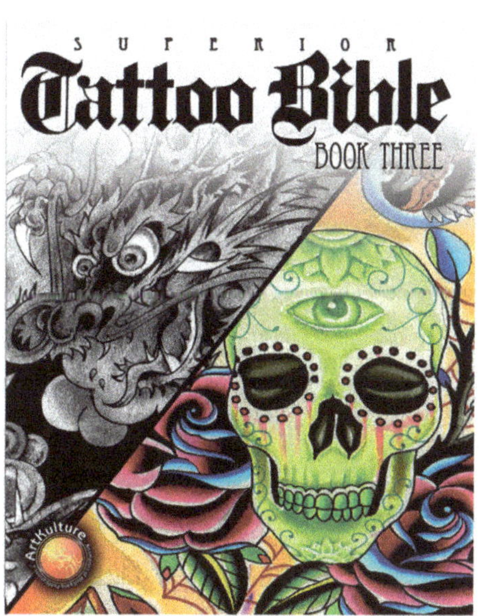

Five Tattoo Books
from
Jim Watson & Superior Tattoo
Published by ArtKulture/Wolfgang
Available @ Barnes & Noble and 'Net

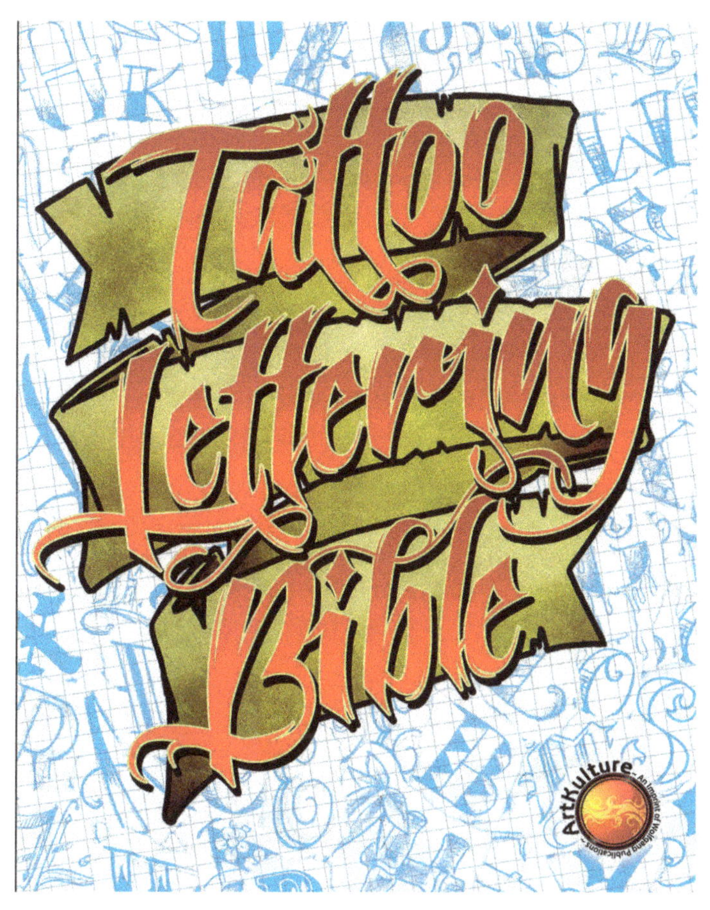
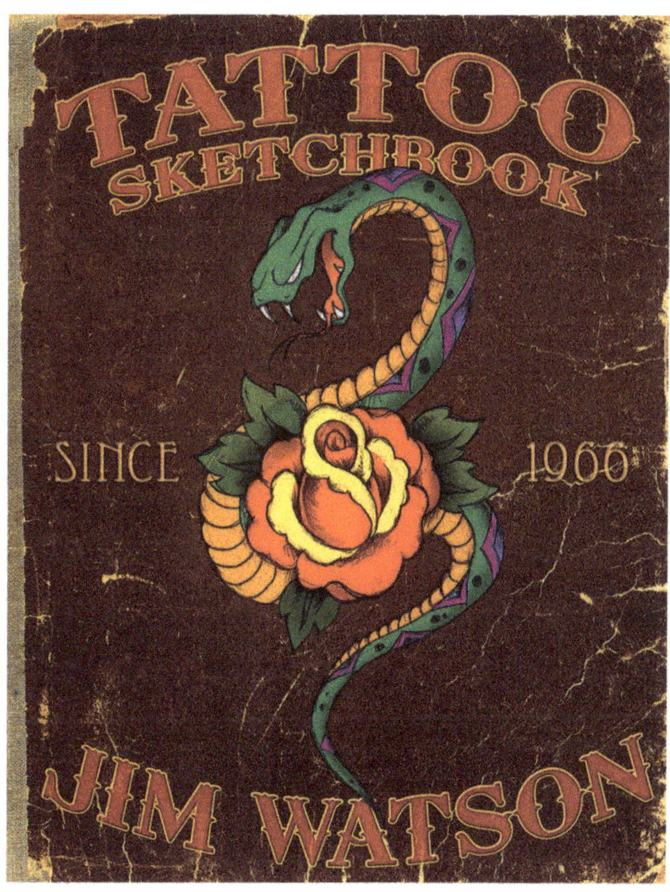